C000294609

Stu Hardin

2017

PORTALS
OF DISCOVERY

GEORGE NORRIE

The Book Guild Ltd

First published in Great Britain in 2016 by
The Book Guild Ltd
9 Priory Business Park
Wistow Road, Kibworth
Leicestershire, LE8 0RX
Freephone: 0800 999 2982
www.bookguild.co.uk
Email: info@bookguild.co.uk
Twitter: @bookguild

Copyright © 2016 George Norrie (2nd Baron Norrie of Wellington New Zealand)

The right of George Norrie (2nd Baron Norrie of Wellington New Zealand) to be identified
as the author of this work has been asserted by him in accordance with the
Copyright, Design and Patents Act 1988.

All rights reserved. No part of this publication may be
reproduced, transmitted, or stored in a retrieval system, in any form or by any means,
without permission in writing from the publisher, nor be otherwise circulated in
any form of binding or cover other than that in which it is published and without
a similar condition being imposed on the subsequent purchaser.

Typeset in Aldine401 BT

Printed and bound in Great Britain by CPI Group (UK) Ltd, Croydon, CR0 4YY

ISBN 978 1911320 128

British Library Cataloguing in Publication Data.
A catalogue record for this book is available from the British Library.

For Rose,
who cared for me during my formative years

CONTENTS

FOREWORD

SIR CHRIS BONINGTON CVO CBE DL

During my time as President of the Council for National Parks I worked alongside CNP Vice President George Norrie in a common endeavour to ensure new legislation for the Parks. I'd signed up for the role because of my love for the hills – I've lived in the Lake District nearly all my life – and because of the chance to act as an ambassador for them. Despite travelling all over the world – to its highest peaks as a climber – I still revel in the joys of the landscape at home, its people and history. George comes from a very different background but we had a shared passion and determination – we wanted to leave the National Parks with the most robust framework in law. We succeeded in that legacy but it wasn't without its challenges.

George and I – together and separately – toured round all the National Parks in England and Wales. While he was in a snowstorm on Dartmoor I was facing farmers in Northumberland who thought our quest to protect the National Park from military training was a threat to their livelihoods. While George beavered away seeing the legislation through the House of Lords, I was appearing on TV and radio to argue the cause.

We loved our walks through these beautiful landscapes with some of the most expert conservationists in the country. These were far-sighted people working for the parks, or supporting them as volunteers, who really got that we can't protect the environment unless we can also enjoy it. And that the future of the planet is really our future – our health, wealth and quality of life are inextricably bound together. George was a champion of that philosophy and when he had to leave the House of Lords he also left behind a legacy for the Parks: new purposes; new independent bodies to run them and a new consensus about their protection.

FOREWORD

DAME FIONA REYNOLDS DBE
MASTER OF EMMANUEL COLLEGE CAMBRIDGE

Of all the members of the House of Lords who spoke up for National Parks in the 1980s and 1990s (and there were many) George Norrie was by far the most assiduous. He never missed an opportunity to raise a concern, move an amendment or speak about why National Parks matter. But by far his most important intervention was to secure the delivery of the recommendations of the Edwards Committee, the 1990 National Parks Review Panel of which I was a member, and whose ideas laid the foundation for a much better future for National Parks. But without George's efforts they would have been simply yet another worthy report sitting on a shelf. His determination, supported by the energetic and diligent staff of CNP, led first to his Private Member's Bill and thereby to the securing of Government commitments to legislate. As a result, the 1995 Environment Act established independent National Park Authorities and ushered in a new, more confident and better funded era for National Parks. Today, as I described in my book *The Fight for Beauty*, National Parks are a beacon of hope for a more sustainable future. They have demonstrated how to achieve the protection of beauty and public enjoyment while also meeting the needs of the local community and encouraging appropriate and innovative forms of tourism and other rural businesses. In fact, so successful are they that I argue they should be a model for managing all our beautiful, lightly populated rural areas. George Norrie, in his calm but passionately-felt devotion to National Parks, represents the best of Parliamentary advocacy, and is a reminder that if we care enough, and work hard enough, we will succeed in defending the values and places that we love, which bring such benefits to the people of this country.

PREFACE

There has been a lot of encouragement from my family to chronicle the various episodes in my life and to write something of a family history. After my retirement, I decided to make the effort and it has been an interesting and rewarding exercise. This book is not an autobiography in the conventional sense but more of a reflection of my journey through the years. It is supplemented by vignettes of family life up to and during the Second World War and the years that I spent with the family abroad in Australia and New Zealand. I have had the good fortune to have been engaged in a number of careers and different interests, all of which are recorded.

Reliving my life by writing these reflections has been a worthwhile experience and I do so in a contented and relaxed frame of mind. This is not a serious literary work but a story simply told for my own and my family's enjoyment. It has been a productive exercise being reminded of so much that otherwise might be forgotten. Twilight years are not to be feared if one can live with the companionship of such stimulating and happy memories and this I am now able to do. I am happy that the book also encompasses my life as a parliamentarian and some of the important issues in which I became involved, primarily my concerns for the environment and for National Parks. Dame Fiona Reynolds, with whom I have worked closely, makes some very salient points in her book 'The Fight for Beauty' which closely reflect my own opinions, that our incessant demands for materialistic gain are in danger of undermining not just the resources of this planet but our understanding of the importance of beauty and the spiritual gains to be won by its nurturing and simple contemplation.

If my children and grandchildren can have some of the fun that I have been privileged to enjoy, I shall rest content. As life comprises fun and sadness, some of my experiences may serve as a reminder that they too may find they will have to face up to the same sorts of challenges from which they will not escape! I hope they will regard some of these challenges as lessons rather than errors and be reminded of the quotation from James Joyce: 'a man's errors are his portals of discovery'.

ACKNOWLEDGEMENTS

This book would not have been written without the months of work and research put in by Vicki Elcoate who, in my eleven years as a working peer, drafted up my speeches in environmental debates and legislation. I would like to acknowledge too the contribution of Deborah Maby, Ruth Chambers, Amanda Nobbs and Alistair Black who researched and commented on more recent issues. Also, Susan Biggs, Maris Warrior and Valerie Gilkes each spent long hours typing at home. Brian Sherman has restored some wonderful old photographs.

I am indebted to Alison Chapman who, despite the daily responsibilities of her organic farm, gave many evenings to honing the text, and later to Nigel Goodrich. The last lap was completed by Hugh McMillan who ultimately brought the book to its colourful conclusion.

I would like to thank Sir Chris Bonington and Dame Fiona Reynolds, with whom I worked so closely in the 1990s in support of National Parks legislation, for writing forewords for this book.

Above all, I would like to show my immense gratitude to my wife Annie for the endless hours she has put in and her never-ending encouragement. She has helped me to see the pitfalls of overexposure to the general public and hopefully saved me from writing something that might prove disconcerting for my family, friends, business colleagues and fellow peers. As a published author, she has helped me to see how this whole unfolding experience became an unseen learning curve but also a lot of fun.

Finally, thanks go also to my publisher Jeremy Thompson and his team at The Book Guild Ltd for their patience and lasting faith in me.

MEMBERS OF THE NORRIE FAMILY REFERRED TO IN THIS BOOK

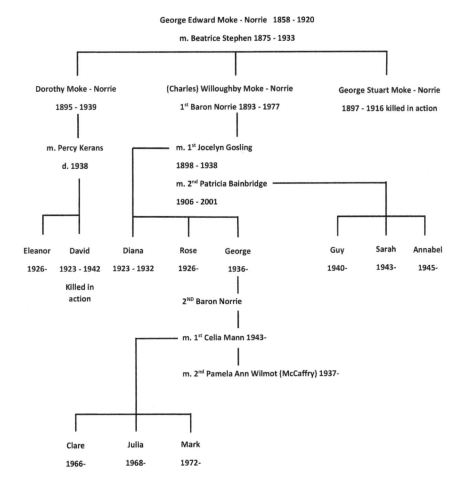

George Edward Moke - Norrie   1858 - 1920

m. Beatrice Stephen 1875 - 1933

Dorothy Moke - Norrie

1895 - 1939

(Charles) Willoughby Moke - Norrie

1st Baron Norrie 1893 - 1977

George Stuart Moke - Norrie

1897 - 1916 killed in action

m. Percy Kerans

d. 1938

m. 1st Jocelyn Gosling

1898 - 1938

m. 2nd Patricia Bainbridge

1906 - 2001

Eleanor   David   Diana   Rose   George   Guy   Sarah   Annabel

1926-   1923 - 1942   1923 - 1932   1926-   1936-   1940-   1943-   1945-

Killed in
action

2ND Baron Norrie

m. 1st Celia Mann 1943-

m. 2nd Pamela Ann Wilmot (McCaffry) 1937-

Clare   Julia   Mark

1966-   1968-   1972-

A MAN... MAKES NO MISTAKES; HIS ERRORS... ARE THE PORTALS OF DISCOVERY.

JAMES JOYCE

1

FACING A NEW REALITY

The telephone rang. I knew exactly who it would be. I lifted the receiver to hear the familiar voice of one of the clerks in the House of Lords.

'I promised to ring', he said. 'The results have just been read out in the Chamber. You were one vote under the cut. It was that close. You recorded eighty-eight votes. Eighty-nine would have secured you a place.'

I thanked him for his call, put the receiver down, and sat there numbed to the core. At the age of 63, and recently remarried, I reckoned I had just reached the most productive stage of my life, living and doing the things for which, it seemed, my earlier years had prepared me. My first marriage and home had already gone, and now my parliamentary career, office and secretarial support would follow suit. I would somehow have to accept that the familiar structure that had supported me for more than a decade had now come to an end. I was being compelled to leave the comfort zone to which I had become so accustomed, to face a disconcertingly uncertain future which I had made no plans at all to deal with.

From that telephone call, and through the weeks that followed, countless memories began to flood back of the last eleven years. I had to admit to myself that I would miss the House of Lords a great deal. It seemed like only yesterday that I had made my maiden speech. Mentally I rewound the hands of the clock back to 1977 when, three months after my father had died, I received the letters patent. This allowed me the customary right to enter the Palace of Westminster and sit in the House of Lords Chamber. Little did I think back then that all this would be cut short, leaving me to face another fundamental upheaval.

All the profound wisdom and knowledge of my fellow peers, from all sides of the House, was no longer there to support my ideas and decisions.

Gone were the immeasurable support from the clerks with their wise counsel on procedural matters; the librarians with their research skills; the friendly and efficient staff from the dining room and bar; the administration staff who ensured that mail and messages reached me; and, lastly, the 24 doorkeepers, in their distinctive attire of tail coats, white ties and a gilded chain, who maintained the decorum of the House at all times, and who had become a constant aid to my life in Parliament. Most were retired and of warrant officer rank from the services, so as a former army officer myself, there was a mutual respect.

Gone too was the coveted perk to invite guests to attend House of Lords Question Time, organised through Black Rod's office. The position of Black Rod is chosen from a selection of recently retired generals, air marshals or admirals. He is responsible for all non-parliamentary administration in the House of Lords, including the State Opening of Parliament, and the security that accompanies it. This aspect has become much more necessary since 9/11, the London bombings and now the terrorist threats of ISIS. When on duty he is always attired in black: a cut-away coat, knee breeches, silk stockings, shoe buckles and sword. A black wand, or rod of office, signifies his appointment, and hence gives him his name.

Lastly, I would miss immensely the incomparable sense of place that I was privileged to have experienced as a parliamentarian. More than just a building or workplace, the Palace of Westminster had become my second home. As a part of the State Opening of Parliament, the Queen passes through the Queen's Robing Room, the Royal Gallery, the Prince's Chamber and the House of Lords Chamber itself. Over the years I found that the more I accompanied guests invited to view this royal 'line of route', the more I began to feel a deep wish to pass on what I had learned about the history and traditions of this remarkable place, including many anecdotal stories, so often gleaned from the doorkeepers and official guides.

One of the more amusing stories told by the doorkeepers concerned Lord Hailsham and his rather scruffy Jack Russell terrier that followed him around the House when he was Lord Chancellor. Only guide dogs and police sniffer dogs are normally allowed in the Palace of Westminster, but I supposed that from the seniority of Black Rod downwards, the thought of asking Lord Hailsham to remove his dog from the Palace was unthinkable. The story goes that His Lordship entered the Chamber one day, followed by the dog, looking for papers he thought he had left by the Woolsack, on which he would sit and preside at Question Time later that afternoon. The terrier jumped on to the Woolsack and busied himself sniffing around, before following his agitated master as he left. On the days when the House sits, the doors of the Chamber are locked whenever a sniffer dog is brought in to search for bombs or other explosive devices. The dog had been trained by his handler to jump onto the Woolsack and sit facing the Chamber door, emulating the Lord Chancellor. This spectacle would cause great amusement to any other member of the police or staff present. On this particular morning, the dog in question, a black Labrador, jumped onto the Woolsack, sensed the very recent visit from the Jack Russell and, as if to reaffirm sovereignty of its own perceived territory, cocked its leg several times in quick succession. Whilst the red cloth of the Woolsack may have looked dry on the outside, the reality was the opposite. At the end of Question Time, the Lord Chancellor rose from his seat, bowed to the chairman of committees, and left. As he did so it was clear that in feverishly rubbing his posterior, his breeches and black robe had been penetrated by rising damp!

In the era before 9/11, guests wishing to sit in the public gallery simply had to sign a book giving their names and addresses. Nowadays, however, photographic identification and a thorough airport-style security check is required. This story tells of a well-dressed young man, who prior to Question Time, signed the book as 'Prince Charles, Buckingham Palace' and took a seat in the front row overlooking the Chamber. During the second question it looked as though this imposter was about to stand up and speak. One of the two doorkeepers on duty had the presence of mind to step forward and say in a quiet but resolute voice, 'Your Royal Highness, I have just received a message from Her Majesty the Queen requiring that you return to Buckingham Palace immediately'. He rose straight away, politely thanked the doorkeeper and walked sedately from the public gallery. A possible intervention and embarrassment had been averted.

One evening I found myself being the object of amusement. I was having a leisurely dinner in the Peers' Dining Room located within a minute of the Chamber. Several amendments tabled in my name were due to be debated in the course of the evening. I was carefully watching the closed-circuit television monitor which showed numerically which amendment was being debated. When the House sits late, I was soon to learn to my cost, peers have the habit of deciding not to move their amendments, waiting instead to debate them at the next stage of the bill. This is what happened that evening. Watching the monitor suddenly became like watching the Tote screen at a racecourse showing the swift accumulation of stakes placed on horses fancied in the coming race. The numbers on the monitor increased in quick succession from 150 to 175 in a matter of seconds.

I remember running from the table at breakneck speed to the entrance of the Chamber where, breathless, I heard the words 'Amendment 197A – Lord Norrie' called out. I hurried to the first available Conservative bench. In my haste I tripped and fell headlong, scattering my briefing papers in all directions.

I can remember shouting in response, unseen at floor level from under the bench: 'Speaking to Amendment 197A now I have finally found my f... f... four pages of notes.' Thankfully the TV crews had gone home. There were smiles and muffled laughter from the benches on all sides of the House. That same incident today would have been in danger of appearing live on the BBC TV Parliament channel.

One recorded incident I would dearly liked to have witnessed concerned the infamous Section 28 of the Local Government Act 1988, which some interpreted as being a dishonourable piece of homophobic legislation. It was an attempt by the Conservative government to suppress the growing visibility of lesbian and gay culture and to stop the so-called promotion of homosexuality through teaching or publishing. The original legislation began as a Private Members' Bill introduced in the House of Lords by Earl Halsbury in 1986. When the bill was passed in the House (with 202 votes for and 122 against) protestors in the public gallery began heaping abuse on those present, whilst three lesbians clad in black abseiled down into the chamber, shouting *'Lesbians are out!'* Three House of Lords doorkeepers tried to quell the protest, and in the chaos two of the three abseilers managed to walk out of the Chamber unchallenged. Irritatingly, I was not there at the time to see the fun and had to be satisfied with watching the spectacle on television that evening.

Now looking back on my time in the House, I do so with feelings of warmth and appreciation towards an institution that gave me great confidence in myself and my abilities. This feeling was shared by many other hereditary peers, whose recorded votes also remained below the cut and, like me, knew that they had to leave. I hoped at least that I had done justice to my father's legacy, whose valiant defence of and service to his country had been honoured by the granting of a hereditary peerage. Those of us not elected were given three weeks in which to empty our offices, say goodbye to all those faithful staff, and leave the Palace of Westminster for good. I vacated my desk to Lord Lamont, the former Chancellor of the Exchequer. My children have often asked me how I felt when I left on that last day. Above all, I had a profound sense of powerlessness, as if my legs had been cut off at the knees.

2

BIG BOOTS TO FILL

As the elder son of a distinguished desert general, later Governor General of New Zealand, I grew up ever conscious that I had very large boots to fill. Charles Willoughby Moke-Norrie, known as Willoughby, and sometimes 'Widdy' as a nickname, was born on 26th September 1893 at 62 Queen's Gate, London SW7, a substantial four-storey Georgian house which he shared as the family home with his parents, brother and sister until he left to join the army. My paternal grandfather George Edward Moke-Norrie was a Boer War veteran and a well-known big game hunter. My grandmother Beatrice was descended from the family of Glasgow shipbuilders Alexander Stephen & Sons.

I never knew the house, but fondly remember a story told by my father about the dining room. At some stage in his life, my grandfather had shot an elephant, the huge head of which had been superbly mounted by Rowland Ward the taxidermist. Its trunk, quoted my father, extended well out over the dining room table and required a steel-backed support to strengthen the holding. Guests would walk into the dining room without noticing it and then suddenly look up from their seat at the table and exclaim, 'My god, I have seen an elephant!'

My father was educated at Summer Fields, a preparatory school near Oxford, before going to Eton. In 1964, he dictated a story to his secretary about his first school:

I found golf, which I had learnt under Pierre Chevalier at Saint Briac in Brittany during the holidays, very useful at Summer Fields. I reached the final of the school golf championship against Eric Ednam, now the Earl of Dudley. Eric's father, who had been Governor General of Australia, was a keen golfer.

6

As we went round the course, Eric said: 'Look, Willoughby, I am going to have the devil of a bad report this term.' He paused and glanced at me. 'I suppose – you wouldn't …'

'You mean let you win?'

He nodded, rather embarrassed. 'Well, you see, it's more important for me than to you, isn't it? It would make all the difference in my standing with my father if only I could win this championship.'

As it happened, I did miss a 12-inch pot at the last hole and Eric was victor by one stroke.

The then Lord Dudley was more than delighted and went round his London clubs saying, 'My son has won the boys' golf championship at Summer Fields and I am going to present a silver medal each year to perpetuate this competition.' Alas, when he died in 1930 he forgot to leave any money to pay for this annual trophy, which is still known as the Dudley Medal. Consequently, it was Eric who found himself having to reach deep into his pocket and pay out a substantial sum for the medal each year. Supporting the competition came at a cost!

After attending Eton and completing his officer training at Sandhurst in 1914, my father was commissioned into the 11th Hussars. Later that same year on 1st September he helped make his name by capturing the first German guns of the Great War in a cavalry charge for which he was awarded the Military Cross. The story, with a sequel, deserves telling.

At the time, the British Expeditionary Force was falling back towards Paris. On 31st August 1914, British units crossed the River Aisne to the south between Soisson and Compiegne. The 1st Cavalry Brigade, consisting of the 2nd Dragoon Guards (the Queen's Bays), the 5th Dragoon Guards, the 11th Hussars and L Battery Royal Horse Artillery bivouacked in the village of Néry barely 40 miles north-east from the outskirts of the capital, with orders to move at first light. A dense summer mist, which occasionally cleared mid-morning, usually kept visibility to a minimum. Although contact with the enemy had been lost, a German patrol had reported the existence of a sizable British force without any obvious defence. During the night, as a result of this information, an artillery regiment from the 1st German Cavalry division placed 12 of its guns with six machine guns in support, on a plateau only 800 metres from the village.

The night prior to the ensuing battle, L Battery had been the last unit of the 1st Cavalry Brigade to arrive at Néry and had been billeted in an open field without any protection. Thus when the German artillery, had opened fire at 0540 hours through the thick mist, the effect had been devastating as shrapnel exploded in-between horses and men, ultimately killing or maiming 5 officers, 49 other ranks and 150 horses. L Battery's six guns were soon reduced to three and after two more direct hits, only one gun remained in action. It was manned by three brave men for more than an hour until the last round had been expended. All three of these men were awarded the Victoria Cross, one posthumously. The German artillery were beginning now to find their position on the plateau rather vulnerable. L Battery had caused considerable damage to their guns and they also found themselves within range of the accurate fire from the British machine gunners, which prevented the horse teams from withdrawing them to safety. Three German counterattacks had failed in taking the village and their own flank suffered severe casualties from an assault by the 5th Dragoon Guards. As the supply of ammunition was running low, the German battery was ordered to withdraw to safety, and it was then that my father was given orders to charge the gun position.

In the 1950s Southern Television ran a series of First World War programmes in which he participated, which included the Battle of Néry. Long afterwards, he was invited to present a paper on the battle to senior officers of the Royal Artillery at Woolwich because of the brave role played by L Battery of the Royal Horse Artillery. In the text of his presentation my father said:

> With drawn swords and a rousing cheer, No. 3 troop galloped through the enemy. Quite a few shell-shaken German personnel were about at the end and one of them had been run through by my troop sergeant, Sergeant Hailey, for failing to put up his hands or shout 'Kamerad'.
>
> When I was invited to speak about Néry on Southern Television I included the reference to the sticking of the unfortunate German by Sergeant Hailey. Later, I received quite a large batch of fan-mail but also two letters protesting about the cruel use of the sword and signing themselves as members of an anti-blood sport society!

Amongst prisoners taken in the battle were two civilian German doctors, with whom my father had to converse in French. One of the doctors had protested strongly that my father was contravening the Geneva Convention by confiscating his handsome grey mare and his brand new pair of Carl Zeiss field glasses which had been given to him by his Berlin mistress. On being shown a copy of the Convention printed in French, my father retorted that doctors had no need to possess loaded revolvers or the three boxes of ammunition found in an ambulance. There was no argument, and he would take both! My father always said that their conversation was quite amicable, the German doctor hoping his charger might be repatriated and his field glasses returned after the war. Much to my father's annoyance, he was unable to stop the grey mare from being transferred to the 13th Hussars, a regiment now desperately short of horses; but he made sure that he kept the Zeiss field glasses. Years after the war ended, the field glasses and their leather case went missing or were stolen. About ten years ago I was telephoned by a friend, who had discovered on eBay a pair of Zeiss field glasses for sale, inscribed with the words 'Captain C.W.M. Norrie, 11th Hussars (PAO)'. I agreed to a substantial bid on my behalf. Just before time ran out, a new bid for the field glasses appeared on the screen, twice the figure I was prepared to offer. I discovered later that the new owner lived in Germany. I believe today that the Zeiss field glasses are back in the hands of the German doctor's family, and that at some moment during their conversation, my father had revealed his name. Modern technology and the Internet accounted for the rest.

I was invited to the centenary celebrations at Néry, and before the church service on the very ground where L Battery had been decimated, I stood on the edge of the ravine looking down at the spot where my father and his troop had waited for the command ordering him to prepare to charge the guns. On the far side of the ravine, a white screen marked the position of the German guns 800 metres away. My father and his troop would have had to dismount and lead their horses up the steep side of the ravine. They would have had to remount, line up on the plateau without any form of cover, and gallop over 300 yards of open country. As I stood, the sun broke through and lifted the mist just as it had done over a century ago. That precise moment, for me, said it all.

Whereas my father had all the luck in surviving the war, my father's younger brother, Uncle George, was less fortunate. He was killed in an assault on the German trenches during the Battle of the Somme on 7th October 1916, just before his nineteenth birthday. He had been commissioned as a Second Lieutenant into the East Kent Regiment (The Buffs), an infantry battalion. The premature end to his life must have caused great pain for my grandparents, and understandable concern that their eldest son Willoughby might suffer the same fate. When my father received the fateful telegram from my grandfather, he wrote letters to both my grandparents. These were dated 18th October 1916 and written from HQ 73 Infantry Brigade.

My darling Mummie,

Poor little Georgie. I got Daddy's wire after lunch yesterday and before I had opened it, I felt I knew what it was. I tried to write to you yesterday – I know you must be heart-broken and so am I. Nothing in the world can make up for him but you and all of us must be brave and bear it, for his sake. I loved Georgie very dearly and I cannot believe we are not going to see him again or get his letters.

When I returned there were several letters from Georgie, all of them full of happiness and life. It is of great comfort to know that Georgie died as happy as this and I am sure he was very brave. My Darling Mummie. I am so frightfully sorry for you – I know how perfectly devoted Georgie was to you and how much you will feel it.

I am so thankful I saw Georgie near Albert last August – he was looking so well and enjoying it all. I am sure he was as brave as any man, as far as the fighting and shelling was concerned. Georgie said he liked it and I am sure he meant it. This is the last letter I had from him dated 6-10-16.

The letter from Uncle George to my father read as follows:

My Dear Widdie,

We go over tomorrow at 4 p.m. 'A A A'. We first take the Hun trenches 200 yards in front, then go for 1,000 yards and build a new trench just below the ridge – so will gain nearly a mile!

I don't like the idea of building ourselves in, do you? We don't expect much opposition from the Hun in front of us: my platoon is third over in my company: every third man carries a pick! We are still in the reserve line and go up to the front line tonight! I have to go on patrol tonight to find out how strongly held the Hun trench is!

The whole of the 4th Army has a stunt on tomorrow afternoon and also part of the French. It is fairly fine today. A Hun aeroplane has just had the cheek to come right over the reserve line at a height of about 400 feet. It did not stay very long but we expect to be shelled now any moment. We had two killed and several casualties while digging a communication trench. No other news – we only knew this morning the division was going to attack. Where are you now?

Best luck.

Your loving brother
Georgie

My father had added a footnote to the letter, saying:

If it had to be, I am sure Georgie would have chosen this way to die – the most glorious and the only way to die in war: actually being killed did not frighten him, his only thoughts being for the sorrow it would cause you.

Georgie has now done his duty and I am certain he is now in God's hands. It is our duty to Georgie to be brave, to follow his quiet example and to think that we will one day all meet again in a better and more peaceful world. My poor Mummie, I feel utterly helpless to do anything for you but I know you will be brave. The General has been very kind to me and so has everyone else.

Best love to Daddy, Dorothy and yourself

Your loving son – Widdy

My father wrote to my grandfather the same day:

My dearest Daddy,

I got your wire yesterday afternoon: poor Georgie has died the most glorious death a man can – one ought to be proud of his example but it is hard to bear the aching loss.

He had done so awfully well out here and all the experience was doing him such a world of good. I used to get letters from him every week, all of them full of happiness and life. George looked so splendid and well when I saw him near Albert in August.

Georgie knew what a good Father you have been to us both and it is a great comfort to think that Georgie died so happily and bravely. I am sending you his last letter written the day before he was killed: this shows you what a splendid son you had. I feel so sorry for you and poor Mummie but I am sure you will both be brave about it. I am sure poor Georgie would have wished this.

Best love and let me know any details when you hear. Georgie was killed the day we took Le Sars.

Your ever loving son
Widdy

The year 2014 marked the centenary of the beginning of the Great War, when television and radio considered in depth the personal accounts of inner and outer conflict facing young soldiers of Uncle George's age in the trenches. Anyone reading his letters would naturally be struck by his boyish enthusiasm, expressed with a flurry of exclamation marks, 'all of them full of happiness and life', as my father put it. Despite his outward jollity and verve, he must have hidden his innermost anxieties and kept them to himself. At the same time, my father writes that the experience was 'doing him a world of good', but was he truly convinced by his own upbeat correspondence to his parents? Certainly, Uncle George must have experienced a harsh transition from youthful innocence to an enforced maturity. He was in awe of his elder brother, who had already proved himself a gallant soldier, and perhaps George hoped to have the opportunity to make his own mark. When the whistle blew for his platoon to climb the ladders and advance 200 yards to the first German trench did he really believe that the artillery barrage that accompanied their advance would silence the German machine gunners to their front? The moment of truth must have been terrifying. I just pray that this experience was as brief as possible. His platoon was virtually wiped out within minutes of their advance.

Uncle George is buried in Bancourt British Cemetery near Calais, which was designed by Sir Edwin Lutyens. Bancourt was occupied by the Commonwealth forces in March 1917. I often wonder, looking at a photograph of my uncle, how he must have felt prior to leading his platoon to certain death under the merciless fire of the German machine guns just

200 yards in front. Writing this book and considering the teenaged uncle, whose Christian name I carry but whom I never knew, casts a long shadow over me.

★★★

UNCLE GEORGE, 1914.

My father returned from the war with an MC and bar as well as a DSO. He had been mentioned in dispatches twice and wounded four times. He also returned with a desire to change the family surname by deed poll to plain Norrie. Three years later he met and married my mother. Jocelyn Gosling, known to her friends as Jo, was the youngest of four sisters. Before her engagement to my father, two of her sisters had already married serving cavalry officers, and the remaining one a Cheshire landowner. Jocelyn was a keen horsewoman much encouraged by her father, Richard Henry Gosling of Hawthorn Hill Bracknell, a joint master of the Garth Fox Hounds. The prospect of marrying a dashing young cavalry officer who shared the same interests would surely have been a strong draw to her. Her lively personality would stand her in good stead as an army officer's wife and she proved to be a huge support to my father until her early death.

Jocelyn was a direct descendant of the Gosling banking family. Goslings Bank was established in 1650 by Henry Pinckney. Until its merger with Barclays in 1896, its London premises remained at 19 Fleet Street. From 1822 the printed bank cheques were distinctive with a three-squirrel motif, a design copied from the fan-shaped window over the bank's front door. The bank expanded enormously at the time of the Industrial Revolution and Britain's interest in India. George Clive, one of the partners, was related to Robert, Lord Clive of India and had been introduced to Warren Hastings, India's first governor general. As a client, Warren Hastings would have brought in a great deal of business. The firm became one of high standing and Francis Gosling, the alderman, whose portrait I have, was knighted for his services to banking in 1760.

Before marrying my mother in 1922, my father had already become an acclaimed amateur rider, winning many point-to-points and steeplechases. When stationed with the army in India in the 1930s, he became a four-goal polo player, reduced his golf handicap to five and was well known for his pig-sticking exploits (a somewhat graphic term probably offensive to modern sensitivities). There was one occasion when he was hunting buck close to the River Ganges when a large boar broke from the high reeds to attack him. After splintering his lance in wounding the animal, he grabbed a rifle from his groom waiting nearby before the animal was able to gore him. He cracked the rifle butt over the boar's head with such force that the weapon broke in two. The boar lay dazed for some moments and my father finished the job by removing a stirrup iron from the saddle and beating the animal on the head until it lay senseless. The boar's head now hangs menacingly in the hallway at my home, with the bent stirrup hung over its neck. This incident certainly became a topic of conversation for some time afterwards and the event was reported in the British press.

My father, who had been originally commissioned into the 11th Hussars, had the honour in 1931 of being asked personally by King George V, then Colonel-in-Chief of the 10th Hussars, to command that regiment in Meerut, India. By this time my parents had two daughters, Diana and Rose, aged seven and four. It was decided that both would remain in England, looked after by a nanny known as Nanny Wiltshire.

They lived in rooms in Swanage, moving later to Weymouth, where the accommodation was even more spartan. There were two bedrooms, one of which Diana and Rose shared; Nanny Wiltshire occupied the other. There was no heating, the furniture provided was minimal and the floor was laid with bare lino. The bathroom, where a large hot water geyser had been installed, was the only place that offered any warmth. Meals were prepared and cooked by the owner's staff and brought up to the nursery.

At the age of eight Diana was sent to Lytchett Manor boarding school in Dorset. With their parents abroad, unless the girls had been invited to stay with friends or relatives elsewhere, their holidays too were spent in Weymouth. Sometimes aunts and close friends of my parents went to visit. I expect they felt it their duty to write and report to my parents in India to say that both girls were alive and well.

My mother apparently was paranoid about Diana and Rose picking up germs, especially when Diana went to Lytchett School. For this reason, Nanny Wiltshire was instructed not to take the girls into shops or even to meet the owners of the house living in the basement. The school insisted that Rose should wear winter vests all through the summer term to reduce exposure to infection.

Life for my parents, meanwhile, in Meerut proved a social whirl from noon till night. Polo matches were played in the cool of the evening, bringing families together. Friends and relations of many army officers visited India during the temperate months when England was so cold. Known in my father's time as the 'the Fishing Fleet', bevies of young ladies would arrive with their parents, searching for suitable husbands. There was no shortage of dashing young bachelors ready to court them. My parents were friends of the Vaughans, whose nanny, Nanny Batty, looked after their only daughter Joan. The complications of living abroad, children's welfare and education were freely discussed amongst them all, whilst watching the polo.

These exchanges, particularly with Nanny Batty, were later to prove a solace for my mother after receiving the devastating news in December 1932 of Diana's death from pneumonia at school. It was during Rose's first term at Lytchett that the headmistress called her to the office to tell her of the death of her sister. She said 'Rose, come and sit down, I have some very sad news for you so you must be brave. As you know Diana has been sick in hospital. She has now gone to heaven. Here is a chocolate biscuit.'

The school staff and boarders were deeply shocked. Rose only remembers leaving the school in a daze clasping the hand of her Aunt Beryl, her mother's sister. In the back of the car was Diana's trunk with all her belongings. There was no mention to Rose of Diana's funeral. My parents must have been devastated at the loss of their elder daughter, there having been no prior warning of her illness. Due to their being in India, they could neither attend their daughter's funeral nor comfort Rose. The journey home by ship from Bombay, via the Suez Canal and Marseille to Southampton, would have taken at least three weeks.

My mother and the teaching staff became so concerned that Rose might also become ill that it was decided that, rather than board in school, she should remain in Weymouth for the following term. On returning to school in May, she was segregated from her friends to sleep in total isolation, to prevent her from catching any infection from the other children. I am sure that this would have emphasised Rose's loneliness and vulnerability.

Three years later, in 1935, my father's tour of duty in India commanding the 10th Hussars came to an end. My mother decided to precede my father back to England. She was accompanied by Mrs Vaughan. Joan had already returned, accompanied by Nanny Batty, in order to start boarding at Lytchett herself. In the course of the journey my mother asked Mrs Vaughan if she could approach Nanny Batty with a view to employing her. Mrs Vaughan was enthusiastic, but not as much as my mother, who was by now expecting her third child, me.

3

BIRTH AND DEATH

Although my parents may have returned from India under the threat of impending war, their arrival back in England coincided with a patchy but steady upturn in the economy. What was really underpinning economic recovery was the manufacture of arms. Between 1933 and 1938 the government spent £1.2 billion on defence. By 1936, despite this massive expenditure, output was climbing, wages were stable and unemployment had fallen to under 2 million. For the white-collar workers and skilled men, life had become quite rosy.

Many families could now afford to buy their own house, a semi-detached with bathroom, garage and garden costing something in the region of £450. Mortgages were cheap enough at 4.5 per cent interest and tax as low as the £500 a year income level, with the Chancellor imposing less than 10 per cent in direct taxation. It was possible now to afford a vacuum cleaner, radio, gramophone, refrigerator, electric fire, washing machine, and even a Morris car for the princely sum of £150. On the farm there were changes too in the form of new machinery such as tractors, the first combine harvesters, and milking machines that a man and boy could operate. Britain was changing rapidly. My parents must have felt strangely out of touch with the economic change in England. Life based in India had been routine, slow-moving and easy-going.

The good news of the economic upturn also heralded my arrival in the world at 6.42 pm on 27th April 1936, at Pax Hill in Hampshire, the home of Lord Baden-Powell, a retired general and the Chief Scout. My father had rented the house to enjoy his two months' leave after serving in India, and before taking up his next appointment as a brigadier at Aldershot to command the 1st Cavalry Brigade and to live at Anglesey

House. I was christened George Willoughby Moke Norrie. Princess Alice, Duchess of Gloucester, a close friend of my mother, was among my many godparents, her husband Prince Henry being an officer of the 10th Hussars, which regiment my father had just commanded in India. Both families, were living in Aldershot, the Gloucesters in the wooden Royal Pavilion originally built for Queen Victoria to review troops of the British Army.

Although less private, Anglesey House was more spacious than Pax Hill. In 1936 a brigadier was entitled to quite a sizeable staff. Two ex-11th Hussars looked after my father's needs as civilians. Hunter, with his well-Brylcreamed short black hair, used to valet my father's uniforms and breeches, polish his boots, as well as drive the official car. Blythe, also short but with considerably less hair, acted as the major-domo in the house and was responsible for its smooth running. Once established, the staff had increased to include a bad-tempered Irish cook with curly red hair, who apparently used to hurl abuse and sometimes any kitchen utensil to hand, at the kitchen maid. Nobody seemed to mind much!

An addition to the staff, who acted as a four-legged security guard, was Remur, a Belgian barge dog who belonged to Hunter, black and very furry with a white patch on her chest. Whilst normally docile, she had the habit of stalking anything unfamiliar, including visitors. She would lie close by when I was asleep in my pram. I learned to walk and keep my balance by holding on to the scruff of her neck. Remur's companion, Rags, was a male Sealyham white wire-haired terrier who was utterly devoted to my mother. He disliked letting her out of his sight. My mother enjoyed sitting peacefully on the oak bench in the garden with the dogs running around. I can picture her with her head bent in contemplation, possibly considering Rose's future now that Diana had died. Nanny Batty, now happily installed *chez* Norrie, took on responsibility for looking after Rose's young friends, including Joan Vaughan who often stayed for much of the holidays. My mother was very aware of Joan's attachment to Nanny, and included her whenever possible.

In those days, Nanny remembered us both regularly walking to the stables to see my father's horses, cared for by Hyde the groom, who would lift me up on to the largest one, some 16 hands high, leaving the ground a terrifying distance below. During this period cavalry regiments were undergoing mechanisation, having to relinquish their horses for armoured cars and light tanks. Hyde also doubled up as an extra valet, looking after the numerous pairs of hunting boots.

There was apparently a small metal model of a Vickers Mark IV light tank, which had been lent to my father, and used to sit on a table at home and for which I had a fascination. At a later stage, I was taken to see a military display of operational light tanks on the parade ground at Aldershot. I suspect that this was a show of force to impress the general public. My father had been stationed here before the First World War when the 11th Hussars had been part of the 1st Cavalry Brigade. One story he used to tell concerned Viscount Allenby, the Inspector General of Cavalry, who at that time took the brigade's annual inspection. One mounted squadron represented each cavalry regiment. Known as 'The Bull', Lord Allenby's fierce reputation terrified many officers before they had even made his acquaintance. In an old file my father had written:

> When he had reached my squadron, he turned to Jeffrey Lockett, the officer commanding, and pointing to a soldier he said:
> 'Why has that man got no socks on?'
> Jeffrey, red in the face, replied: 'I think he has, Sir.'
> General Allenby ordered the soldier to dismount from his horse and take off his right boot. No socks!
> Jeffrey kept his head and said: 'How on earth did you know that, Sir?'
> The Bull replied: 'He was my servant for four years and never wore socks then.' Whatever his threatening exterior, The Bull had a sense of humour.

It was my father's sense of humour and fun that prompted him to practise Rose in the basics of public speaking, bemoaning that it was not a subject taught at school. As a circus act for friends, she was encouraged and rehearsed by my father to speak on such off-beat subjects as the merits of the mechanisation of the cavalry regiments, followed by a short dissertation entitled 'Eat more fish – it's good for the brain', for which occasion my father made her dress up in a mackintosh and sou'wester. Rose says today that these early experiences proved to be good grounding for her public service in later life. Her skills were tested at the age of 18 when, as the eldest of the family, she made a speech on opening a new extension to Adelaide Zoo, extolling the alluring virtues of the native koala bear.

MY FATHER WITH THE DUKE & DUCHESS
OF GLOUCESTER.

Nanny sometimes took me for a walk to the Royal Pavilion to see Princess Alice. On one particular day Prince Henry was in the garden sweeping up leaves. Whilst Nanny and Princess Alice were talking, unnoticed I was busily dismantling Prince Henry's heaps with a second rake which I had found on the grass.

Seeing me prompted him to shout, 'Take that boy away and do something with him – show him the parrot.' I was lead off to see a pink-grey parrot, already of an age, that had been inherited from King George V. I often wonder now if this was his much-loved African grey parrot Charlotte, that been bought in Port Said when the King had been serving as a midshipman in the Royal Navy. I admired it in its cage at a distance, remembering I had been nipped on a previous occasion by a green parakeet.

My father was always a practical joker and thankfully my parents shared each other's humour. I can see this trait in myself. My father loved dressing up. He arranged a dinner party, so the story goes, for close friends and, with my mother's collusion, pretended that he was unable to join the party until after dinner. Whereupon, with the help of someone from a local amateur dramatic society, he successfully disguised himself as an Indian manservant, complete with *puggree*, a colourful turban. For half an hour he served cocktails to the assembled company with great decorum and on the dot of 8.15 pm, bowed and announced dinner. As the guests filed in to the dining room, he disappeared to the kitchen area. Next – within minutes – the sound of shattering china on a hard floor rather indicated that the entrée might never reach the dining room. The guests held their breath until the main course was brought in. My father, now fed up with domestic service, attempted to join in the conversation around the dinner table. The guests sat tight, not wishing to offend, even though the situation appeared to be getting out of hand. His costume and make-up were so convincing that no one recognised him until he removed his *puggree*, whereupon the entire dinner party dissolved into laughter.

He seemed to enjoy the element of danger in balancing risk with fun. A further example of this was during the colourful event of the annual Aldershot Tattoo, which was held in the summer, lasted a week, and although not a dressy affair attracted many people. In fact, through its scale and spectacle, Aldershot remained the premier tattoo in the UK during the intervening war years. For a bit of fun my mother suggested to Nanny that she might like to see one of the afternoon performances, but

21

with a twist – the idea was to dress Nanny in a shawl-sari so that she would appear to be an Indian dignitary. My mother then sent Nanny off to the event, ensconced in the back seat of the staff car, with Hunter at the wheel, and my father, as the princess's personal escort, dressed in civilian clothes in the front. As the car approached the entrance, they were stopped by two sentries. My father wound down the window, winked, and pointing to Nanny in the back saying 'Princess Chickybooboo', whereupon both men saluted smartly and promptly lifted the barrier. Nanny swept through, and escorted by my father to her seat in the royal box, sat down to enjoy the spectacle of 1,500 musicians from the massed bands of the Aldershot Command playing and marching in front of a full-sized model of Caernarvon Castle.

In March 1938 my parents were preparing to attend a 10th Hussars warrant officers' and sergeants' mess dance in Aldershot. My mother had not been well for the last month or so, and was suffering from a chest virus, but she was insistent on accompanying my father. The evening was a roaring success, and everyone enjoyed themselves. But my mother's health did not improve. Within a few days her condition was very much worse and she appeared to be going downhill fast. Prince Henry as a close friend suggested that his doctor, Lord Horder, could give further advice. He arrived promptly from London and spent considerable time with my mother and father. Everyone was very worried.

On leaving the bedroom, he met Nanny on the stairs and said, 'I am so sorry – there is nothing more I can do for her.'

Within twenty-four hours my mother had died of pneumonia, and the household descended into gloom. My father had thus suffered a third family death: he had lost his only brother George during the Great War, then his first-born Diana, and now his young wife Jo. How would he deal with this overwhelming despair?

Once again, Rose was left in the dark, nothing was said in case it upset her. She was despatched to stay with Aunt Beryl whilst Nanny and I – aged 18 months – remained behind at Anglesey House. My mother was buried at Lytchett, the village she knew so well, and next to Diana. Many officers and other ranks of the 10th and 11th Hussars attended the funeral. This must have been unbearably harrowing for my father.

My own health during this period was causing alarm. Since birth my digestion had always been weak, and caused Nanny a lot of worry. Like

FRONT ROW: MY MOTHER, NANNY AND THE AUTHOR.
TOP LEFT: ROSE.

everyone else, I was reared on Cow & Gate powdered milk, most likely too rich for my constitution. I was duly taken to see Dr Dewsbury in Harley Street, who confided to Nanny that my sickness could have been directly connected to my mother's low physical and emotional state during her pregnancy. There were occasions when my very survival seemed to be in doubt. Prince Henry came to visit one evening.

'Come up to the nursery and see Boy,' (as I was nicknamed), my father said proudly.

On arriving somewhat breathless at the top of the stairs he viewed me in Nanny's arms for a few moments, and retorted, 'He doesn't look very strong, does he?'

His observation proved to be accurate, as the following week I was back in hospital with Nanny in the room next door. After copious tests the doctor concluded that my digestive difficulties would settle down by the age of four. This actually did happen.

After my mother died, my father seemed to lose his zest for life. According to Rose, Jocelyn had said that should she ever die, in her opinion, the as yet unmarried Patricia Bainbridge would be an ideal wife and stepmother. As it was, she died on 7th March 1938, and my father did indeed marry Patricia on 28th November.

We all moved into her house, Upton Grove in Gloucestershire, now to be our new home. Set in parkland about 2 miles north of Tetbury, it was a nineteenth-century house built of traditional grey Cotswold stone. The formal garden, partly bordered by clipped yew hedges, had two ornamental ponds full of white water lilies and goldfish. I smile remembering the mulberry tree on the lawn in front of the house, bearing abundant fruit whose staining powers defeated the wits of even the best dry cleaners! A semi-circular ha-ha wall divided the garden from the park, and to the south the high spire of Tetbury church was just visible above the trees. The first-floor chapel was converted into a bedroom and there was a cellar reputed to be the original entrance to a priest hole constructed during the Cromwellian era. I recall it being cold and damp, and firmly out of bounds for young boys.

Adjacent to the house were a number of two-storey outbuildings that included garages and stables with converted flats above. The farm at Upton was some distance from the house, and was surrounded by 500 acres of good-quality agricultural land. There was also a herd of 40 milking cows and a large poultry enterprise. Whereas tractors were used minimally, two black Clydesdales, Prince and Danny, pulled their respective carts and carried out the ploughing.

When I was young I was unable to pronounce my 'p's or 't's very well, and the name of my new stepmother – Patricia – was quite tricky for me to say, so it got reduced to Risha. In time I gave up the struggle and just called her 'Mum'. It must have been daunting to inherit an instant family of two stepchildren, two dogs and a nanny, not to mention my father, to which were added three new children, but she rose to the occasion seemingly effortlessly. At a later date Eleanor and David Kerans, wards of court, joined the family too, after both their parents, Dorothy and Colonel Percy Kerans, died. Eleanor, who was the same age as Rose, came to live with us on a permanent basis, becoming another older sister to me. David had just left school and was called up for military service, so I saw little of him.

Patricia's father, Emerson Bainbridge, became Liberal MP for Gainsborough from 1885 to 1900, following a successful career in mining. As a quintessential Edwardian country gentleman, he divided his time between political duties in London and his estates in Scotland and Northumberland. From her father Patricia inherited her positive attitude to life and a deep love of the countryside, and especially Scotland. It was here that he had taught his daughter to cast a fly for salmon, a sport she shared with my father and us for many years. The beautiful villa at Roquebrune on Cap Martin owned by the Bainbridges boasted a spectacular western panorama of Monte Carlo set against the rugged escarpment of the Alpes Maritimes. The villa's acclaimed gardens exhibited a mix of shady emerald green foliage and colourful flowering plants, providing a vivid contrast to the azure blue of the Mediterranean. No wonder it was a treasured asset for memorable holidays during my teen years.

Patricia's mother was born a Merryweather, and the family firm of that name, based first in Clapham then Greenwich, was famous as one of the earliest and greatest British manufacturers of fire engines with turntable ladders. Merryweathers produced the first motorised fire engine in 1904 for the Finchley Fire Brigade, commemorated in 1974 by the issue of a 3½ pence Royal Mail postage stamp. The country would soon have good cause to appreciate Merryweather fire engines: war was imminent.

4

WHISPERS OF WAR

In the summer of 1939, just before the outbreak of the Second World War, fearing the Germans would drop poison gas from aeroplanes, the government issued 40 million gas masks to the population. This included everyone in the house at Upton. Mine was red and had been thoughtfully designed to look like Mickey Mouse. I remember being coaxed by Nanny into having the straps adjusted to fit my head. I hated the feel of it and did everything I could to avoid having to wear it. It had the unpleasant smell of rubber and disinfectant, and made me feel very claustrophobic. I certainly struggled not to breathe once it was in place and tore it off at the first opportunity.

The government provided Anderson bomb shelters for householders earning less than £250 per annum. I remember being shown into an Anderson that had been built in the garden of one of the farm cottages. All that showed above ground was the curve of the corrugated iron roof. It was being now used as support for a crop of marrows. The fact that many people grew vegetables on top of their shelters to catch the maximum sunlight led one journalist to comment that people were in greater danger of being hit by a marrow falling off the roof than being struck by a German bomb!

Once we had adjusted to our new home, Patricia decided that the family would take a break in North Cornwall. Clutching our gas masks, we set off to catch the *Cornish Riviera* from Swindon to Bodmin Moor. To reach Swindon, however, we had to catch the train from Tetbury to Kemble. On the day of departure we were running very late, and although it seems almost inconceivable in today's world, the Tetbury stationmaster was telephoned and agreed to hold back the Kemble train until our arrival.

This was not strictly on our behalf, but because my father joined by two generals had to catch the same London train from Kemble to attend an urgent meeting at the War Office. They were being driven to Tetbury from the Bath area and were running a few minutes later than us. The Tetbury train arrived at Kemble in good time for the connection. Whereas the three senior officers travelled first class to Paddington, we changed trains at nearby Swindon travelling third class in the opposite direction. I remember that the *Cornish Riviera* was very crowded and we squeezed into the only remaining seats in the compartment. Passenger services had been cut enormously to enable goods trains to carry materials to support the war effort. The Great Western Railway was short of both coal to fuel the steam engines and staff to operate them.

Two taxis took us from Bodmin Moor to our destination of Corncockle Cottage near Trebetherick. From here we could see the entrance to the estuary and the town of Padstow. At the very time we arrived at Corncockle Cottage that year, German troops were crossing the border into Poland. By the time we packed up the cottage to return home, the map of Europe had changed dramatically. Meanwhile, our greatest excitement on arrival was that a coaster had been blown onto the rocks just below the cottage, its engines having failed. It remained almost upright with little structural damage. At low tide Nanny and I were able to clamber down the rocks and climb up the metal ladder that led onto the deck. The seaweed on the rocks was very slippery and so Nanny attached me to her belt with a cord to prevent me falling. Boarding a shipwreck was a most exciting adventure for a three-year old.

Unaware of the build-up to war, I can remember Nanny and Patricia listening to the radio. What was said was obviously incomprehensible to me so I would then beg Nanny to change the programme. Sometimes at night she would leave the volume on low, the music having a soporific effect, sending me to sleep. I found this very soothing and have loved music ever since.

After our Cornish break we returned home to find strict blackout procedures being observed everywhere. Rumours had it that when walking in the dark, local Tetbury men were encouraged to leave their white shirt tails hanging from their trousers, and it was even reported that a farmer painted his herd of cows with white stripes in case they ventured onto the road in the dark. The Churchill government had recently established the

Local Defence Volunteers, more commonly known as the Home Guard. Local groups of men were raised throughout the country and this included Tetbury. At first, neither uniforms nor weapons were provided. Volunteers might turn up with an ancient shotgun or even knives attached to metal poles. Men between the ages of 17 and 65 deemed unfit for enlisting into the armed forces were able to join them.

One of the Home Guard's first jobs was to pull up all road signs throughout the entire country, so that in event of an invasion, the German troops would not be able to find their way around. However, the removal of the signposts and the destination boards from buses proved a double-edged sword. Some of the general public, when lost in the countryside and seeking directions from the Home Guard, were thought to be spies.

The very best example of wartime defence measures coinciding with peacetime leisure was set by the mid-Devon hunt. In the south-west of England, the Home Guard in mid-Devon were keen followers of the local hounds. And so, mounted with shotguns, hunting continued as usual under the pretext of targeting German parachutists rather than stags or foxes.

Our return home also coincided with some severe measures taken by the government on rationing. Fuel was the first target, and rationing came into force on 16th September 1939. The monthly allocation of petrol for our car was very small. Preference was given to doctors, vets and people whose wartime employment necessitated the use of a car. Somehow Patricia's entitlement managed to fall into this category. Around the country, horses and carts were soon used again for basic transport, and the pony and trap at Upton was used frequently on our return.

The 29th September was National Registration Day for rationing. Application forms had already been sent out to every householder and the government issued a ration book and identity card for each person registered in Britain. The government controlled prices of all food items so that the prices were the same in every shop. The scientific division of the ministry promoted ideas for people to eat healthily. Its principal recommendation was 'the basal diet'. This had been worked out on the availability of food in general and how its nutrient and calorific values could provide maximum energy. The basal formula, although never introduced officially, included a basic minimum of bread, potatoes, oatmeal, vegetables and milk. Other suggestions might have gone down well today with vegetarians and vegans: nettle toast and dandelion fritters. Winston Churchill thought little of the basal diet and wrote to Lord Woolton at the Ministry of Food, saying: 'Almost all of the food faddists I ever knew, nut eaters and the like, have died young after a long period of senile decay. The way to lose the war is to try to force the British public into a diet of milk, oatmeal, potatoes and washed down on gala occasions with a little lime juice!'

Special arrangements were made for young children. Babies up to the age of two were given blackcurrant syrup to provide vitamin C, and cod liver oil to provide vitamins A and D – all free of charge. I felt it was a treat to go to Tetbury hospital with other local children and sit in my underpants under an ultra-violet lamp. We wore Biggles-like goggles with dark lenses to prevent damage to our eyes. It was lovely and warm. The reason for all this was that the government believed that children might be deprived of vitamin D through lack of sunlight by spending an inordinate amount of time in the darkness of air-raid shelters.

As from June 1941, clothes, materials and footwear were also rationed. This was one of many areas where Nanny showed her resourcefulness. As a seamstress, old overcoats and baggy trousers belonging to my father were cut and redesigned as clothes for me. Rose, Eleanor and I were all therefore fortunate to have sufficient clothes to avoid having to buy from the government's range of utility sales. Clothes were simple, and strict rules were introduced to minimise work on buttonholes, pleats, seams, hems and collars; fashion remained low on the agenda.

In spite of all these restrictions, children's parties still took place. When it was our turn Nanny would organise party games of which the most popular was a blindfold competition. Nanny, being quite an artist, in readiness sketched on cardboard from an old box a life-size portrait of Hitler. Using drawing pins, the paper was secured to a large board. We children were then blindfolded and invited one by one to try and pin on his moustache. The inevitable inaccuracy in choosing its location caused great amusement.

Nanny and I, on the whole, lived almost independently from the rest of the family at Upton. We were very much confined to the nursery wing upstairs. From this wing there was a separate, rather steep and dangerous back staircase that led down to the kitchens, pram area and garden.

Living in self-contained flats over the stables and garages were Edward, a retired chauffeur, Box the head groom, and Billy Lea, the under-groom, who was, amongst other duties, charged with looking after Rose's pony and taking her riding every day. Amos, the rescued donkey who had been given a home by Patricia, was usually relatively friendly until the blacksmith came to trim his feet. This was the only time I was kept away from the stables as Box could, on occasions, express his full repertoire of swear words. On one occasion during the trimming operation, Amos reared up. Box, who was holding him, was caught unawares as Amos lashed out with his hind leg, scoring a direct hit. Box was seen to be bent double for several minutes.

Griffiths, doubling as the housekeeper and parlour maid, was in overall charge of the staff. Mrs Brown, the cook, was a chain-smoker even during the preparation and cooking of food. When there was a danger of ash falling into a saucepan, she would scream for Beryl, the kitchen maid. Beryl would then remove the cigarette from her mouth, dispense with the ash and stick it back in her mouth again. Dorothy was the nursery maid, and so an extra pair of hands for Nanny. As Nanny and I ate in the day nursery, Dorothy brought up all the meals on a tray from the kitchen and was responsible for keeping the fire burning with wood or coal. She had lived a sad life. Her father was a merchant seaman who drowned at sea, after which she was put into care by her mother. When Nanny read to me at night, Dorothy often used to come and sit on the bed and listen to the stories too.

There was a time when I lay in bed with concussion for a fortnight, having fallen off the top of a farm cart pulled by one of the Clydesdales. The wheel hub caught the gatepost, which brought the cart to an abrupt halt, catapulting me over the side. I lay motionless on the ground with the cartwheel ending up perilously close to my neck. Thankfully, I was saved from decapitation. Nanny read to me constantly whilst I was confined to my bed in a darkened room, which gave Dorothy an excuse to delay the routine chores so that she could come and join us.

Nanny and I would go for long walks, sometimes as far as Chavenage, a nearby Elizabethan manor. Queen Mary was invited to lunch there one day, and this marked my first recollection of waving a Union Jack. Nanny supported me standing on a farm gate opposite the drive entrance as the car departed, but there were no waves or smiles from Queen Mary on this occasion. Sometimes we would go on to visit the hermit's cave in a wood, hidden under thick ivy, uninhabited for many years. I imagined it was the home of an old, old man, with a long, long white beard, a wizened face, friendly to children like me. In summer we sometimes passed, on the route home, a small settlement of Romany gypsy caravans. The families came as casual labour and in their spare time produced wooden clothes pegs to sell.

Around the age of five I began to express my fears and dislikes. I certainly experienced some aversions. Why did I hate so much the sound that came from a lovely Victorian musical box which Patricia had given to my father, or the sound of an accordion? Of what episode in my life, I now wonder, did it remind me? Hunter was an accomplished accordion player and at the very sound of him playing I could be seen to run away with my hands clapped over my ears. Was it to do with Hunter? Oddly, I now very much enjoy listening to recordings of the late Sir Jimmy Shand, still considered by many to have been Scotland's best ever accordionist and dance band leader.

Other senses conjure up childhood memories for me. I found the smell from Tetbury gasworks repugnant, as I did the similar odour from a gas fire about to be lit. Even going to the dentist was terrifying, since I recall being forcibly held down in the chair whilst gas was administered through a mask. By coincidence in the dentist's surgery a gas fire was burning in the grate. Were these two things connected? I resisted breathing the anaesthetic mixture of gas and air for as long as possible, feeling as though I was being forced into a state of unconsciousness through suffocation. The experience gave me ongoing nightmares for weeks. It was reminiscent of me trying on my Mickey Mouse gas mask for the first time, where I got my first whiff of gas. As a young boy, all gas meant the same thing: panic.

I must have been a constant worrier. I can remember one evening taking careful aim at the full moon with my popgun out of the nursery window. After I had fired the cork, which was attached to a piece of string, it seemed, as I looked more closely, that I had created an enormous crater in the moon. This brought on an immediate panic. Who would punish me for this heinous crime? God, the Tetbury police, or (worst of all) my parents? Maybe Nanny could think of a way to fill up the hole? Even after she had explained that the cork, which was still attached to its string, had travelled a maximum of 4 feet and the distance to the moon was like walking to Tetbury 232,000 times, I remained unimpressed by her mathematics, convinced that I had caused the moon serious irreparable environmental harm. Perhaps this was the origin of my later interest in protecting the natural world!

All the Upton staff were beyond the age of call-up, so the authorities seemed satisfied that their contribution to the war effort should be confined to working locally. It was made clear to Patricia, nevertheless, that either she or Nanny would be required to aid the war effort. Patricia had no hesitation in deciding that it should be herself. So every day she went to the servicemen's canteen in Tetbury to make sandwiches, saving Nanny from the certain fate of working in a munitions factory. Despite Patricia's daily absence, she would give us children lots of quality time in the evening, playing such games as cards, I-Spy or Snakes and Ladders.

As I grew older, my dislikes and fears were taken more seriously by Patricia, which helped me to gain in self-confidence. I was unsure of my father, however, perhaps because I saw so little of him at that time. Whenever he was able to spend more time at Upton, his way of communicating with me was for us to start the day with exercises in his dressing room, both dressed in vest and pants. He would wind up the gramophone and play 'Colonel Bogey' and we would attempt to keep our exercises in time with the music. Whether his daily routine kept him fit was debatable; it didn't do much for me, but my own efforts to emulate him gave him much amusement. I relished his sporadic approval.

The first three days of September 1939 marked a massive evacuation of children from cities mostly likely to be bombed. One and a half million people, mostly children but some mothers and teachers too, were transported to stay with families throughout the country. Some evacuees settled in happily but others were miserable and returned home. But when the Blitz started in earnest in 1940, a second big evacuation had to take place. The government offered a financial incentive to each householder of 8 shillings and 6 pence per child per week.

Many of the evacuees who came from deprived areas in towns and cities had suffered poor hygiene and were troubled by infections. Some of the new arrivals found it difficult to adjust to eating meals at tables, having hot baths or using a lavatory in the home. Their behaviour must have often been difficult for the foster parents to manage. But equally there were many incidents of child exploitation, where they were subjected to primitive living conditions and made to work all hours. When some evacuees eventually returned back after the war, their homes had been destroyed by bombing. In other cases the foster parents were preferred: for some of them it must have been a soul-searching moment when they realised their foster children, whom they had treated as their own with love and affection, were about to experience a quality of life considerably worse than they had enjoyed for the past few years. Patricia agreed to take in two families who had been bombed out of their houses in the East End of London. On arrival they were in a very nervous state. They moved in to two converted flats on the top floor, but could not settle in the country, and so moved to Tetbury.

I was, of course, blissfully unaware of any of this. Our house became the safe haven for close relations, friends and their families, whose homes were under threat. Mothers, nannies and children arrived in droves and I did not enjoy this influx of people. It meant sharing my toys, for which the other children showed little respect. I had a unique set of about 50 lead soldiers, attired in battle dress and carrying weapons, which I loved deploying in combat on the nursery carpet. These suffered a very high casualty rate from the incomers and were of course never replaced; I would have to wait a few more years before I commanded a real troop of my own!

The year 1940 saw two important events in the family. Firstly, Patricia gave birth to Guy, who was born at Upton in May. Then in August my father was promoted to Major General and given command of the 1st Armoured Division which had recently returned from France. It had landed at Cherbourg without its infantry to take the pressure off the evacuation at Dunkirk in France which took place from 27th May to 4th June. Once back in England, it formed part of VII Corps and was scheduled to undergo two years of strenuous training, developing efficiency and team spirit. It was then split into two armoured brigades. But training posed a major problem as all the modern tanks were withdrawn in readiness for shipment to the Middle East for the 'desert build-up' and the general protection of the Suez Canal.

In a very short time soldiers of the 1st Armoured Division, bearing their new motif – a charging white rhino on a black oval background – and still relatively untrained, embarked for Suez. One brigade sailed with 155 Crusader tanks and the other sailed one month later with a further 124 Crusaders and 60 Stuarts. Due to enemy control of the Mediterranean, the division sailed by the long sea route around the horn of Africa, a haul of some 12,000 miles, with the ever-present threat of German U-boats.

My father spent a great deal of time before departure visiting the contingents of the entire division, which were widely spread through England. Whereas he was able to keep in touch with Patricia by telephone, he was never allowed to divulge his secret location. However, by means of veiled speech which alluded to friends' houses, hotels or landmarks with which both were familiar, Patricia made successful attempts to join him when time allowed. As soon as the last shipment had left, my father prepared to fly to Cairo in readiness for the arrival of the 1st Armoured Division in Suez.

IN 1940. LEFT TO RIGHT: MAJOR GENERAL MARTELL, GENERAL SIKORSKY, C-IN-C POLISH ARMED FORCES, WINSTON CHURCHILL, GENERAL DE GAULLE AND MY FATHER, G.O.C. 1ST ARMOURED DIVISION.

5

WAR AT HOME AND ABROAD

On the day of my father's departure for Egypt there were hurried goodbyes and much suppression of tears. He was driven to a secret airfield where two Dakotas had been fuelled and were ready for take-off. The first carried a full cargo which included all of his luggage. He boarded the second plane to travel with his staff officers, carrying only his briefcase. The first plane, it was said, broke down in Malta, where it had landed for refuelling, and remained there for repairs. He therefore arrived in Cairo with only the clothes he stood up in, and had to be escorted immediately to the souk for a hurried appointment with an Egyptian military tailor, who worked throughout the night to replace the clothing in his missing suitcase.

Included in this new wardrobe was a camel-hair coat suited to the cold desert nights. The coat became a real favourite of his, as shown by the many photographs of him wearing it. In a letter dated 15th April 1942 to Patricia, who clearly didn't share his enthusiasm, he wrote:

How dare you criticise my coat! I designed it myself, and it is the pride and envy of all in the Western Desert, made of Senussi camel hair. It is not an overcoat, but a tunic, allowing me to wear my medal ribbons! The press out here call me 'the General in the Teddy Bear Coat'.

Now I have the coat at home, I love it and wear it continually. It brings back childhood memories of comments from people such as, 'Your father is fighting in the desert'. These remarks meant very little to me at the time as a four year-old; I just knew that he was not at home. I was too young to comprehend that my father was about to command an armoured division in the first Libyan campaign, which would be fought in a desert the size of

India. I now can imagine him carrying out his duties in that stiflingly hot, barren, inhospitable terrain.

Many of his troops were seasoned veterans of desert warfare who had been frustrated by the year-long ebb and flow of battle, so as the new divisional commander he also had to consider how to get the best out of these soldiers. In their view, no leader would be able to scotch the myth of invincibility that surrounded General Erwin Rommel, who although the enemy, was greatly respected as a colourful and intrepid commander. I am sure my father was uncomfortably aware of the paradigm shift that had to be made: he needed to sow the seed of a new narrative into the minds of his men so that Rommel could be defeated. This task was made easier when the shipload of Crusader and Stuart tanks finally arrived in Port Said on the Suez Canal.

The 8th Army comprised two Corps: XIII commanded by Lieutenant General Godwin-Austen and XXX Corps led by Lieutenant General Pope. Pope and his chief of staff, Brigadier Russell, were acknowledged experts in the handling of armour, but disaster struck early on when both Pope and Russell were killed in the same air crash, leaving XXX Corps without a commander. A new successor was needed immediately. My father had only commanded an armoured division for a year but he, unlike many other generals who were becoming weary, was fresh to the scene. Considered an expert on tank warfare and experienced in battle, he was readily available. Thus he was chosen to take on the new command, handing over his former division to Major General Lumsden.

In many ways he was well suited to a position of leadership. Later, I found amongst some press cuttings an article written by a desert war correspondent, who described my father as 'an enormously equable man, who wore his hat with a Beatty slant and talked in that gentle smooth way one does when standing in front of the roaring fire watching the butler pour out a glass of port'. Another correspondent had written: 'He managed to avoid capture several times in spite of his inspiring habit of tearing over the battlefield in an unescorted 1500 cwt truck cheering on his men.'

In his book *Dilemmas of the Desert War*, Field Marshal Michael Carver wrote: 'Norrie was a charmer, a most persuasive and likeable man, at his best dealing with awkward characters'. He goes on to say that my father could also be indecisive, for example giving precedence to the advice of his old friend XIII Corps Commander Lieutenant General Strafer Gott.

By contrast the author Adrian Stewart, in *The Early Battles of the Eighth Army*, cites *The Official War History* which notes that the C-in-C Middle East, General Sir Claude Auchinleck, took a number of measures which 'seemed to the men in the ranks inconsistent with a firm determination to fight'. This referred to Auchinleck's consideration of a general retreat and evacuation of Egypt. Stewart states that my father had put forward a number of valuable suggestions that his superiors had rejected to their cost, and it was the memory of these that probably stiffened his resolve to stay and fight. Instead of being discouraged by Auchinleck's bleak 'provisional orders', he simply ignored them. According to Stewart, he took the action that the Official History believed Auchinleck should have taken: my father had simply made up his mind about the matter and told his subordinates that this was the last ditch: XXX Corps would fight and die, if necessary, where it stood. This resulted in Rommel calling off his offensive, complaining of the increasing strength of opposition, the depleted strength of his own forces, and the vulnerability of an overextended supply line.

Interestingly, my father's letter of 13 June 1942 reads:

The battle has now being going on since 26 May with both sides beginning to become a bit exhausted. We gave him [Rommel] a really bad knock during the first two days, but he recovered himself and the issue is still in the balance. The next three days will bring forward something definite as one side or other will have to give way or get isolated. I hope it is not us. The bigger decisions are not mine to make and very heavy responsibility falls on the Commander 8th Army [Major General Neil Ritchie]. I don't always agree with his views, but it is my job to see that his orders are carried out even if I am not d'accord.

Commenting on the campaign generally in a letter on 5th May, my father wrote:

I think WC [Winston Churchill] would like to shoot any general, air marshal or admiral who does not succeed. Like Admiral Byng if you remember some history. I don't mind, but I am not too keen that a start should be made on Strafer [Lt Gen. W. Strafer Gott] or me. I am still rather rankled over our last offensive – it was badly handled by our own propaganda – that the public were seen to believe that we would have a walk-over, that our tanks were more numerous and better than the Germans. Everyone knows that neither is true and that the Germans have a gun which fires effectively at exactly double our range and shoots a shell four times as heavy as our own. In spite of all these disadvantages both in numbers and equipment, we have captured 35,000 prisoners, destroyed 400 of his original 470 tanks and relieved Tobruk. Yet instead of being hailed as a success, it was greeted as a disappointment in that we did not capture Rommel's army and go as far as Tripoli. At least this was the attitude the press educated the public to believe. Rommel is not a BF and it would take an army twice as strong to eliminate him altogether. But he is nothing like as good as he himself thinks and we are looking forward to having another crack at him at some future date.

On 29th June, my father wrote to Patricia saying: 'There was chat of my getting to command a corps in England. They wanted someone with experience. I thought it probably a polite way of saying that they had had enough of me.' The rumour became reality and he duly returned to England to become GOC Royal Armoured Corps from late 1942 to 1943, where his knowledge and experience of armoured warfare could be put to good use.

His new appointment coincided with events in August when it was announced that Auchinleck would be replaced by General Alexander as commander-in-chief of Middle East Command, and General Montgomery would assume command of the 8th Army. Lieutenant General Strafer Gott, my father's great friend and ally, had already been chosen to take up this appointment. A pre-war Bombay Transport aircraft, carrying him to Cairo to meet Churchill, was shot down by two pairs of Messerschmitt 109s. Although the pilot managed to crash land the plane, a third pair of fighters set the aircraft ablaze on the ground. Seventeen men including Gott died in the inferno.

Before leaving the desert, my father had to experience two further losses. Firstly, my half-brother Andrew died at birth. Soon afterwards David Kerans, his nephew, was killed in a tank battle. He had gone to corps HQ to visit my father, and confided in him that for 36 hours he had completely lost his way in the desert. My father thoughtfully gave him a compass. After his death Patricia received a letter:

By now you will have heard that David was killed in action on 27 May. He was commanding a troop of our big tanks when his turret was hit by an 88-mm (big shell). He died instantaneously. I am sorry for Eleanor, please tell her so. This is a bloody war and one gets callous out here about death.

MY FATHER AS COMMANDER 30 CORPS,
LIBYA, 1941. DRESSED IN HIS TEDDYBEAR COAT.

In a letter several days later he also wrote: 'It is an extraordinary coincidence that I should have motored straight up to David's tank and grave. I did not know we were within 15 miles of where it occurred.'

Back at Upton, to support the war effort, the park had become a concentration area for troop movement for days at a time. Convoys would arrive and camouflage up in the woods. They would depart before dawn to avoid being an obvious target for enemy bombers. The Battle of Britain was now in full swing, although living in Gloucestershire we were not immediately aware of it. Upton did seem, however, to be astride the bombing route to Bath, Gloucester and Bristol and we were also close to RAF stations, such as Kemble and Hullavington. The melancholic wailing note of an air-raid warning became a regular occurrence. Once the all-clear had sounded, we would all breathe a sigh of relief.

As the bombers passed on their way to raid those cities, searchlight batteries stationed around the Tetbury area would illuminate the night skies, silhouetting some of the barrage balloons around the town. The anti-aircraft guns would attempt to locate a target and open fire, but as the maximum range of the searchlight was only 12,000 feet, and the bombers were flying at more than 20,000 feet, the chances of anti-aircraft guns bringing down enemy aircraft were small. At least it was reassuring to know that efforts were being made to retaliate against the enemy. On occasions, the Germans offloaded their bombs prematurely, as on the night that a 'stick of eight' fell into the 40-acre grass field between Upton and Tetbury, only some 500 yards from the house itself. The series of explosions woke us up in the middle of the night. The only fatality was one unfortunate Friesian cow. With the Sunday roast in mind, local bush telegraph travelled fast even at the dead of night and in the morning people with carving knives, hacksaws, pots and pans arrived from nowhere. By midday, there was scarcely a sign that the cow had ever existed.

Though it was never verified Nanny remembers a further incident during that time which was the surrender of a Luftwaffe pilot who had crash-landed his plane some miles from Upton. The crew had all survived. Three of the four had been captured almost immediately but the pilot had hidden under cover during that day. Suffering from severe hypothermia, he wisely decided to give himself up. He rang our front door bell and was met by Griffiths the housekeeper who opened the door dressed neatly in her black dress, white pinafore and cap. How I would have loved to have witnessed that sight! He could not speak a word of English and could only point to his mouth indicating his hunger and thirst. Griffiths apparently gesticulated that she would fetch help, and after firmly bolting the front door ran to the back door shouting in alarm at the top of her voice for Edward, Box or Billy Lee, other members of the household staff. They all appeared within seconds and then escorted the German from the front door around the house to the back and into the kitchen, where he was politely asked to remove his revolver from its holster. Only then was he given a large bowl of steaming soup by Mrs Brown the cook. The police arrived shortly afterwards to take him away, but not before he had bowed and clicked his heels in thanks to each member of the Upton staff. The whole affair seems a perfect setting for an episode from *Dad's Army*.

It was decided that it was time for me to start daily lessons at Dr Braybrook's house in Tetbury. He was our GP who had delivered Guy, Andrew and Sarah. He also had two sons close to my age. Their rather formal governess taught us to read and introduced us to elementary maths. It was fun for me to meet other children.

To travel anywhere was difficult due to petrol rationing and I remember being taken to children's parties by pony and trap. I attended dancing classes at Burton House in Malmesbury, but on those days we went by car as it was too far for the pony. Whilst the dancing teachers put us through our paces our mothers did the shopping. Princess Alexandra was in my class and one of my partners. She was always being told to keep her head up, I remember, instead of gazing at my bright red shoes. I was unaware that the colour was more suitable for the fairer sex.

On my eighth birthday I was ready to board at Beaudesert Park, a preparatory school owned and run by the Richardson family near Tetbury. The staff there did their best to create a homely atmosphere, and for this reason we new boarders were billeted in the homes of some of the teachers and their families in the area. I and five others stayed in in the cottage of Vincent and Enid Keyte in a wood in the school grounds. The headmaster, Austin Richardson, spent most of his spare time encouraging boys to catch moths and butterflies, or taking parties by bus to watch birds at the Severn Wildfowl Trust. Barton Richardson, Austin's brother, preferred horses to teaching so he used to scurry off racing at Cheltenham or watch the Cirencester polo matches. When I arrived in 1944, there were 108 boarders, all boys. Nowadays there are some 380 day boys and girls. At one stage that included a grandson and granddaughter and, before that, both of the children of the Princess Royal. Although homesick, I was happy at Beaudesert, where cricket during the summer became quite an addiction for me. Little did I realise that I would spend such a short time there.

My father's movements after his return from North Africa were something of a mystery and not talked about, and his time at Upton was spasmodic. There was a rumour that he was in the process of heading up an important French military mission with General de Gaulle, visiting Algiers, Madagascar, Lebanon and Syria. By September 1944, a few months after my eighth birthday, my father was officially appointed Governor of South Australia with orders to take up his appointment as soon as possible to succeed Sir Malcolm Barclay-Harvey, who was retiring prematurely due to ill health.

The new governor, Sir Willoughby Norrie, freshly knighted by the King at Buckingham Palace, would now have to leave Upton with all his family and some of the staff. I remember feeling a heady mix of apprehension and excitement about this impending adventure into the unknown.

6

NANNY

Maude Florence Batty was the daughter of a landscape architect from Sussex who had been invalided out of the army with trench fever during the First World War. By the time he had completed his convalescence he was too old to re-enlist. Nanny was his only daughter. By 1940 his work had somehow caught the eye of the then Lord Mayor of London, for whom he began to work exclusively. Wartime conditions certainly made this a challenging prospect. He found himself responsible not only for growing a variety of suitable plants for Mansion House functions, but also for designing and arranging the displays.

Nanny, who had left school at the age of 14, inherited a lifelong love of gardening from her father and gave her care and advice to our gardens in England. She lived with my stepmother until her death, and though no longer sufficiently agile to carry on such work, Nanny became an avid reader of gardening books and publications, continuing to have an unquenchable thirst for plant knowledge even in her tenth decade.

The traditional English nanny nowadays has changed her spots, and her characteristic uniform is no more. Most people in Britain today would probably know of *Supernanny*, a TV series first broadcast in 2004 and subsequently aired in many other countries. Here the role of the nanny is not so much nurturing a child as providing parents with strategies to modify their behaviour. *Supernanny* has a philosophy of never smacking a child; mine had that too. Maybe she was ahead of the game!

My sister Diana died three years before I was born, my mother died 18 months after my birth, and my father remarried Patricia within the year. This was quite an adjustment for the family. I was too young at the time, of course, to be conscious of the effect on us all of those traumatic months. Looking back now I realise how Nanny did her best to protect me from the worst of the blows during the first seven years of my life. She became the secure and constant lynchpin of my early life by standing between me and the real world.

So many memories of that time are still prompted by incidents that involved Nanny, and her alone. My mother suffered greatly after Diana's loss; hence Nanny looked after my likes and dislikes, my moods and my behavioural patterns. It was Nanny who told me, when I was researching this book, how much my mother enjoyed seeing me tucking into Farley's rusks mixed with a little milk before I had cut my teeth. Perhaps she would have been as surprised as me to learn that all these years later they have acquired cult status amongst university students, as a cure for hangovers! Little of the first eleven years of my life recorded in this memoir could have been written without Nanny's crystal-clear long-term memory and the hours we spent together recalling my childhood.

Both she and my parents had been brought up to value Victorian traditions. Each had an autocratic outlook on life. Expressions such as 'Little boys don't cry!' or 'Be brave!' were frequent and had a marked effect on my life in early age. As a child, I now realise, I never learned how to express deep-seated emotions of anger, fear or sorrow. Instead I subconsciously developed the habit of denying that these feelings existed. This habit, repeated time and time again, of obeying without question what I was told to do, served to mould my character. What a contrast this is with the current 'Facebook' generation, where someone may announce almost hourly to the cyber world what they are feeling. If there had been such a thing as Facebook during my childhood, my home page would have had only one status which would have remained the same for decades: 'numbed out'. It was not until my much later years that I have been able to own my feelings, and express them, much helped by writing this book.

Nanny was a person for whom nothing was ever *that* good or *that* bad. She was like a rock: plain-looking, with her straight hair seemingly always arranged the same way, lacking in outward emotion, but unerringly consistent and reliable. In a world where I would experience so much change, she never appeared to change. She made sure that my youthful energies were guided and diverted into necessary creative activities, reflecting her imaginative and inquisitive spirit. Nanny had won a scholarship to an art college in London as a teenager, but could not afford to go. Not unduly deterred, she continued to dabble in watercolours and produced many sketches, nearly always of the natural world. I came to see the world through her eyes. She had the knack of making life enthralling and stimulating for me, no matter where we were living.

During my pre-school years at Upton Grove, Nanny encouraged me to appreciate the natural world in all its forms by stimulating my interest in animals, birds and flora. She took me on nature walks and drew attention to things that I would not otherwise have noticed. She taught me in a practical way about all the creatures of the universe. We even dowsed for water and iron ore, an ancient practice in which I still maintain an interest. Significantly, she did not just impart facts; she brought them alive. Alongside the farm, the family kept many animals including numerous dogs, cats, caged birds, rabbits, tortoises, goats and ponies. I learned, through Nanny, to see that life is bittersweet: alongside the joys of watching pets being born and grow is the gnawing sadness of knowing that one day they will die. This pain has been a familiar companion at most stages of my life, and as a boy, on reflection of these early losses, I kept my feelings to myself.

My parents – my father and mother, and then my father and stepmother Patricia – led very full lives, so it became the pattern that the time they shared with me was usually confined to after tea, before bedtime. Although I had a very close relationship with my stepmother, somehow Nanny always remained my surrogate mother. She caught my imagination in *Treasure Island*, *Gulliver's Travels* and one book I remember in particular: the seventh book in Arthur Ransome's Swallows & Amazons series, *We Didn't Mean to Go to Sea*. The plot here involves a young man, John Walker, and his sisters who end up adrift at sea, their father being abroad on military service, and ending up with the family eventually being reunited with their mother. Having lost my mother and eldest sister, and then being separated from my father, that story must have been, unconsciously, very poignant for me.

Nanny had been with the family for a full 65 years when Patricia died. She asked the family to be excused from the funeral and remained in her room with the cat, armed with, as was her custom, the ongoing bottle of Amontillado, for many years her fortifying tipple. Later, after my stepmother's house, the 'Old Vic', had been sold, Nanny chose to move to a nursing home within a short distance of my sister Sarah's home in Derbyshire. I used to visit her and take her out to lunch at the Bull's Head, Ashton-in-the-Water.

Only at this time, now in my seventies, did I feel able to readdress some of my buried childhood feelings and ask her about my mother. How did

Mum compare to Patricia, I asked? What were things like between Mum and Dad? I never received a satisfactory answer to either question, although I received a clearer picture from my father just before he died.

Nanny had sought little outside of our family; we had been her whole life and, as I saw it, her devotion to us had never faltered. She and I had developed a deepening friendship over the years, albeit one wherein she allowed little room for emotion; I understand that well now. Our family was still her world, including attending to my needs, perhaps still protecting me, in this case from the inevitable sadness of losing her too.

The family contributed to a fund for her retirement and care, allowing her to be well looked after. She died peacefully in the nursing home a few days before her ninety-ninth birthday. All of us attended her funeral. Her ashes were interred in Great Longstone graveyard, close to the nursing home where she had spent her final years. A recurring feature of my life has been facing up to dealing with loss. Now Nanny has gone too, I can feel a great sense of gratitude for her compassion, kindness, and care for a lonely little boy; she seemed always to understand me. It is with constant appreciation that I revere her memory.

NANNY BEING INTERVIEWED FOR THIS BOOK BY THE AUTHOR.

7

HIGH HOPES DOWN UNDER: A NEW START

The first concern, before departing for Australia, was letting rather than selling Upton Grove and ensuring that its remaining staff were cared for in our absence. As the new Governor of South Australia, my father was responsible for providing and paying for the outward journey of any Government House staff that accompanied him, which cost him £1,400, a considerable sum in those days.

This story was substantiated from a most unexpected source, Field Marshal Lord Alanbrooke's diaries, which record a meeting at the War Office between him and my father prior to our departure, when the subject of my father's heavy expense was lamented. The new staff would include two aides-de-camp (ADCs), a butler, under-butler, footmen, two cooks, ladies' maids, housemaids and chauffeurs, the total number being about 16 in all. I did wonder whether my father would have to ante up again when seven years later he moved on to New Zealand as governor general. A copious number of permits were required for the family to leave the country, and special coupons were needed for clothing, books and bikes. Receipts and private correspondence were vetted and documents from the Ministry of Labour were required for us all. Further papers for specific goods necessary for Australia were issued by the Ministry of Supply. On top of this a special licence had to be obtained to move the packing cases and luggage from Upton to Liverpool by road. Finally, Neville Chamberlain, our yellow canary, had to have his own permit for a 'one-way ticket'!

At last we were on our way to London, en route to Liverpool and the ship. There was a big send-off at Euston from friends, many armed with small presents. I was even offered a piece of banana, almost never seen during the war. Nanny said later that I was confused by having to peel it.

On arrival at Liverpool Docks we boarded the elegant liner formerly known as the *Empress of Japan*. In October 1942, after the Japanese attack on Pearl Harbour, Winston Churchill personally ordered that the *Empress of Japan* should be renamed the *Empress of Scotland*, although it operated under its wartime codename J1. This ocean liner was built and completed in 1930 at Govan on the River Clyde and before the war regularly traversed the trans-Pacific route between the west coast of Canada and the Far East, setting a new speed record for the route from Yokohama to Vancouver on 7th August 1930.

Space was limited and Guy and I shared a minute, cramped cabin. All portholes were painted black and were permanently secured. Every morning there was compulsory lifeboat drill undertaken by a contingent of the Royal Marines. We had access to a very small private deck as the main decks were covered with depth charges and large boxes of cargo destined for Australia. On both sides of the deck anti-aircraft guns were mounted and the crews practised their drills with regularity. Each morning there was a series of PT classes for all personnel, and I was invited to join. Boxing was a compulsory sport for the ship's crew, and I got in on this one too. Armed with full-sized boxing gloves I sparred with a tough marine, who knelt on the deck with his hands behind his back ducking and weaving his head, at which I ineffectively aimed blows.

Everyone rested in the afternoon but things livened up around 5.00 pm for a *thé dansant*. There were quite a number of women on board – nurses, Wrens and members of the Voluntary Aid Detachment (VAD) – who had volunteered to do basic nursing for the armed forces, giving them exemption from less desirable work such as the munitions factories. I was taught to dance by one of the VADs who was about my height, and learned to waltz, foxtrot and quickstep before reaching Sydney. Smoking being forbidden on deck, people would light a cigarette to smoke between dances. Very strict blackout precautions were always enforced throughout the ship and all entrances to the deck were draped with heavy tarpaulins to exclude the slightest sign of light.

By the time we reached the tropics the cabins had become stifling and airless. This was made worse by the rationing of water. No showers or baths were available and fresh water was rationed to 1 pint per person per day. Nanny, however, was allowed 2 pints for baby Sarah, just sufficient for her bottle and other odd things. A clothes line was rigged up on deck for her. She underwent a lot of ribbing from the sailors, who wished to know what signal the washing on the line indicated. The days for me seemed very long, hot, and somewhat monotonous in such a confined space. Apart from meals in a tiny wardroom, we were limited to our small deck or our own cabins. Nanny religiously did her best to keep us amused with stories, books, card games and drawing, though she sensibly gave herself time off in the afternoons, when Rose and Eleanor agreed to look after Sarah, Guy and myself.

One afternoon when it was particularly rough weather, Nanny, who was prone to seasickness, had taken to her bunk, leaving Rose and Eleanor to keep an eye on Sarah, then only 18 months old. The ship was pitching and rolling and Sarah was propped up on the lower bunk against some pillows. Suddenly the ship lurched, so that Sarah rolled across the pillows, landing head first on the floor. Whether the fall knocked her out we shall never know, but she uttered not a sound. This put the fear of God into Rose and Eleanor, who were convinced they had caused her permanent brain damage. This fear was further compounded as Sarah took some time to learn to walk. It was not until she could talk coherently that they let go of their fear and guilt.

The weather grew hotter as we approached Panama City at the Atlantic entrance to the Panama Canal, where the crew took on fresh vegetables, fruit and salads. None of these delicacies had been seen by the passengers since leaving Liverpool. The journey seemed slow, but it actually only took a day to cover the 50 miles, the ship travelling through a series of locks which raised and lowered the vessel when necessary, as the canal is, at its highest point, 85 feet above sea level.

As we journeyed on, we left the canal in darkness behind us, travelling towards the brightly illuminated city of Colon, at the Pacific end of the canal. The dazzling lights seemed strange after being so used to the constant blackout drills. We were now set to travel across the Pacific to Sydney.

Due to the continuous intense heat, Nanny had dug out some cooler clothes for us from the trunks in the hold. No sooner had she descended to the bowels of the ship on that day than there was a red alert from the bridge, following the possible sighting of a Japanese U-boat. Panic! We abruptly changed course, thereby avoiding the danger. Before long, however, we were given the all-clear and so sailed on peacefully towards our destination. The J1 safely docked at Sydney harbour to be greeted by the Governor of New South Wales, Lord Wakehurst.

Most of our staff, plus luggage, continued from here by train to Adelaide. The family, together with ADCs, spent the first day at the governor general's house in Sydney, a castellated gothic mansion whose turrets and towers looked to me, as an eight-year-old boy, to have come straight from a book of fairy tales. Impressively situated next to the Royal Botanic Gardens, the building looked out across the panorama of Sydney harbour.

The following day began with a car trip crossing the magnificent Sydney Harbour Bridge. I remember it was very sunny and warm, and Nanny remarked later what a delight it was to drink a cup of tea once more made with fresh milk. That same evening we clambered aboard the overnight train, *Spirit of Progress Express*, bound for Melbourne en route to our new home in Adelaide.

After spending the next day in Melbourne in the company of the Governor of Victoria, Sir Winston, later Lord Dugan, in his lovely home, we boarded our second overnight train, this time to Adelaide. It was wartime, so there were no sleepers. We sat up all night, my father and Patricia in one carriage, whilst we children and Nanny – doing her level best to read to me until I could fall sleep – were in the compartment next door. Early next morning, tired but relieved, we arrived and were met at Adelaide station, which was within only a short distance of Government House. Our route passed the Olympic swimming pool, for which I showed my immediate enthusiasm, to be later rewarded with swimming lessons there. By midday, my father had been sworn in at Adelaide Town Hall as the next Governor of South Australia. A new life had begun for us all.

★★★

In 1836, 100 years before I was born, Colonel William Light had chosen and surveyed the site for the new South Australian capital, Adelaide. The centre was sited 7 miles inland from the port of Adelaide and within good agricultural land. To me it seemed large and important. Although life there seemed quickly to fall into a routine, it was full of unexpected excitements, which made the three years that I spent in Australia pass all too quickly.

I was now living in a new environment in constant sunshine, and in a country where there seemed to be no restrictions on me or my life. I was to attend a new school where I could, amongst other things, pursue the sporting activities that I most enjoyed. My favourite sport had been cricket, but I was given excellent coaching and encouragement in tennis and swimming. I felt fit and warm after the cold of England. Apart from periods of extreme heat, the only unpleasant weather I can recall were the dust storms of 1945, which according to the meteorologists were the worst ever recorded in South Australia. The red dust was picked up by the winds from the Nullabor Plain and at night the moon, silhouetted against a dark sky, transformed in colour from gold to blood red. This unfortunately meant staying indoors to prevent inhaling the fine dust into our lungs.

There was no air conditioning installed in Government House. In the most intense periods of extreme heat we all moved, with a skeleton staff, up to Marble Hill, a vice-regal residence that had been completed for Governor Sir William Jervois in 1879. The house stood some 2,000 feet above sea level and was about 13 miles by car from the heart of Adelaide in the Mount Lofty Ranges, between Ashton and Montague. We all remember the terror of bush fires approaching in our direction. On each occasion, luckily for us, the wind would change direction and the fire crews were able to cope with the ensuing danger. The flames were a magnificent sight, particularly at night. In 1912, when the MCC was touring Australia, they found themselves amongst "ashes" that they had not anticipated. The team had been invited to lunch by the then governor and his wife, Sir Day and Lady Bosanquet. It was a stifling hot day and bush fires were breaking out and raging all around the property, requiring the cricketers, it was said, 'to drive between two walls of fire' before they were able to help save Marble Hill from destruction.

I can remember that the danger of bush fires was carefully instilled into Australian children's minds from an early age. One of our favourite family pastimes was a picnic out in the bush where marinated lamb chops were grilled on the dying embers of a eucalyptus wood fire. The chops themselves always seemed to turn out charcoal black on the outside but the eucalyptus certainly gave the meat an aromatic flavour. After our meal the fire was extinguished with great care: just out of sight lay the remains of some unfortunate sheep whose charred carcases were a reminder of what otherwise could happen.

There was no electricity there in our day: the lighting was provided by acetylene gas which was piped from a gas bunker built into the side of the nearby hill. The gardener operated the system, the workings of which were beyond an eight-year-old, but I seem to remember that gas pellets were pressurised under water in a metal cylinder. My imagination ran wild: due to my early experiences gas in any form remained anathema. I therefore became convinced that the gas which I could smell in the garden was definitely responsible for the gigantic worms I found there. They were abnormally large and unlike the little worms I was used to in England. I imagined that they were inhaling gas, which vastly blew them up in size. At the same time I saw plagues of locusts, which looked like giant grasshoppers to me, rapidly descending on the plants and vegetables around me. Here too, I felt that the gas might mysteriously account for their voracious appetite.

Each night the staff at Government House had to light, and later extinguish, at least 40 gas lamps. Heavy opaque glass shades had to be lifted off to reach the gas tap which, when turned on, had to hiss for a few seconds before ignition would take place – gas again! We children used to sing a made-up song to the tune of 'Lily Marlene':

Underneath the gas light, home at Marble Hill,
Boys when I am reading, you must keep very still.
The gas light it flickered and nearly went out,
Dad gave a shout, while Mum rushed about
To find a box of matches,
Now the darned thing's out.

On looking back, it was here at Marble Hill that I first became aware of feeling my explosive anger. I had a serious disagreement with Guy followed by another with my parents. In the nursery I had laid out a display of Hornby trains. Guy, who was bored by not being involved, kicked the engine and coaches from the track. I became wild with rage, and as I lashed out, hitting him in the face, my father walked into the room. Dad shouted loudly at me, and told me to come to his study immediately, where he struck me several times across my bottom with a wooden map case. By then I was so consumed by my own rage that I picked up a paperweight and hurled it straight at him. Luckily it missed. Was the gas responsible for this too? At the precise moment that the paperweight hit the glass French windows, Patricia rushed into the room shouting, 'What on earth is going on?'

Dashing out of the room, letting loose my full vocabulary of expletives which I had so carefully learned at my new Australian school, I sped across the garden and clambered up into the tree house, and stubbornly refused to come down. From the safety of my eyrie a little later I watched as my father, dressed in the uniform of the South Australian Chief Scout, with my stepmother beside him in full Girl Guide regalia, came out of the house and climbed into the official car en route to a jamboree in Adelaide. As he got into the car my father, still incensed at my behaviour, bellowed to the off-duty ADC: 'Catch him and beat him!' Of course, he never did. My subsequent apology, nevertheless, had no mitigating effect on his decision to dock my weekly pocket money for several months to pay for the reglazing of the shattered French window.

Our other escape was to a house we rented on the coast at Henley Beach. 'Lausanne' was a simple five-bedroom bungalow with a view across the esplanade to the beach, where we swam and enjoyed long afternoon picnics. Much of the Henley Beach activity centred on the pier, which was constructed on wooden piles and ran for some 50 yards from the shore out to sea. At high tide, with my local friends Mervyn, Phil, Doug Allen and Sydney Cook, an Aboriginal named after the explorer, I would spend the afternoon diving off the end into the deep water. This pastime was soon considered too risky, as a number of grey nurse sharks had been sighted in the area. At other times we would simply visit some of the more colourful individuals living in homes along the Henley Beach esplanade, who were always welcoming and overgenerous, offering copious amounts of Coca-Cola and ice creams. One of these was a well-known 1930s Australian test cricketer called Nitschke, and another character called Johnny Ryan who kept a pet boxing kangaroo reputed to have chalked up two knockouts.

Life could scarcely have been better at this point in my life. Here under sunny skies I was happy at school, made a lot of friends, played tennis and went swimming and diving to my heart's content. The whole way of life suited me admirably. I was able to toughen up a little by playing a full role in competitive sports, something Australians take very seriously indeed. I felt I was gaining in confidence. My days glided along as smoothly as if on rails.

THE AUTHOR AND KOALA BEAR.

8

SWEET AND SOUR

With the long hot Christmas holidays over all too soon, I started as a day
boy at Palm House, which was the pre-preparatory school of St Peter's
College, Adelaide. On looking back, Palm House certainly conjures up
some strange memories. Nearby was the Rosella factory with its pungent
smell of tomato sauce: Australia's answer to Heinz! I can smell it as I write.
Evidence of loyal allegiance to King and Country was shown in many ways
across Australia. Before classes commenced in the mornings, the national
anthem was played on a gramophone. We all stood strictly to attention and
were made to look at the top of the blackboard until the last bar of music.

Recreation during the break between classes was usually spent collecting
the fruit from the Buri palm trees, from which Palm House took its name.
During the lunch break, when we consumed our home-made sandwiches,
we would play marbles together. This was very competitive. Games were
set up on the bare sun-hardened ground. Many marbles changed hands.
Most of us were reluctant to part with any of our collection. Three marbles
could be lost to an opponent in a single game. I would never risk playing
with my favourite multicoloured marbles for fear of losing them forever.

I could already read and write before arriving at Palm House. Once
there I was taught by Miss Ferris and Miss Berry, and later, when elevated
to the top class, by Miss Prickett, the head teacher. The method she taught
us was to hold the pen so that the cap pointed to the middle of the right
shoulder. Neat writing and good spelling was rewarded by the page in
question being stamped with the word 'Excellent', something we all
aspired to and would show our parents. My father decided to inspect Palm
House and was greeted by Miss Prickett who brought him in to my class.
I was relieved that he did not ask any questions. Instead he told a story of

another school in Whyalla, now the third-largest city in South Australia, where the teacher had asked one eight-year-old boy if he knew the name of the visiting governor. He replied, 'Is it Sir Wallaby Nirrie?'

After two terms, I was old enough to become a weekly boarder at St Peter's. Pioneer churchmen founded St Peter's in 1847. It was a Church of England institution, a school based on religious foundation. It aimed to produce 'Christian gentlemen' on the lines of the great English public schools. But a somewhat different curriculum was needed for the colonies, and the original proprietors hoped to promote a sound classical, mathematical and commercial education. Although Latin and Greek formed the basis for the early curriculum, by 1857 these subjects were dispensed with once any boy had reached the age of 13. French and German were also taught and at this time a small chemical laboratory had been set up for those 'who evinced a taste for such pursuits'. However, neither Latin nor French appeared on the curriculum at St Peter's Preparatory School. This was a major concern to my parents, who knew that these subjects were an integral part of the Common Entrance Examination to all English public schools.

I felt smartly dressed for school in cap, white shirt, grey flannel shorts, and grey jacket embossed with the school motif of a crown and gold cross keys on a dark blue background and its Latin motto, *'Pro deo et patria'*. I preferred to travel to and fro by tram, or if taken by the official car, I asked to be dropped off round the corner from the school gates, to avoid being teased. There were a few permanent boarders, whose homes were in the more remote areas of South Australia and Victoria and so found themselves often remaining as inmates at weekends. The dormitories we slept in were large enough for 12 beds and named after the ships of well-known explorers – *Endeavour, Victory, Buffalo* and *Investigator*. The teaching staff and their lessons encouraged all forms of sport, and most of them had been fine athletes themselves in their youth. In the case of cricket coaching, I was too young to appreciate that I was being taught to bowl by Tim Wall, a former New South Wales cricketer who had once taken ten wickets in an interstate Sheffield Shield match.

Our housemaster was the Reverend Rufus Ray, known as Red Ray because of his mop of thick red hair. The only time I recall him being angry was over an incident in the dining room. The teaching staff used to sit and eat with the boys for breakfast and lunch. One boy, who claimed an allergy to fried eggs for breakfast, surreptitiously removed the egg from his plate and threw it under the table, where it landed sunny-side up on Red Ray's shoe. The culprit owned up and was given a few weeks of chores, which included weeding the vegetable garden, cutting up kindling wood and sweeping the shelter shed. This building had a corrugated roof, one open side with high wire and a dusty concrete floor. It was used as an outside venue for assembling the boarders and day boys, but it also doubled for recreational activities. A battered dark green rubbish bin served as a wicket. The batsman batted until he was either bowled or caught out and queues of boys waited to bowl at the batsman with their own tennis ball – a good game! I made many friends at St Peters, and still maintain contact with some of them to this day. Several of whom went on to earn their blues at Oxford or Cambridge.

Being a weekly boarder as I was kept me in touch with home life, but I saw little of my parents. When I was younger our time as children with them was slotted into a period during the early evening, when we would play some sort of family game. Their official duties seemed onerous, from time to time including children's fancy dress parties to which we would go along, my father insisting on taking an active part in the frivolities, whether at home or other venues. His favourite guise was as Al Jolson, the white Jewish American singer who would 'black' himself up, as did my father. I can remember my him standing in his slippers on the state banqueting table, diligently polished by Rushden the butler, who would then stand in the shadows near to tears and wringing his hands as my father cavorted up and down his precious polished table, amidst squeals of delight from young party-goers. To the accompaniment of a 78 rpm gramophone record he would croon to the strains of 'Swanee, how I love ya'.

Sarah was still in a pram at this time, Guy was on his tricycle, and they would go off with Nanny along the track by the River Torrens to the botanical gardens. It was highly convenient. I would join them after school if I was not swimming or playing tennis. It was at this time then that I became a sea cadet, and I used to join others of my age on the *Wongala*, a retired and engineless old coaster, moored near Adelaide's outer harbour. We also found a riding school and so I could ride in the park in North Adelaide most Sunday mornings. On one occasion the pony ran away with me, I remember, and I found myself galloping out of control across a main road. Thankfully there was no Sunday traffic. I managed to hang on like grim death until we arrived safely back at the stables. This episode may well have put me off ever wishing to follow in the footsteps of my father's successful racing career.

In 1946, Rose, Mike Farebrother (one of my father's ADCs) and I went off to ski at Mount Kosciuszko in Victoria. This mountain stands some 7,000 feet high and at the time was considered the best-known Australian ski resort. My stay was short-lived and I never skied because I was diagnosed with appendicitis, and the following morning was transported by horse-drawn sleigh 2½ miles down the mountain to a waiting ambulance which transported me to the provincial town of Cooma. Whilst the ambulance men enjoyed a lengthy breakfast en route, I remained tossing and turning in some discomfort in the ambulance. We finally reached Canberra Hospital at about 3.30 in the afternoon. Prince Henry, Duke of Gloucester, came to my rescue. As the recently installed Australian Governor General at Canberra he arranged for Mr Poate, the royal surgeon, who luckily was travelling from Sydney to Canberra that day, to perform the appendicitis operation. As it was too far away for me to go home, he and Princess Alice kindly had me to convalesce for two weeks afterwards in the comfort of Government House. What an account I had to share with my school friends!

I loved being in the company of my father's two ADCs when they were off-duty. Mike Farebrother, an exceptional pianist who played by ear, encouraged me to do the same. He could play anything from Grieg to Gershwin. Philip Kirkpatrick had brought to Adelaide one of the earliest forms of recording machines, which used blank 78 rpm records on which sound was recorded. This fascinated me. This was how my parents practised their official speeches. Patricia hated speaking in public and announced to my father that she would rather have another baby … On December 1944, Annabel was born in the Calvary Hospital in North Adelaide. Patricia's wish had come true.

As part of their duties, the ADCs were responsible for arranging Government House receptions, banquets and less formal dinner parties, and making them fun. For the less formal dinners they devised a game of indoor cricket in the ballroom. Divided into two teams, the fielding side were strategically placed on chairs around the room, which they were not allowed to leave. These formal wooden chairs were a bit fragile for the game, with their wicker seats and spindly legs. The batsmen and bowler, also on chairs, were given a miniature cricket bat and a soft woollen ball. Runs were accumulated by boundaries only: whenever the ball reached the walls or skirting boards. The game broke the ice for the more reserved guests, and also broke a number of chair legs. I was allowed to watch the match from the balcony in my dressing gown and pyjamas.

The MCC arrived in Adelaide for the 1946-47 test series against Australia and this was one of the most exciting events that I can remember as a ten-year-old. The Adelaide Oval hosted the fourth Test match and two days before it my father held a large reception for the whole team. The Ashes had already been lost. The ADCs had erected a cricket net on the Government House lawn and I nervously donned a pair of pads. As a somewhat unsure batsman I faced some gentle bowling from Alec Bedser and Norman Yardley. Afterwards I realised what a privilege it had been.

For the match itself, the English team, captained by Wally Hammond, featured many other post-war cricketing icons such as Compton, Hutton, Edrich, Bedser, Washbrook, Evans and Yardley, whilst the Australian team included Bradman, Hasset, Morris, Miller, Harvey, McCool and Lindwall, who seemed to bowl at the speed of light, taking three wickets in four balls at the end of England's first innings of 460. It was a high-scoring match which ended in a draw, but not before Compton had scored a century in each innings with 147 and 103 not out, with Hutton also making a good contribution of 94 and 76. For the Australians, Morris and Miller both knocked up centuries and Hasset made 78.

My father had generously allowed me to invite at least ten of my school friends to the vice-regal box at the Oval for this five-day test match. I was very popular with my friends despite the fact that the great Don Bradman was bowled for a duck by Bedser in the Australian's first innings! The Test series also triggered boys' cricket matches held on the lawn at Government House, which caused an embarrassingly long waiting list of hopeful potential invitees from St Peter's.

Whilst I was very happy at St Peter's, my parents had to make a decision about my future education. I could remain there until I was 18 years old; I could go to Geelong Grammar School, considered to be the cream of Australian academia and situated near Melbourne, or I could go back to England and follow in my father's footsteps at Eton – although I had not yet learned the obligatory Latin or French. Finally, opting for Eton, they decided that I should return to England and spend 18 months back at Beaudesert, and with some extra cramming during the holidays I would then be in a position to sit the Common Entrance Exam for Eton.

FAMILY GROUP, GOVERNMENT HOUSE, ADELAIDE 1946.

BACK ROW: ELEANOR (KERANS), MY FATHER,
PATRICIA HOLDING ANNABEL, ROSE.

FRONT ROW: THE AUTHOR, SARAH AND GUY.

All too soon I reluctantly boarded *Orion*, the first luxury Orient Line passenger ship to sail from Australia after the war. I travelled back along with Patricia, Rose, Eleanor Kerans and Mike Farebrother, whose parents were to be my guardians in England for the next five years. So in 1947, much to my consternation, I left my wonderful newly found world, Nanny, and all I had grown to love, to become an 'abandoned child' for four years, when the only contact with home would be by letter and a solitary telephone call on Christmas Day.

I remember our departure vividly, although I must have unknowingly blocked out my feelings of sadness and bewilderment. With three blasts from the ship's siren, *Orion*, festooned with red, white and blue streamers, gently edged away from the wharf, pulled by two tugs and headed for the open sea, taking the most direct route across the Great Australian Bight to Fremantle, and on. There was sufficient time during our stopover in Perth to visit the lovely city before sailing on to the port of Colombo in Ceylon, modern Sri Lanka. On arrival there, the resident Orient Line representative entertained us to lunch and later took us to the exclusive Mount Lavinia Hotel and its private beach. In the foyer of the hotel, Ceylonese waiters smartly dressed in white tunics and red turbans served us freshly cut cucumber sandwiches with crusts aptly removed. Tea was served from a silver urn into delicate china cups. All this was redolent of Victorian times.

Enduring some very hot and airless days without modern air conditioning en route to Aden for refuelling, making sleeping under such suffocating conditions nigh impossible, we passed through the Suez Canal, spending a whole day at Port Said. On disembarking here, passengers made straight for the souk, engaging in a massive shopping spree, buying everything that appeared to be a bargain: leather goods, basketware, trinkets, as well as fine jewellery. Upon re-embarking once more, the *Orion* became surrounded by a multitude of traders in small boats, crammed with goods. Passengers lined the rails on the deck. There was a bustle of activity as ropes were thrown and secured to the ship's railings to haul up the new purchases. Haggling took place for a host of different things: bananas, dates and oranges, and assorted carpets, rugs and mats. We bought an enormous wicker laundry basket which remains in use at home. Adding spice to this entertainment was a gully-gully man standing on the wharf by the gangplank. Passengers and children were waylaid, becoming engrossed in his conjuring tricks. Like a forerunner to Tommy Cooper, he wore a red fez and was dressed in a voluminous cream-coloured robe, producing a seemingly endless number of live baby chicks from the clothing of any one of his captivated audience.

Finally, after a month at sea, we docked at Tilbury to my relief but trepidation. Travelling on to London by train, Patricia and I stayed first with her mother, Granny Warre at 54 South Street in Mayfair, residing in some comfort. Later on my father flew back to join us for a holiday at Beaufort Castle, overlooking the river Beauly in Invernesshire. I will never forget the thrill of landing my very first salmon at the age of eleven, ably assisted by Matheson with his net. His family name epitomises a long line of ghillies on that estate. The river had been in spate and was now dropping, so conditions were perfect on a dull September afternoon to have a decent chance of landing a fish, something that had eluded most of the house party during the preceding weeks. Matheson had offered me a choice of flies. I chose a Thunder & Lightning, tied it on myself, and was relieved that my blood knot held good.

Prior to going on down to Sussex to meet my new guardians and prepare for the 18 months I would spend back at Beaudesert before going to Eton, I had to be taken to Billings & Edmonds in Hanover Square, the school's nominated supplier of uniforms. None of the school clothes that I had worn when there before aged eight would now fit me as an eleven-year-old: I had grown tall in Australia. My new grey jacket appeared to accentuate my bony shoulders, and my new trousers had been duly sewn up inside the trouser legs, allowing for further growth in the years to come. I felt rather more like a wartime refugee than a smartly turned-out new boy. Patricia packed everything into a trunk in readiness for the Michaelmas term. The following day she drove me down to Sussex to meet the Farebrother family, my guardians-to-be. I was beginning to feel the familiar sense of unease. My parents were shortly to return to Australia, leaving me feeling abandoned again, with no friends or relatives nearby. I had never even met the Farebrother parents, with whom I was to stay when not at school. I felt somewhat insecure.

9

RETURN TO THE LAND OF CAPTIVITY

Canon Felix Farebrother was Rural Dean of West Sussex, living with his family at Warnham Vicarage near Horsham. He was light-hearted, avuncular and kind, preferring to wear a bow tie rather than his requisite Sunday dog collar. He was much loved by the inhabitants of Warnham and seemed to be involved in endless village activities, ranging from umpiring village cricket matches to judging the cake stall at the annual village show. There was always at least one good story used as an illustration for his sermon. Never did I ever feel religion was thrust down my throat, though lunch and dinner always commenced with grace. Margaret Farebrother, his wife, was the power behind the throne. Whilst being kind to me, she stood no nonsense from anyone, could be very bad-tempered and was a compulsive chain-smoker, which sadly contributed to her early demise in 1952 from lung cancer.

The Farebrother children were all grown up and the sudden appearance of an eleven-year-old interloper could not have been easy for a busy parson's wife. Being left alone for long periods didn't help because I was not naturally good at occupying myself. There were no kindred spirits of my age in Warnham village with whom I could share my teenage years. I was not an avid reader of books and my single hobby was limited to stamp-collecting. Occasionally we played cards or games such as Monopoly. Happily for me, I was given a BSA bicycle as a late eleventh birthday present and there were occasions when I was allowed to ride it to visit friends of the Farebrothers in the outlying villages, sticking rigidly to the country lanes. What I would have given, though, to have been back in Adelaide riding that bicycle with my school friends under the glorious Australian sun!

I still had a connection of sorts with those friends – from them I had acquired an Australian accent together with some fairly undesirable expressions. Furthermore, whilst I had received a basic grounding in Latin and French in Adelaide, both learned under private tuition rather than at school, I had to accept that there was going to be some very hard work ahead in order to pass the Common Entrance Examination to Eton. Those two subjects themselves, let alone history, English, geography and maths, needed constant work and considerably more revision. I didn't like the thought of this at all.

Thus, on returning on holiday from a term at Beaudesert, I was to find myself with a resident tutor at Warnham, a bachelor master from Malvern College, who set about this task in a professional and thorough manner. Maths proved my weakest subject and algebra in particular. The thought of having to understand the supposed simplicity of simultaneous and quadratic equations filled me with despair. However, the tutor's patience and my perseverance improved over time. I found I was able to laugh at some of my mathematical blockages. I have now learned that by laughing at seemingly irresolvable problems, it is often the case that a way through becomes apparent.

To raise my morale and create a new interest over this period of such intense intellectual concentration, I was encouraged by Felix Farebrother to take up archery. I was given a bow, carved from yew, a quiver that held 12 arrows, a wrist guard and a standard round straw target with a stand. Thus well equipped I was able to set up the target at one end of the Vicarage lawn, which gave me a range of about 50 yards. Even if my arrows strayed well over the target, they fell short of the hedge, thus the likelihood of losing them was minimal.

I could not resist extending my newly learned skills to firing arrows at live targets in Warnham Park. Through a gate beyond the churchyard, some 200 yards distant, were two large clumps of trees, thickly underplanted with rhododendrons, each clump being surrounded by metal railings. In front of these were numerous rabbit burrows. The scourge of Myxomatosis had not yet been deliberately introduced. Rabbits were always grazing, playing or sitting within a safe distance of their home. Rather like the game of Grandmother's Steps, I would walk towards them, stopping whenever a rabbit looked in my direction. If it sensed danger, it sat upright and pricked its ears. When within 60 to 70 yards I would aim and fire an arrow in the direction of the target. The higher and more vertically the arrow travelled, I discovered, the more amusing it was to see the rabbit's reaction. The arrow would strike the ground with a light thud, quivering for a few seconds on impact. The rabbits could not identify the danger and would go on grazing. I never ever scored a bull's eye, but there were some near misses. I just became fascinated and amused by the rabbits' reaction to circumstances that were abnormal to their living environment.

In 1949, meanwhile, my father's governorship of South Australia was extended for a further three years. He had become well known for his interest in sporting activities and particularly in the racing world. Horses running in his colours of black, with claret sleeves and cap, were a familiar sight on the South Australian racecourses. Fixed in my memory from Patricia's weekly letter, however, are two pieces of news about his sporting activities, one involving a camel and the other a White Pointer shark, also known, in UK waters, as the Great White shark.

My father had been on a visit with Patricia and Guy, then aged eight, to Marree in the Broken Hill area and was introduced to a man who owned a number of working camels. Camels are a not uncommon sight in Australia. The first camel imported to the country was from the Canary Islands in 1840. I can only surmise that my father had a yearning to ride a camel, perhaps because the opportunity to do so in North Africa in the 1940s never arose. Having watched Guy being given a ride on a frisky male, my father settled for a ride on a more docile female. The camel's movement on rising caught him unawares and there was a crack as their respective heads made sharp contact. Momentarily stunned, my father fell to the ground, landing heavily on his back. He was transported to the local hospital where an X-ray revealed he had broken his sacrum. The incident caused some amusement in the local press. Instead of Sir Willoughby Norrie, my father became known as Sir Wibbly Wobbly, and a cartoon depicting the female camel rising from the ground showed my father being catapulted from the saddle with the caption: 'Will Her Be Sorry'.

Between 1950 and 1952 two stupendous catches landed my father in the world class of big game fishermen. The practice in shark-fishing is to trail a dead seal behind the boat, a lure that a shark will follow for miles. On reaching the boat, the shark circles it warily for a while, before making a rush for the dead seal. As the shark rises to take the meat, it is the job of the skipper to drop a baited hook into the gaping mouth. For the fisherman, the few minutes that precede the taking of the bait are as tense and exciting as any part of the struggle with the shark. My father would have experienced all this from the deck of a 48-foot yacht called *Nyroca*, at sea just east of Port Lincoln.

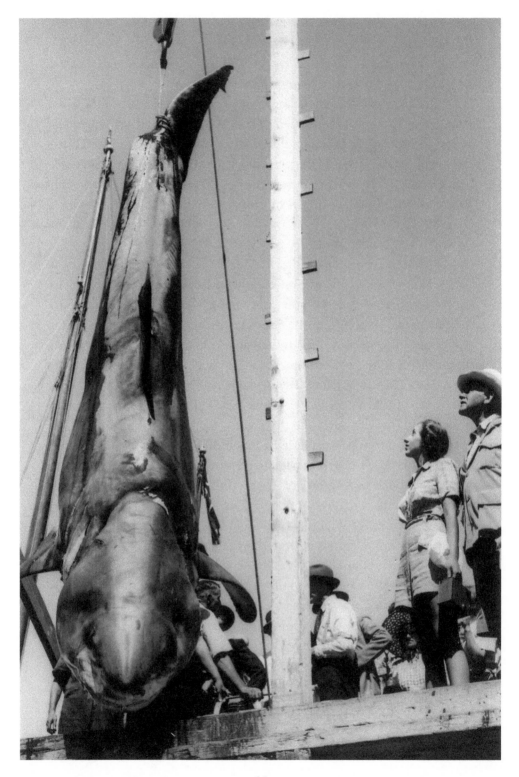

**WORLD RECORD SHARK
CAUGHT BY MY FATHER, 1949. INSET LEFT, WITH
VISCOUNT ALTHORP, LATER TO BE EARL SPENCER,
FATHER OF PRINCESS DIANA.**

The yacht was owned by the Tostevin family, who were Adelaide friends of my parents. Also on board at this time were my sister Rose and one of my father's ADCs, Viscount Althorp, later to be Earl Spencer, father of the late Princess Diana. My sister said that after the shark had been weighed and cut open on the beach, in its stomach were the remains of a half-eaten collie dog that they discovered had been owned by a local farmer on a nearby island. The dog was old and had been put to sleep by the local vet. The owner was so sad that he had decided to give it a sea burial. The owner, needless to say, was contacted by the national press and due to this episode the dog became famous overnight.

At this time, Patricia, Sarah and Annabel were on their way back to England on board the *Orcades* and had shared the excitement, listening to the record shark story as it was reported on the World News. Later, in a *Country Life* article, my father wrote:

> The shark looked from above not unlike a midget submarine. Proud and arrogant it came straight to the dinghy behind the yacht, shook it and bit it viciously. Then it circled the yacht before going straight for one of the dead seal lures hanging over the stern. The others on board begged us for time to get the cameras ready but the shark was hungry. We shouted and made a noise to keep him off for the cameras. But he came in with his jaws wide open and the skipper Jim Green dropped the bait into his mouth as he rose to within a few inches of the deck.
>
> As he started to make his run and I felt the first pressure on my line, I struck vigorously and was confident he had been well and truly hooked. He went out 400 to 500 yards and then followed a long hard tussle. He was hooked at 2.58 p.m. and brought along side at 4.50 p.m. When weighed at Port Lincoln, the shark tipped the scales at 2,225 lbs.

It would have been a world record at the time, but for a small technicality. During the battle, skipper Jim Green helped to adjust the drag on the reel, while the rules demand that fish should be landed singlehanded. My father's second huge catch at the time was also a White Pointer shark weighing 1,713 pounds. This was recognised as an Australian record in the 80-pound breaking-strain class by the Australian Game Fishing Association. It was also recognised as the largest shark or fish ever caught anywhere on a 24-thread line. So our respective sporting activities at the time differed wildly, from untouched rabbits to record-breaking sharks.

Back in England, my last year at Beaudesert passed quickly. If I tried to explain to my grandchildren some of the barbaric behaviour that many boys like me had to endure in schools such as mine, they would probably think that I was making it up. Two particular members of the teaching staff at Beaudesert were feared by the boys. Their behaviour was renowned, and we all prayed that we would never be taught by either. One was a fierce and unforgiving spinster who held classes for the eight- to nine-year-olds. She had an abusive habit of administering punishment by cracking our knuckles with the sharp edge of a wooden ruler. It was demeaning, and it hurt. I am sure her intentions belonged to the 'this will hurt you more than it will hurt me' category, but they proved counter-productive.

The maths teacher who took the top set for boys taking the Common Entrance Examination had little patience for his less bright pupils. The lifeless stare of an ill-matched glass eye was somewhat unnerving, and I was never sure whether he was looking at me or the boy sitting next to me. I remained unable to understand simple geometric calculations on graph paper, and he would grasp the short hairs on my neck and twist them in a clockwise movement, whispering menacingly, 'Do. You. Understand. Now?' One day, however, he was to have a real shock. I had a leg set in plaster after I broke it playing football. I hobbled at school with the help of a stout pair of crutches. After one assault too many, I waited with resolution for him to come within range. I plucked up enough courage to hit him smartly across his shin with one of my crutches. He immediately lost his cool and stormed off out of the room to report me to Austin Richardson, the Headmaster. I was regarded as a hero by the rest of the class, but in a state of terror I waited to see what the consequences of my action might now be.

I was summoned to the headmaster's study. Although it was known that he too beat boys with a cane, that was a rare occasion. Rather than administering a further dose, he merely questioned my problems with maths, and soon changed the subject completely to that of sport and the school's football team's home match to be played that afternoon. The matter appeared to be forgotten – but not by the boys. After this episode that teacher's attitude curiously changed for the better, and no boy in my year suffered again at his hands. In today's world I reckon he would have been arrested and eventually had his teaching registration removed.

The most feared disciplinary punishment for bad behaviour was the boxing ring. The gymnasium at Beaudesert was run with military precision by Sergeant-Major Miller, who had retired from the army, smoked like a chimney and suffered from emphysema. Simple misdemeanours would attract a round in the boxing ring with a boy considerably larger and stronger than oneself, so to exit from the ring with a bleeding nose was a not uncommon occurrence.

Perhaps all this helped me to focus on passing the Common Entrance Examination. I was very conscious of the fact that my parents were clearly worried that I might not get through, their concerns being frequently expressed in their weekly letters from Adelaide. That in itself did not imbue me with confidence. I worried that I would be letting my father down if I was unable to follow in his footsteps to Eton. All was well in the event, and I would indeed follow in his footsteps. Mercifully for me the exam was easier than I had anticipated. The relief of my success was bolstered when I received a congratulatory telegram from Australia.

As my arrival at Eton loomed, Margaret Farebrother threw herself wholeheartedly into preparing me. Shopping began. One whole day was spent in Eton High Street. The tailors Denman & Goddard measured me for two sets of Eton tailcoats and trousers. White shirts, strange little white ties, underpants, vests and socks were purchased from New & Lingwood and black shoes from Ganes. Since all boys had rooms to themselves – only brothers ever shared – I was permitted to choose matching fabric for room curtains, easy chair and ottoman, a simple wooden box with a lid to hide dirty clothes and sports gear. Margaret seemed happy that I should take full responsibility for my choice and did not interfere. All these items were delivered to South Lawn – the school house in which I was to live – prior to the beginning of the term, known at Eton as a 'half'. Outwardly, then, all was set for my arrival at perhaps the most famous public school in England. Secretly, I wished I could be on the other side of the world.

The half began with a housemaster's tea party for new boys and their parents. I arrived with Felix and Margaret and remember clearly the scrumptious chocolate cake more than the impressive college buildings, or any of my new contemporaries. There was no time for any tears when the Farebrothers all too soon said their final goodbyes and drove off. New boys (including me) were immediately bundled off to the music school to find out whether our angelic voices came up to the standard required for the Lower Chapel Choir. None of us were on the side of the angels on that occasion, probably for me because my voice was in the process of breaking. The chapel was just 30 yards away from South Lawn (my house), but the classrooms on the other hand could be as much as half a mile apart!

The senior boys in my house, known in other schools as prefects, had the title of 'Members of the Library'. After the first three weeks they arranged a 'colour test' for new boys, where we had to learn the colours and designs of more than 40 school caps awarded for house colours and other school sports. We also had to know some of the school customs and strange colloquialisms. I think I got five out of six questions correct; I found this quite easy and the older boys, in any case, were reassuringly understanding if we did not get them all right.

Eton is well known for the now defunct custom of 'fagging', whereby members of the library were entitled to send the lower boys like me out on their errands. They had only to stand outside their door and scream '*Boooooy!*' at the top of their voices for every faggable boy to hurtle down the stairs at breakneck speed to the source of the scream. The last to arrive was fagged to do whatever duty was required, the most common being taking notes to boys in other houses. I suspect that today this would be done by mobile phone.

I made many friends at Eton, but the strongest bonds were formed with five boys who arrived on the same day as me. We all boarded at Fred Coleridge's house, soon becoming firm friends, which we remain to this day, meeting from time to time afterwards, as was the tradition, for an FJRC Old Boys' Dinner in London, where friendships were renewed and tales of times past fondly recounted. Sadly, in 2015, only three of the six now remain alive.

The first month or so at a large boarding school, accommodating 1,100 boys, was an awesome experience for me, despite all I had been told about it. I was uneasy in case I could not find the right classroom at the right time. Boys five years my senior towered above me; most, I noticed, would now be shaving every day. I felt strange in my new black tailcoat and pinstriped trousers, and unable to tie the white tie, which was effectively a strip of cloth folded over into a starched, detachable collar. On my first morning I was helped by the 'Dame', the matron in my house, and I soon got the hang of it. Luckily for me I was above the magic height of 5 feet 4 inches, below which I would have had to suffer the ignominy of wearing a 'bum-freezer'.

This was a short black cut-away jacket that scarcely covered the buttocks. I always felt blessed not to have to start my Eton days wearing one.

Fred Coleridge was my much-respected housemaster. He had the ability to get the best out of us boys in his house. During my final year, Coleridge's won a plethora of major sporting events. Ten days before I left Eton forever, a final trophy was added to the shining array of silverware displayed on the tables in the house dining room. Playing as a second pair in the school tennis team, my partner and I surprisingly defeated the first pair in the final of the school doubles, thereby winning the championship.

Most of my contemporaries in Fred's house who chose not to go to university would go on to pursue successful careers in many different fields. I considered myself somewhat academically idle, and unless boys of my vintage were particularly bright, higher forms of education were not pressed upon them. Compared to modern standards, Eton did not often produce large numbers of Oxbridge candidates during my time. Going to university was in general not a priority. Today, by contrast, there are few who do not take up a university place.

I carried out only what was required of me, to the extent that it would not bring me to anyone's undue attention. One notable exception to this was my performance in 'trials' (school exams) during the shorter Lent halves. To my utter amazement I achieved several 'first classes'. This augured well if all I intended to do was swot like fury for the next few months before sitting my O levels. I fretted, however, since I knew that I could not – or would not – keep that effort going during the summer, whose glorious delights tantalisingly included a surfeit of tennis, cricket, swimming and many other activities to choose from. I applied myself to academic work only as far as was needed, passing my O levels in the summer of 1952 at the age of 16.

By now I had been separated from my parents and Nanny for the four long and crucial years during which I made the painful and emotional change from boyhood to young manhood. I was longing to see them again, but wondered what difference this gap would make to our relationship. I would not have to wait much longer to find out: my father had arranged for Guy and myself to return to Australia for our summer holidays. Although born in England, I felt Australia to be my home.

Guy, now at prep school in England, was to accompany me on the Quantas flight from Heathrow all the way to Darwin. The plane, a Super

Constellation, was very comfortable, if a bit noisy due to being propelled by four large piston engines. Unlike modern air travel, the journey to Darwin had several overnight stops. We arrived first in Rome at lunchtime, and enjoyed a bus tour of the city with a picnic lunch. We returned to the plane for a short flight to Cairo, where we spent the night at the Heliopolis Palace Hotel. We arrived the following day in Karachi, in time for dinner. The third day took us for a night in Singapore, after a break in Calcutta. Finally, from Singapore, we reached Darwin on the fourth evening, tired but happy to be home and reunited with our parents. We both remember it fondly as a great adventure for two teenage boys.

In his position as Governor of South Australia, my father was also the administrator of the Northern Territory. The family spent a week in Northern Territory from time to time which included a visit to a buffalo station near Adelaide River, some 70 miles south of Darwin. The station, if my memory is right, was on land owned by the multinational company Vestey Brothers Ltd, who from their beef operations processed the hides into leather. In the case of buffalo it was only the hides that were of interest. Buffalo (*Bubalus bubalis*) were first imported to Australia from central India in 1854. As the buffalo population expanded and dispersed, from the 1890s seasonal shooting licences were granted to individuals to supply hides and horns to local industries. Three years after our visit there, the buffalo hide industry collapsed and the buffalo population began to pose a serious threat to the beef industry and agricultural development, penetrating new areas of wild grazing destined for beef cattle. But buffalo hide was still in demand on our visit to Adelaide River, and we watched two buffalo 'runs', one in the early morning and one in the late afternoon. On each occasion, a herd of several hundred beasts moved at considerable speed across the plain with crews of hunters on horseback in hot pursuit. There were three or four Aboriginals on horseback armed with .303 rifles with short stocks to make it easier to fire from the hip.

As they galloped alongside the herd, they would select a bull and fire a round into its shoulder or its back. As one animal fell, another hunter would quickly dispatch it. In what seemed like a long drive, as we followed in an open jeep, at least 30 buffalo lay on the ground. Following behind our vehicle were more Aboriginals on horseback. The animals were skinned while still warm, leaving the carcasses where they lay for the predators and birds of prey to scavenge. What an unforgettable spectacle all this was.

ETON, WINNING HOUSE CRICKET TEAM, 1954.
THE AUTHOR BACK ROW, SECOND LEFT.

THE NEWLY APPOINTED GOVERNOR GENERAL OF
NEW ZEALAND: MY FATHER AND PATRICIA, 1952.

On returning to the base camp, we watched Aboriginal women wash, scrape and salt the hides, after which process they were hung out. Once the hides had dried they were folded, then despatched to trading stores in Darwin or exported by rail from the station at Adelaide River. One of the Australian daily papers reported that my father had shot a buffalo. He had indeed – not with a rifle, but with a cine camera!

The landscape near Adelaide River was stunning. The billabongs were generously populated with so many different varieties of duck that the entire area of water was hidden from view. On arrival, in addition to the billabongs, we found that torrential rain had left large areas of flood water about 2 to 3 feet deep. As the spring and summer weather returned these areas began to dry out, trapping any fish now unable to escape back to the safety of the rivers, particularly barramundi fish, which were a staple of the Aboriginal diet. We all watched as the local people walked in line very purposefully and slowly through the flood water in bare feet with nets and spears at the ready. Half a dozen sizeable fish weighing about 5 pounds were taken and the catch was divided between our party and the local Aboriginal families. Had I been standing there 1,000 years earlier, I am sure that I would have seen fish being caught and shared in exactly the same way. On returning from a visit to Australia in 2006, I was interested to read an article in one of the national newspapers about barramundi being fish farmed commercially on a site in the New Forest.

That autumn, we were given special dispensation to arrive back at school three weeks late, returning with Patricia by sea on that occasion. We found ourselves travelling on the Orient Line; this time it was the *Orcades* that brought us back to English soil. I had held back on opening a letter from Fred Coleridge, containing the results of my O levels, lest this information might cast a blight over the holiday. Inside the envelope was a postcard upon which Fred had written 'Passed 6. Flopped Maths'. The relief of hearing that I had passed rather than failed was so exhilarating. When the *Orcades* reached Aden I sent the postcard to my father in New Zealand, saying that I would give maths another shot the following year. On that occasion I was indeed able to put two and two together successfully.

Though Warnham with the Farebrothers was regarded as home, my godparents were also particularly hospitable in having me to stay. My royal godmother Princess Alice would invite me to stay at Barnwell Manor near Peterborough during the Easter holidays. My elder sister used to come as well. Rose saw to it that I arrived with clean clothes and polished shoes.

I would have another two years at Eton, the first of which coincided with the Coronation of Queen Elizabeth II in June 1953. My father, then into his second year as Governor General of New Zealand, arranged with the New Zealand High Commission that Rose, Guy and I be allocated seats in a covered stand erected for foreign ambassadors and high commissioners on the edge of Green Park, overlooking Buckingham Palace, to view the procession. It was wonderful. To our left we could see the colourful uniforms of soldiers, sailors and airmen impressively lining both sides of The Mall. As the procession approached the cheering became louder and the waving of Union Jacks more frenetic, including mine. I remember vividly seeing Princess Elizabeth travelling in the Gold State Coach on her way to Westminster Abbey and return as Queen. We listened to the Coronation service transmitted through loudspeakers and celebrated with other guests around me the newly crowned Queen, soon to return to Buckingham Palace. I also recall Queen Salote of Tonga in an open coach, smiling and waving to us, quite unfazed by the pouring rain.

Meanwhile in New Zealand preparations were being made in Government House Auckland in readiness for the impending royal visit. Government House Auckland probably reached the zenith of its importance during the Christmas of 1953.

The Queen and Prince Philip reached Auckland harbour aboard the SS *Gothic* on 22nd December, staying at Government House, which had undergone considerable refurbishment ahead of their stay. A garden party for 2,000 guests was held under unseasonably wet conditions, followed by a reception for 1,500 guests the following day. Soon after their arrival, my father had the responsibility of breaking the tragic news to the Queen about the Tangiwai rail disaster in which 151 people lost their lives. Although this understandably dampened the festivities, my parents worked tirelessly to ensure that Christmas lunch was a joyous affair and retained its traditional form with roast turkey, Christmas pudding, and crackers that had been flown out especially from England. It was from Government House Auckland that the Queen delivered her first Christmas broadcast to the Commonwealth and Empire, as it was then.

Around this time I was preparing to leave Eton, accepting the inevitability of following my father into the army. Some aspects of my school days might have prepared me, so I thought, for such a disciplined career. In my first two years at Eton I was beaten with a cane three times. On these occasions the pain was perfectly bearable. However, my luck later ran out when John Bingham became the new captain of the house. He had a vicious temper and aimed his cane with great accuracy. Nine strokes felt painful enough and my posterior remained multicoloured for most of the holidays. We, as boys, considered beatings at school to be par for the course and nothing unusual. It had happened to our fathers when at school and they had taken it in their stride, so why not us? As he grew older John Bingham developed a strong taste for gambling, spending much of his time at the Clermont gaming club in London. Years later, he was suspected of murder, disappearing without trace in 1974. He is better known as Lord Lucan.

MY FATHER WITH THE QUEEN AT WELLINGTON RACES, 1954.

10

WELLINGTON BOOT

Over the past few years, a series of letters had gone back and forth with my father concerning my next move. This continuing correspondence had been with both me and Fred Coleridge, and was along the lines of, 'What will be a suitable career for George?' followed swiftly by, 'I think he should go into the army.' To me, my father wrote, 'I strongly advise that the army would be the best career for you. I have fixed that you spend a year in New Zealand, and then when you go back to England, you can go to Sandhurst as a New Zealand Cadet, which exempts you from having to take the army exam.' I did have confidence in my ability to pass the exam, but I dared not argue the point, since I thought it was to my advantage that I obey his plan. I was not at all certain that I wanted to be a soldier, and nobody had ever asked me that question. At least he had accepted my request to work outdoors on sheep farms for the year in New Zealand, rather than luxuriate within the confines of Government House.

It was ultimately decided that over the next six months I was to remain in New Zealand and work full-time on three different sheep farms, one in the North Island and two in the South Island. The first farm, Overton, belonged to the Arkwright family and was located in attractive undulating landscape near Marten, some 100 miles north of Wellington in Rangitikei County. This holding was originally 1,200 acres and had been bought by John Arkwright's great uncle, who had married a daughter of Viscount Sidmouth, Prime Minister of Great Britain from 1801 to 1804. The family had moved to New Zealand in 1882. Once again, as at St Peter's in Adelaide, I remember being self-conscious about arriving at Overton in a highly polished Government House car driven by Macdonald, the chauffeur. Was I ever going to get used to being singled out as different?

Turning off the main Wellington to Auckland road, Macdonald and I were unaware that we had to cross the single-track railway line connecting those two cities. We stopped at the unmanned crossing. As we ventured slowly forward, there could only have been inches to spare us from certain disaster as a 'jigger', a maintenance truck which ran on the rails, physically propelled by the backward and forward movement of a central lever operated by a crew of two, moved silently at speed across our front. It was a narrow escape. In hindsight, I should have got out of the car to look down the track in both directions, as the line of sight was marred by high banks. If I could have spoken to that young man all those years ago, I would have advised him against taking things for granted. There would be other times, however, when I would have benefited from heeding my own intuition, as I would discover.

On my first day at Overton I was thrown in at the deep end, starting work at 5.30 am by dagging 20 Romney-Southdown ewes, entailing the removal by clippers of the more disagreeable parts of the fleece from their rear ends. During my second week at Overton, I had to face up to slaughtering a ewe for home consumption. I was taught how to skin it, remove its intestines and prepare the carcase for butchery. Preparing the various cuts and joints was fascinating, and by the end of my stay I would have felt confident to work in the meat trade, but that opportunity never arose.

At the beginning of the third week, my responsibilities increased as I was given the task of cherishing a prize Aberdeen Angus bull that was as docile as a black Labrador, relishing constant pampering. I used to groom him twice a day with a stiff brush, and kept his hooves clear and polished. He could scarcely wait for the arrival of his daily supplement of egg yolks and beer, poured down his throat from a bottle. This concoction, which was intended to ensure a shiny coat, was clearly considered by him to be bovine nectar. This daily routine paid off, as when I proudly displayed my protégé at the local agricultural show he won his class handsomely. On leaving Overton, I remember being paid by cheque for my services which, taking into account my board and lodgings, worked out at about £8 a week. Even in 1954 as an 18-year-old, I felt excited to receive my first ever salary, which seemed to me like a fortune.

After a short stay back at Government House, and with a suitcase full of clean clothes, I took the ferry from Wellington across to Christchurch in the South Island from whence I was given a lift to my second billet, the McKergows' home, Horsford Downs, where I would continue my employment. It involved a drive of 40 miles on shingle roads. The nearest town was Rangiora and the nearest community was an isolated hamlet called White Rock. Mount Karetu formed a backdrop to this wild 3,000-acre farm, located in the picturesque foothills of the Southern Alps. John McKergow had been commissioned from Sandhurst in 1922 and joined the Royal Scots Greys. He retired in 1935, emigrating to New Zealand, buying Horsford Downs which he farmed until the outbreak of war in 1939. He then re-enlisted with the New Zealand Army, eventually to command the 26th New Zealand Battalion. He was wounded in 1944 which permanently impaired the use of his right arm. This did not, however, prevent him from riding with his pack of beagles on his return after the war. Rather than following his pack on foot, he hunted with the beagles as one might with a pack of harriers. There were plenty of hares to chase.

The farm was predominantly sheep but over the years would also include some beef cattle, pigs and a dairy herd. Much of the land had been reclaimed from the bush and the lambs risked being taken by wild pig if they strayed too close to the thicker vegetation. When I was there, a total of more than 200 had been recorded as shot. Red deer were also in abundance. It is said that Captain Cook can be blamed for this, as some of the domesticated pigs and deer kept on board his ship for food were taken ashore and escaped into the wild. Both species have been breeding successfully ever since, much to the vexation of livestock farmers. Rather than using a 4x4 vehicle, the entire farm could be covered on horseback, which I loved and of which I took full advantage. Most of the farming activities in which I was involved took place under the eagle eye of the shepherd, Ernie Hunt, who regarded my knowledge of sheep farming as suspect after only two months at the game, but even more so because my sole experience had been on a farm in the North Island. This was an early insight for me into inter-island rivalry.

On leaving Horsford Downs, I travelled further south to my next destination, Mount Possession near Timaru, which was then the third-largest sheep farm in New Zealand after Molesworth and Glenaray. Mount Possession at the time was owned by the Australia Land Company. Sam Chaffey, the manager, took me out the very first day to look at some sheep that had been marooned on an island surrounded by floodwater some 30 miles from the homestead. The place was called Erehwon – 'nowhere' spelt backwards! Being somewhat overconfident when driving through the water to the island, Sam and I very quickly sank into a hole some 4 feet deep. The vehicle needed to be winched out, so we attached it by a hawser to what we took to be a sturdy tree nearby. We soon noticed, unfortunately for us, that instead of the tree remaining firmly anchored and our vehicle moving as anticipated, it was the other way round. Tree and roots were on the move, whilst we remained well and truly stuck. Eventually, some Maoris on horseback passed our spot, and reported our plight when they reached the nearest telephone some 20 miles away. It took until the early hours of the next morning for rescue to arrive. This being New Zealand there were, not untypically, two crates of beer in the back of our vehicle. The following morning they were empty. The night must have passed very quickly, for I have no memory of it at all!

Mount Possession marked the end of my sheep farming experiences, but before returning to Wellington I enjoyed a series of wild parties in Christchurch, meeting members of the Elworthy family from Timaru. I was immediately invited to Craigmore, their estate of 4,500 acres with a mix of cattle and sheep. In the 1920s American elk – wapati – had been imported and released, but the area had proved to be too wet an environment for them. In the 1980s they successfully took advantage of the boom in Germany of imported venison. The Craigmore Estate became one of New Zealand's venison pioneers, capturing live deer and farming them extensively. In order to satisfy the European market, stock numbers rose from a mere 300 to more than 3,000.

My last two months in New Zealand were an absolute breeze and I enjoyed the very best of Government House life. I fished for trout on Lake Taupo and visited the Bay of Islands to try big game fishing, where I hooked a striped marlin which exercised me for 49 exhilarating minutes until it spat out the bait and hook. Had I managed to land it, I doubt that it would have been even a quarter of the size of my father's world record shark. Having only recently passed the New Zealand driving test I took every opportunity to attend parties, using a Government House car, sometimes quite irresponsibly, much to my parents' exasperation. It was without any doubt a wonderful, wonderful world, but I knew it could not last forever. My final departure from Auckland Airport back to the UK came round all too soon. I had fallen in love with a beautiful girl, and it was clear that this budding relationship could not blossom from 13,000 miles away. The pain I felt when parting from that marvellous life was more sorrowful than sweet. When I arrived at the airport it was with a deep sense of trepidation. For all I knew, I would never taste such happiness again.

In 2002, I decided to return to New Zealand and then Australia in order to research material for this book. My wife Annie had encouraged me to travel back alone on a journey down memory lane. My plan was to revisit the three Government Houses where I had lived, beginning with Auckland and going on to Wellington and Adelaide. I discovered that the university had made so many changes to the old Government House in Auckland, now part of the university campus, that there was little that I could remember of the original layout. I noticed immediately, however, that the fire escape outside my old bedroom had been removed. I had many happy memories of creeping down it with regularity after my parents had retired to bed, using a spare key to borrow a government house car in order to further my romantic relationship. Arriving at Wellington ten days later I was, by contrast, immediately familiar with every room in Government House, which I found had hardly changed at all. The sights and sounds greeted me like an old friend, and I felt warmly accepted.

It was my arrival in Adelaide a week later, however, that triggered powerful feelings and emotions which I had, unconsciously, kept safely buried for half a century. Even though I had left Adelaide so many years before, Adelaide had in truth never left me. After all, some of my most formative years, between the ages of eight and eleven, were spent there. My several visits to Government House concluded by lunching with the governor, and afterwards her staff presented me with a book containing press cuttings of my parents' official duties during my father's seven memorable years in office. As I leafed through the book, I became submerged in a torrent of familiar recollections. As I walked up the stairs to the old day nursery that day, I felt that I had at last come home. It was as if I was a boy again, dressed in my grey flannel uniform, my school cap in one hand and a small suitcase in the other. I knew as I opened the door that the house no longer held Nanny's reassuring welcome, but I was amazed at what I did find.

After my family had left, making way for the new governor, Sir Robert George, all sorts of changes were made for the first post-war royal visit of the Queen and the Duke of Edinburgh. Due to the reconstruction of the old day nursery, the bathroom had become surplus to requirements. The clerk of works' schedule began to run out of time and with days to go before the arrival of the royal party, panic ensued and the door was hurriedly boarded over, the wall plastered and papered, and new carpet laid. The bathroom might have been hidden forever had not Sir Eric Neil, an architect by profession and governor some 18 years later, noticed one upstairs window that seemed not to correspond to a room. This was indeed the bathroom window of my old day nursery. Sir Eric tapped on the wall in the passage. On hearing a hollow sound, the clerk of works was asked to investigate, and the nursery bathroom was rediscovered. The bathroom is a time capsule, remaining exactly as it was during my time there: the same black tiles surround the avocado green basin, lavatory and bath, whilst the same small white mosaic tiles still cover the floor. Even though the room was used by the governor as a walk-in wardrobe, I was seeing it as I had always remembered it, through the eyes and indeed the emotions of the young boy with whom I was becoming increasingly reacquainted. My trip was turning out to be not so much a research expedition but a voyage through my 'Portals of Discovery'.

My week in Adelaide resurrected deep feelings of the despair that I lived through at the age of eleven, when wrenched from my school, my friends and the security of home life in Australia in order to start a new life back in England. I relived the bewilderment that I experienced because I had not understood why I had to leave. In retrospect, a word or two of explanation from my parents would have helped. I had been taught to be brave, which meant, in our family, expressing no emotion. My way of surviving, as with many of my friends, was to deny the existence of what I didn't want to know or feel. In a flash those childhood feelings of despair returned out of the blue. Up came the outrage and feelings of hopelessness. Tears came to my eyes, remembering the eleven-year-old who had lost so much of the life he loved. My resentment reappeared with the same intensity when I began to write this chapter of the book. I found the process of healing a longer one than I had envisaged, and rather harder work, involving as it does acceptance and forgiveness!

In June 1955 I was about to board my plane at Auckland airport back to England. There was sadness, I remember, in parting from my parents once again, just when I was getting to know them. I was leaving Nanny, to whom I was still very close, for the second extended period of time.

These strong feelings were momentarily forgotten, though, as I stepped on board BOAC's service to the Far East, which had just introduced the De Havilland Comet to replace the Super Constellation. I switched to the Comet flight at Singapore unfazed by the fact that a Comet, only the third one built, had recently crashed off Elba.

After landing at Heathrow I would have only three weeks in London, based at Rose's flat in Lowndes Square, to adjust from freedom of choice to the imminent strictures of military life. Discovering who I really was would have to wait, for now I was more concerned with learning to play the role I was expected to take: that of a soldier.

11

SNAKES AND LADDERS

I arrived by myself at King's Cross in July 1955, my army travel warrant in one hand and permitted solitary suitcase in the other. My departure coincided with a prolonged national rail strike. A state of emergency had been declared by the government, following which Churchill had been forced to announce his resignation to a silent press. Some trains were still running, and so it was that I was able to catch an LNER steam locomotive to Darlington from London. My status as a civilian would end after the next 232 apprehensive miles. I was 19 years old, and about to start once more at the bottom of yet another ladder.

In common with the 80 young men who alighted from the train onto the platform with me, my army career began in the inauspicious confines of the back of an olive green Bedford 3 ton truck. Answering to my name, called out by one of four NCOs armed with clipboards, I found myself segregated from a crowd of nervous chain-smokers to be herded together with 19 other unknown potential officers. We were soon transported from Bank Top railway station to the 7th Royal Tank Regiment at Catterick Garrison, to form one of the four squads taken from the fortnightly intake of recruits. Our squad was to undergo four weeks of basic training, followed by three weeks of potential officer training to give us a head start for our arrival at Sandhurst in September. We each had passed the Regular Commissions Board at Westbury and had been selected as cadets for Sandhurst. The other three squads from our intake were national service recruits who, after basic training, learned a trade such as tank driving, gunnery or signalling, and at the end of their course they were posted to other cavalry or royal tank regiments within the Royal Armoured Corps.

Potential officer training started rather earlier than I anticipated. After lunch in the cookhouse there was an ice-breaking exercise in which individuals from our squad were chosen to give a short talk about their life in front of the entire intake and certain members of the permanent staff. My turn came on the very first day, and I realised then that I was fortunate to have had my horizons broadened at an early age when I had worked on the other side of the world. Some of my new associates found it difficult to relate much life experience outside their families and friends, with some struggling to get beyond their last sunny holiday abroad. Many of us sought to conceal any indication of a privileged background or public school education from such a mixed audience.

Basic training seemed mainly to consist of endless forensic kit inspections. All army issue clothes, ranging from PT shorts to khaki shirts, were required to be displayed on our beds with surgical precision. Many items had to be ironed and folded against a hidden cardboard support cut exactly to the same size, eliminating any hint of creasing. Buckles and other items supposed to shine were vigorously polished with Duraglit or Brasso. Boots were buffed to an immaculate shine. Square-bashing took up two-thirds of the day, intermingled with bouts of PT in the gym; all exhausting for us newcomers. Over the next weeks route marches gradually increased in length to a distance of 9 miles. All 20 of us survived this training with great humour and I cannot recall when I have ever felt fitter or in ruder health. Whereas Eton had focused very much on developing the individual, Catterick fostered team spirit in us all, something I increasingly enjoyed.

My entry to the Royal Military Academy Sandhurst coincided with a welcome change to its curriculum. Our intake was caught between the two stools of the old 18-month curriculum and the new one of two years. The good news was that 'Intake Eighteen' would uniquely have to endure only 15 months of officer training. This would bring forward my anticipated commission to December 1956.

There were three colleges – Old, New and Victory – divided into four companies of approximately 50 cadets in each at any one time. I was posted to Old College and placed in Dettingen Company. This austere white building adjoins the expansive Sovereign's Parade ground. Its Doric grand entrance was surely intended by its architect John Saunders to be redolent of a Greek temple, wherein fearsome titanic gods would be worshipped and appeased by puny mortals. Above the imposing entrance stand statues of two Roman gods, Mars the god of war and

Minerva the goddess of wisdom. I hoped to learn from both, but serve only the latter.

All cadets going through Sandhurst are required to attend an annual Sovereign's Parade. Nevertheless only those being commissioned that day have the privilege of marching up the steps in time to the academy band and through the famous grand entrance into Old College. By tradition the parade ends when it is out of sight and the adjutant then rides his horse gingerly up the steps and into the building. Learning to be a British army officer is a serious business a lot of the time. At least once a year during my innings there was a form of 'students' rag', which had the aim of provoking an unexpected response from the commandant downwards. Prior to my time, a previous rag had boisterously succeeded in its aim of diverting all traffic from the busy A30 through either the Sandhurst main gates from the south or the Staff College gates from the north. Unsuspecting motorists would have been surprised and possibly delighted to find themselves passing through the landscaped beauty of woods and lakes surrounding the campus. Little did they know that they were being manoeuvred into a pincer movement whereby the two columns of traffic would converge unexpectedly on the Sovereign's Parade ground in front of Old College, resulting in chaos, in the diabolical ballet of a massive traffic jam. It was some time before the traffic on the A30 was restored to normal by the police.

Intake Eighteen decided they wanted to better this by causing confusion to our rival colleges. The mission for our rag was for Old College to steal all the cutlery from the dining room shared by New and Victory Colleges and hide it on 'Fornication Island', which was in the middle of the lake. Following the success of this daring raid the press would be immediately informed that the IRA had broken in and were responsible for the theft. We foolishly anticipated that this scoop would make the headlines in the national newspapers. Thus, those about to eat breakfast would buy their papers in the corridor, read the headlines, enter the dining room, find no cutlery, and be forced to collect their army issue knife, fork and spoon from their rooms – usually quite a long trek! My task was to inform the press and ensure that the story appeared widely. I carried this out over the telephone in the middle of the night from a call box in the basement of Old College. All our expectations were high. The result, by contrast, was a very damp squib.

The incident subsequently only made it into the second edition of a few newspapers. The following morning, collecting their papers from outside the dining room door, the cadets of New and Victory Colleges were still quite unaware of who had stolen the cutlery now missing from the breakfast table. The whole episode was accepted by all in good humour until two cadets, who shall even now remain nameless, decided to hold a press conference to discuss the way in which the academy was being run. This subsequent event brought an immediate influx of reporters to Sandhurst, eager to exaggerate the story. Major General Hobbs, the commandant at the time, was very unamused by this development. He exonerated those who took part in the raid, but those involved with the press were by contrast asked to step forward and identify themselves.

General Reginald Hobbs had fought under my father during the war and knew him well. At this juncture my father was on three months' leave from New Zealand and had been invited by Hobbs to lunch the following day. I suspect that my father had written to the commandant and his hopes were to find out first-hand how his son was fitting in to army life. I was invited to the lunch as well. The conversation scarcely deviated from the raid and the consequent adverse press coverage. All seemed to agree that when the culprits involved with the press scandal were caught, they should be dismissed immediately from the army. I can only recall pushing the lamb and roast potatoes round and round my plate in a state of heightened anxiety.

My father flew back to New Zealand the next day without any word to me at all on this subject. That was a relief! I decided that my next move must be to seek advice on how my prospective career stood. I approached a very affable and shrewd civilian senior lecturer, who at least knew who I was. I explained my predicament. He advised me to own up to having telephoned the press, and to say categorically that I had nothing whatsoever to do with criticising Sandhurst. I duly owned up to my company commander as to the part I had played. He was clearly troubled about the situation as he had designated me as the next senior under-officer of Dettingen Company for the following term, and did not want my copy book blotted. News of my situation circulated rapidly. Big doors hang on small hinges: the response of the Sandhurst hierarchy would determine fundamentally the direction my life would take. On looking back upon my earlier years, it is clear to me that my father had in truth browbeaten me into joining the army. His choices became my decisions. If I were to be thrown out, what would be next for me? There was no plan B.

My summons to the commandant's office was swift. General Hobbs was understandably very angry with me, particularly as I resolutely refused to reveal to him the culprits' names. I did not know whether he interpreted this as commendable loyalty or insolent stubbornness. The sentence he handed out was three weeks' restriction of privileges, which included having to wear uniform at all times. I was not allowed to leave the academy grounds, and had to undergo two extra 45-minute drills per day on the parade ground.

One saving grace during these restrictions on the campus was that I was chosen to play in the second pair of the Sandhurst tennis team, and so travelled with the team to play outside fixtures. Through this time my sister Rose brought me surprise picnics to share with my friends and enliven my life. Meanwhile, news of my involvement in the rag had spread through New Zealand, where I heard that my father was shaken by the prospect that I might not now follow in his footsteps as a future general; actually, he was more likely in a panic about an alternative career for me. Government House Wellington was surely filled with doom and gloom. I wished to put the matter to rights, but how? So, needing to make a decision, I began to consider the options.

The wise part of myself said I should write a letter to General Hobbs admitting *mea maxima culpa*. It was as if Minerva herself had spoken. I would acknowledge how embarrassing the whole situation must be for him, my father and the academy. I was now beginning to see the light of my tomfoolery and realised that my sense of fun had prevailed over my common sense. But I would steadfastly maintain in the letter that in no way had I ever wished to be associated with the press interviews. This was the truth. The letter was accordingly written and delivered. Once again I was summoned to the commandant's office.

Contrary to my fears, the General looked affable and relaxed as I entered. I could scarcely believe the change in him from the previous meeting. 'Norrie,' he said, 'thank you for your letter of apology and explanation. The matter is now forgotten.' You could have knocked me over with a feather. I felt as if I had been absolved from a mountain of sin by an unexpectedly benevolent high priest.

Having cleared that up, I was nevertheless surprised to be later appointed the next senior under-officer. There was certainly strong competition from two of my fellow cadets, namely Peter Graham and Bob Hodges. Boasting unblemished records, they deserved the appointment more than I did. Bob Hodges made it to Major General, and Peter Graham would later himself become commandant of Sandhurst, retiring as a Lieutenant General and subsequently knighted.

I learned two valuable lessons from this experience. First, that my sense of fun could run away with me; and second, that it always paid to be honest regardless of the consequences. My father quickly recovered his composure and I was, as planned, commissioned in December 1956, marching up the famous steps as he had done before me.

As I look back on my 18 months at Sandhurst, I see how important this period of my life was. From hereon I had to make my own decisions rather than having them made for me. No longer being young enough to know everything, I now realised that we all take risks and that it is possible and profitable to learn from them. Learning from these different insights I left my teen years behind me and entered young adulthood. The growing-up process had also extended into the periods of leave which divided up the four terms of the Sandhurst year. I had kept up with many of my old school friends. Most now had almost finished their National Service, whereas I had taken some months out sheep-farming in New Zealand before going to Sandhurst.

On one occasion I met up in London with one of these old friends, Robin Newman, who had been commissioned in the Coldstream Guards. We went for dinner, after which we walked back along Piccadilly towards Eros, where we were accosted by a seemingly well-dressed man with a bowler hat and umbrella. I remember the words he uttered to this day. 'What are you two looking for?' he said, 'Wine, women or song?' 'All three,' we laughingly replied, expectantly. He then explained that he was going to a private club off Duke Street, where there were lovely young ladies of easy virtue languishing at the bar. Would we, he said, like to join him? We would indeed!

The three of us walked towards Fortnum & Mason and then down Duke Street, where our new friend announced that as we were not members of the club, he would have to fix the doorman to allow our entry. He disappeared, only to return almost immediately. All was arranged he explained, but the entry fee was £5 for each of us. Taking the money from us, he said, 'I'll be back in a couple of minutes, we can all go in together and I will introduce you to the girls.' We each expectantly gave him a £5 note. He disappeared towards Mason's Yard, never to be seen again. After chatting together for a while, the penny dropped. Robin and I returned home with our tails well and truly between our legs. I was discovering that I needed to be 'as wise as a serpent', not 'innocent as a dove'.

SANDHURST TENNIS TEAM, 1956.
THE AUTHOR SECOND RIGHT, BACK ROW.

12

REGIMENTAL DUTY

Joining his regiment for the first time is a proud moment for every newly commissioned officer. I was accepted into the 11th Hussars, the same regiment into which my father had been commissioned and served with distinction. It was whilst first at Sandhurst that I thought in any depth about this regiment's history, in particular its role as an armoured car regiment in the Second World War. Most impressive to me was their fighting record in the Western Desert, where they served longer and more continuously than any other regiment, winning more battle honours here than any other cavalry or royal tank regiment, and they were mentioned nine times in the official history of the Africa Korps. As a 19-year-old second lieutenant, I wondered how I would have fared under those circumstances of combat. Would I ever, I questioned, find out?

After completing a young officers' course at Bovington in Dorset I joined the regiment in Carlisle in April 1957. Just back from service in Malaya, the 11th Hussars had now taken over from the 67th Training Regiment at Hadrian's Camp. Their next task was to train regular and National Service recruits to the standard of military proficiency which would enable them to join other armoured car regiments of their choice as efficiently trained soldiers.

Fortnightly on Thursdays there would be an intake at Hadrian's Camp of about 60 young men aged in their late teens. For the majority of them it would be their first contact with army life, and for many the first time they had ever left home. Having spent seven years away myself from my parents whilst at boarding school in England, including four years when I never saw them at all, I could empathise with any who might suffer the pangs and loneliness of homesickness.

After five weeks of basic training the new recruits had learned how to be smartly turned out at all times, were able to drill efficiently on the parade ground, could handle small arms and classify on the open range with a rifle. After this, eight weeks were then spent in the wireless wing, which allowed the young soldiers to pass a trade test as signallers. Once this was accomplished it was off to their respective regiments, where they would learn a second trade such as driver or gunner. The onus of training and teaching a trade to the recruits rested on the shoulders of the non-commissioned officers rather than on us officers.

Over and above the usual army sporting activities in which officers like me were involved – typically rugby, cricket, athletics or boxing – we were privileged to have at least one day's leave per week to pursue 'extra-curricular activities'. We were encouraged to accept invitations to shoot and fish from local landowners in Cumberland or nearby Dumfriesshire. Naturally, as a cavalry regiment, many officers including myself kept horses in the regimental stables. Officers chose to hunt with hounds or race in point-to-points, steeplechases or hurdle races at race courses as far apart as Ayr and Kelso. This was great fun. These events were recorded in the officers' leave book and make interesting reading.

The relevant volume, which was kept in the adjutant's office while I was there, shows that during the hunting season of 1957-58, 20 officers serving with the regiment managed to hunt 258 days with 29 different packs of hounds. On one of the most notable days the 11th Hussars Regimental Lawn Meet was held at Knockhill, near Lockerbie, and produced a post-war record of 16 horses out from the regimental stables hunting with the Dumfries.

The local landowners were exceptionally generous with their shooting invitations. For the duration of our stay at Carlisle the regiment took a shoot of 1,000 acres near Langholm belonging to the Duke of Buccleuch. Whilst it could hardly be termed a grouse moor, it held enough birds to give us some very amusing days. I remember we shot 100 brace in our last season there. In addition Ivan Straker, Tim Holcroft and a couple of others agreed to take a 4,000 acre rough shoot close to the Solway Firth which provided us all with plenty of pheasants and wildfowl. The regimental journal records the following three-year summary of game shot by officers whilst at Carlisle: 1,997 grouse, 1,491 pheasants, 238 partridges, 50 woodcock, 102 snipe, 426 duck (consisting of 323 mallards, 71 teal, 10 tufted, 9 widgeon, 7 pintail, 3 pochard, 2 golden eye, 1 goosander), 99 geese (88 pink foot, 11 grey leg), 408 pigeon, 16 black game, 232 hares, 64 rabbits and (intriguingly) 15 'various'.

For those officers who fished, the Eden River offered a serious challenge. In the first year at Carlisle the Parkbroom Beat, an unattractive stretch of water with no holding pool, proved to be disappointing. However, for the following two seasons, through local generosity, there was an opportunity to fish the Warwick Hall and Crosby Beats. Over three seasons 120 salmon were caught – 22 in 1957, 76 in 1958 and 22 in half the season of 1959 – the average weight being 12½ pounds. Not bad, we all agreed.

When I first arrived at the officers' mess at Hadrian's Camp one late April Sunday afternoon, I was met by my cousin Dick Sutton. He was unable to offer me a cup of tea, he said, until the 'rat hunt' was over. Somewhat thrown, I was led into the anteroom, where the sofas and chairs were occupied by more dogs than officers. I remained baffled by Dick's remark until I noticed that an entire ceiling panel had been removed, and from the aperture came muffled yelping. The head of a black and white short-haired Jack Russell appeared at the edge of the gaping hole above us, its jaws tightly locked around a dead rat. The terrier's owner stood on a chair and lifted dog and rat to the ground amidst a furore of howls from a bevy of Labradors behind him, unable to join in the fun. In truth, rigor mortis had already set in and Rentokil, rather than the terrier, had already won the day.

Carlisle boasted a famous greyhound stadium at Harraby Park which could allegedly hold 70,000 people. I have never yet discovered how a black and somewhat vicious greyhound, who seemed to have no owner, found his way to Hadrian's Camp. Digger had apparently been raced several times at the White City track but the trainer had found the dog's temperament too aggressive to want to keep him on. Now settled with the regiment's cook, Sergeant Paddy Byrne, he was duly entered to recommence his racing career at the Carlisle track. First time out he won by a distance, but alas not one officer had supported Paddy by backing him, and they missed the opportunity of making a fast buck.

Digger was entered for his second race two weeks later. Given his unexpected victory the bookies were by this time understandably wary. A bunch of officers went to the race meeting and, as agreed, at a given moment all furtively placed their bets with different bookmakers at 2/1.

All eyes were on Digger. He started badly, got better during the second lap, made up tremendous ground thereafter and looked like he was going to win. Alas, he was pipped at the post. All our wagers were lost. We officers quickly lost interest in Digger. Before running him again, Paddy Byrne made a trip to Ireland and brought back another greyhound called Abbey Street Smasher who was known to be a good runner. Within a week the tide had turned: Digger won again at Carlisle with favourable odds, Abbey Street Smasher went on to break the course record at Gretna Green, we recouped all our losses and morale was high again.

I was having a great time making the most of the sporting activities on offer to me, and also looked forward with relish to the riotous weekend house parties. During the three years we were at Carlisle there was so much happening around and about that we had little need to go to London for our entertainment. In Yorkshire alone there were dances given by generous-hearted parents to celebrate their daughters' coming of age, and also hunt balls. Therefore, with the exception of the orderly officer and dogs, the officers' mess was mostly deserted at weekends. Meanwhile, in the surrounding country houses it was a bachelor's paradise.

In September 1959 the 11th Hussars handed over duties as a training regiment to the 15th/19th Hussars and set off for Northern Ireland. The regiment had last been in Ireland from 1903 to 1908, when it was stationed in the Curragh and in Dublin with somewhat different duties. Our job now was to frustrate the activities of the IRA by supporting the Royal Ulster Constabulary and the Ulster Special Constabulary in the counties of Tyrone and Fermanagh. From 1956 to 1962 the IRA was engaged in its 'Border Campaign'. This entailed carrying out guerrilla warfare against targets in Northern Ireland with the aim of overthrowing British rule and creating a united Ireland. Whilst the campaign itself was considered a military failure, members of the IRA felt that it was a justified cause.

Most of the regiment was based in Omagh, but I was deployed with a squadron detached to Castle Archdale in Fermanagh on the shores of Lough Erne, a camp described to us as little more than a collection of Nissen huts. To me, as someone interested in military history, Castle Archdale was instead a place of great significance and as such I welcomed being stationed there. During the Second World War, Castle Archdale had been used as a large base for Sunderland flying boats. It was from here on 26th May 1941 that a coastal command Catalina reconnaissance aircraft had flown over the

Atlantic and spotted the German battleship *Bismarck* via a trailing oil-slick from the ship's damaged fuel tank. The *Bismarck* had already participated in the sinking of the cruiser HMS *Hood* and had damaged the battleship *Prince of Wales*. She had eluded the British forces until that moment. However, she met her fate two days later when a torpedo crippled her steering gear and the following morning she had to fight for her life and was eventually sunk by the combined efforts of gunfire, torpedo hits and deliberate scuttling 30 nautical miles west of Brest.

As a troop leader my main task was to carry out road patrols in conjunction with the police, from whom we had close and willing cooperation. We would often patrol after dark, spending the remainder of the night at a police station. I can recall only two incidents that disturbed the peace. The first was when an overenthusiastic special constable fired a volley of shots at James Daly's Saracen, which had just arrived to aid the Rosslea police station after a shooting incident involving the IRA. James was in the hot seat once more when his troop was housed overnight in Lisnaskea police station. Here the IRA mounted a mortar attack during the night. The attempt was not very accurate, except for one shell which removed some tiles from the roof. James's main concern was for the safety of his two faithful Jack Russell terriers, Punch and Rags. The dogs accompanied him in his armoured car on every patrol. On this occasion they remained oblivious to all that was going on, curled up at the bottom of his sleeping bag.

Soon after my arrival I was invited by Colonel Johnny Blakiston-Houston to shoot partridge at his Beltrim estate. He also requested that as he was short of beaters for the next day's shoot, would I bring any available soldiers from my troop. Most of the boys had been raised in urban areas in the Midlands and knew little about the idiosyncrasies of the Northern Ireland partridge, but they were all happy to take part in something new, and were briefed beforehand at some length by Johnny.

The first four drives rendered not even a solitary blackbird. The keeper, Johnny Morris, nevertheless remained positive and enthusiastic, intimating that the next drive would produce a mass of birds. As the guns, we were lined up in a deep ravine facing north, expecting to be fully engaged, and after 20 minutes we heard a series of whistles, indicating that partridges would soon be flying in our direction. They certainly did, but not from the north. Instead they came from the south, taking us completely by surprise.

Three coveys of about 15 birds flew straight over our heads and not a shot was fired.

Again thanks to the generosity of the Abercorns, Brookeboroughs, Ernes and Blakiston-Houstons, we fished the best beats of the River Mourne and its smaller but more exacting tributaries. In 1959, five salmon and grilse were caught, and the next year just over 20. Most of the salmon averaged 9 pounds. This kept up the high standard of cuisine in the officers' mess.

Lough Erne had become a centre for sailing and water-skiing and the Army Sailing Association had lent us two Snipe boats at Castle Archdale. As a consequence, Sunday lunch water-skiing parties were hugely popular. A fellow officer Freddie Wills owned a Dowty jet speedboat with a fibreglass hull. Inspired by this, Nick Rayner decided to build one himself inside a storage hut in the barracks. Later, when the trailer arrived to remove it to Castle Archdale, he discovered that it was 2 inches too wide to pass through the large metal doors. The cost of removing and replacing the wood, metalwork and masonry of the hut was estimated to be more than the value of the boat. Nick's boat, it is said, was still entombed as the regiment prepared to leave the barracks for Aden three months later.

On account of the abnormally dry spring and summer of 1959, the water levels on Lough Erne had dropped considerably by the time we were about to leave, but this did not deter our water-skiing escapades. On one memorable occasion at twilight, after a good dinner, Michael Allenby was driving Freddie's Dowty at high speed, 20 knots, across the lough with myself as passenger, towing Freddie Wills and Johnny Lewis on water-skis. The boat suddenly hit an unseen vertical pipe just below the surface, catapulting me over the widescreen. I caught my shoulder en route, landing in a heap near the edge of the lough in only 3 feet of water. I had broken my collarbone and given myself a nasty shock. For some reason an image of Admiral Lord Nelson after his arm had been shot off by a musket ball came to mind. Admittedly, such a comparison was somewhat tenuous, not least because whereas he had resumed his command 30 minutes after having had his arm amputated I, having spent a part of the night in Enniskillen hospital, merely returned to work the following day full of painkillers and with my arm in a sling.

Over the next weeks, the arrangements for our imminent departure for Aden were much in our minds. However, we were given the news that after our tour there was completed, we would become an armoured regiment in Germany. This would entail changing over from Saladin armoured cars and Ferret scout cars to 52-ton Centurion tanks. The agility and speed of wheeled vehicles would be sacrificed for the cumbersome heaviness of metal tracks. This change, although in some ways regrettable, would present a new challenge since switching to this type of equipment meant having to learn different tactics.

Sam Elworthy, our new commander-in-chief (C-in-C) of Middle East Command, had been appointed to the position just prior to our arrival in Aden. He was a distinguished Air Marshal and highly decorated wartime Wellington bomber pilot, born in New Zealand but educated at Marlborough and Cambridge. The regiment was quick to offer to provide him with an ADC. Perhaps because of my age and connections to New Zealand, it was suggested that I should accept the post. My own years in Government House had helped me become well acquainted with the basic duties of an ADC. This position would, amongst other things, entail travelling across lands encompassing the entire Arabian Peninsula, and as far south as Kenya and Uganda. What an opportunity that would be for me to see more of the world! I accepted with alacrity.

13

ARRIVAL IN ADEN

Sam Elworthy, his wife Audrey and I flew out to Aden from Northolt Airfield, West London in a Hastings aircraft that had been seconded to him by the RAF for his tour of duty. It had four engines, and although slow, was surprisingly comfortable. We flew directly to El Adem in Libya to refuel, finally – exhausted – touching down in Aden to land at Khormaksar. A sense of excitement and anticipation immediately filled me at the thought of experiencing something so new and stimulating.

Aden had always been a strategic port, situated as it was on the south-west corner of the Yemen, dominating the entrance to the Red Sea, and was in the early 1960s the third-largest port in the world. It had been controlled by the British since 1839, and because of its position, roughly equidistant from the Suez Canal, Bombay and Zanzibar, it had acted as an important staging-post for shipping. Legends say that Cain and Abel founded it and Cain was reputed to have been buried in a tomb which had been elevated to an inaccessible height by repeated volcanic action. The large port was also known for the Tawila Water Tanks. These were built in a cleft in the volcanic rock which surrounds the city of Crater to collect and store the infrequent rainfall. Some sources refer to them as Solomon's Tanks or Cisterns, and it is said that they were constructed under the orders of the Queen of Sheba to provide a source of water for her armies. Originally 53 tanks were constructed. Today only 13 may still survive.

From Command House, the C-in-C's residence where Sam and his family lived, I could see the officers' club at Tarshyne, where I was to find my living quarters. This Indian-style building had a veranda and open space on both sides, secured by shutters. I was delighted to see two large electric fans hanging down from the ceiling. These features, together with a thatched high-pitched roof, made it comfortably cool for me.

Three years earlier, the perils of bathing at the club beach had hit the headlines when an RAF wife was attacked by a shark in shallow water. Above Command House, neatly tucked away behind the trees and foliage of their gardens and terraces, were the residences of the general officers commanding, a major general and an air vice marshal. Further away beyond the blue waters, one could pick out Little Aden harbour and the BP oil refinery, visible against the peaks of the hills to the west. Nearer by stood the Victorian Custom House on the Prince of Wales Pier, a two-storied building constructed in 'Indo-Colonial' style sporting a Union Jack fluttering from its rooftop. It had been built in 1868, and was now the Secretariat, and headquarters of Britain's South Arabian administration. A feature that will forever remind me of Aden was a tower with an enormous clock face resembling Big Ben. Far from the temperate climes of London, however, Aden had a reputation for a disagreeable climate; but I found this to be unjust. The months from October to February offered a perfect temperature, I thought. To sit under brilliant Arabian stars in the evenings, with a gentle breeze and no insects to annoy one, was sheer delight. Annual rainfall is only 2 inches so there is little risk of an unexpected deluge. March and April become a little warmer. From May to September the average temperature is more than 100 degrees and is therefore the period to avoid. Aden had notoriety as a punishment station for officers of British regiments who had misbehaved elsewhere or who had got themselves into matrimonial difficulties. Happily I was not, as yet, in either category.

Aden in 1960 appeared to be a staging post for anyone in the services whose eventual destination was Malaysia and Hong Kong. Command House, being the official residence of the commander-in-chief, was often full of guests. Some of my more fun duties included arranging lunch and dinner parties for official engagements both military and civilian, producing a list of guests and a biography for each; making sure the transport was on time and that the commander-in-chief knew what the appropriate attire was for the occasion.

When not on duty, there was ample spare time to appreciate the cool of the wonderful Arabian evenings under a blanket of stars and the light of a pale yellow moon. There was something about this heady combination that made any budding romance even more intense. Single girls were much in demand, and some were hoping to find a husband amongst the many single young officers of all three services stationed in the Arabian Peninsula. Somehow I managed to avoid the more obvious traps.

However, I did have an enduring friendship with a lady nine years my senior, until the day she died in her eightieth year. Born in the Western Isles of Scotland, she was a fluent Gaelic speaker and despite a life of extensive travelling she served as a lifelong member of the London Gaelic choir. Accomplished as a linguist in French and German, she joined the Foreign Office after the Second World War. When I announced in 1964 that I was engaged to be married, with tongue in cheek she immediately sent me an appropriate present of one of Graham Greene's bestsellers: *The End of the Affair*! One of her main attributes was her in-depth knowledge of the English language. Renowned for her expertise, during her last few years she was asked to read and critique a number of autobiographies, including the memoirs of a very well-known politician of the 1990s. She was much looking forward to helping me with mine, but sadly her demise took place some years before I had even started writing.

There was a constant flow of guests staying at Command House. I remember a General Richardson, a former Royal Engineer, going to his room to change for an evening engagement to which I was to accompany him. After a period of time he hastened down the steps of the guest bungalow, apologising for his lateness. As we jumped into the C-in-C's car he explained to me that there had been no cold water to cool his bath. 'I ran half-dressed,' he said, 'to the garden to find the hose, in order to put it through the bathroom window and solve the matter. I am a trained plumber, as it happens.' Next day I checked with the works department, and discovered that the Arab plumbers had connected both taps to the hot water system, which explains that!

General FitzGeorge-Balfour had stayed with us on several occasions, and on this particular one he changed his plans after only two days and for some reason decided to catch the earliest RAF flight back to London. In my usual cavalier fashion I had left the journey to Khormaksar Airport with little time to spare. We were of course delayed – by a crash on the Ma'alla Straight dual carriageway – and so arrived 20 minutes late for check-in. Not even a three-star general was able to persuade the RAF to allow him on board under the circumstances, and so keep his meeting with the chief of defence staff on the following day. As a result of my irresponsibility he was fairly wild with me, and I returned to Command House wondering what the consequences of this might be. I had, however, forgotten that as a form of belt and braces back-up arrangement, I had also booked him on an Air Italia flight to London. This should have been cancelled by me 24 hours before, so that the War Office would not be liable to pay for the unused ticket, but I had not done it, so by a mixture of sheer luck and incompetence the general had an alternative flight to London, which surprised him enormously and got me off the hook. I received welcome praise which was later followed by a letter of thanks. No conjuror ever pulled a more welcome rabbit from any hat! In the event, the RAF flight that had taken off that morning got as far as Cyprus, where it broke down, marooning its passengers for three days. The general, on the other hand, flew in first class comfort all the way home.

My forgetfulness played havoc yet again on another occasion. I was to fly with Sam and Audrey Elworthy to Mukalla, the regional capital on the east coast. We left Command House for the airport when, after ten minutes, I realised to my complete horror that I had left the C-in-C's briefcase behind. I had no option other than to tell the driver to return at once. As the Humber Super Snipe made an urgent U-turn on the Ma'alla Straight, successfully traversing the raised central reservation, the Elworthys sitting in the back must have thought that I had taken leave of my senses. When the expletives from behind me had passed, I explained as calmly as possible that I had left his briefcase in the hall. This was not a propitious moment for my future career!

We arrived back at Command House with Sam looking as black as thunder, saying brusquely to me, 'I'll get the thing myself' as he got out of the car. Two hours later, on board the Hastings transport plane, tempers had calmed down. Sam was struggling to read the airmail edition of *The Times*, to which Audrey said, 'Why are you squinting Sam? Why don't you find your glasses?' A search took place but there was no sign of them. He had clearly left them somewhere, which resulted in Audrey giving him a lecture on personal responsibility. That afternoon a follow-on flight arrived at Mukalla with a special delivery: his glasses, found exactly where he had left them in Command House.

Sam and Audrey were good sparring partners when it came to discussions, often on subjects of political history. A graduate of the University of Auckland, Audrey was a perfect match for Sam, and he got away with very little. He had that rare gift of being able to talk to anyone on any subject that fitted the occasion. The only time that Sam and I ever fell out seriously was when sailing. Sam had been a skilled international sailor. He arranged for a Flying Fifteen, an exciting, competitive two-man racing craft, to be shipped out to Aden by RAF transport. He asked me if I would like to crew for him. I explained that I had no previous experience of sailing, so if he wanted to race seriously, I was not the person to be in the boat with him; but added that I would happily come out to christen his new boat as he had suggested. He as usual behaved with charm and decorum throughout that Saturday afternoon, during which my seamanship began to improve, even to attempting the spinnaker drill.

The first race was due the following day and Sam had wisely organised an experienced yachtsman to crew for him, but on Saturday evening discovered by telephone that his new crew member was off sick. So, turning round, he said to me, 'You will have to crew tomorrow, it's too late to find someone else now.' Alarm bells rang loudly in my ears as I said to myself, this is the C-in-C's first race in Aden. He aims to win it. Just to take part is not an option. By next morning I felt as apprehensive as I had been at Sandhurst when summoned to the commandant's office after the rag.

Together we walked to the water's edge and prepared for the race. We got round the first marker in the lead, but from this point onwards, things went downhill. Rounding the second marker, we lost two places; after the third marker we lay seventh. On rounding the fourth marker at the end of Aden Harbour we lay second from last. The wind was getting up and Sam became more boot-faced by the minute. His orders to me came out in sharp staccato tones. For myself, the end of the race could not come soon enough. 'Get the bloody spinnaker up!' he yelled. In my haste I jammed it halfway up the mast, where it billowed hopelessly in one long distended line, failing to open. Sam screamed, 'Take the tiller!' I scrambled over to where he was and took control – I thought – but the boat seemed to have a mind of its own.

We zig-zagged towards the finishing line in last place, the ignominious boom of the cannon signifying that the race was over. I feared Sam that would become the focus of amusement and ridicule amongst his sailing peers. Whereas he never ran me down in public as the most useless crew member with whom he had ever had the misfortune to sail, we hardly spoke until he was safely reunited with his first choice of crew member, who thankfully had now recovered. They won the next race, and all returned to normal: it was as though our old relationship had never faltered. Competitive sailing, I concluded, was possibly a catalyst likely to bring out hidden aspects of people's characters. Was this an example of someone displaying a lack of humour and being impatient, and somewhat overbearing, I wondered? Perhaps the C-in-C revealed himself to be human, just like the rest of us.

Although the regiment was now stationed some 12 miles west at Little Aden, I was able to keep in touch with them. On days where there were no official afternoon duties I found time to join my brother officers in some of their activities. I learned to play polo on a ground of rolled sand, the same venue used for the Aden race meetings which were held from May to October. These attracted large local crowds and were well supported by bookmakers and a tote. The main attraction was a camel race over 3 furlongs, the camels starting in the lying position. The race would start at a cracking pace, but then it seemed that the camels' stamina waned in spite of the frantic urgings of the Arab jockeys, eliciting dismal roars of discomfort from their mounts. For my one and only race, thankfully not on a camel, I mounted a polo pony called Nimbus, a complete outsider, and so was given 50 yards head start. By the time we had gone halfway round the course I had been passed by every other runner, and Nimbus had clearly had enough. I finished last.

The C-in-C packed a lot of travel into his first year. Within a week of arriving, we flew to Amman, Jordan to pick up the new Governor of Aden, Sir Charles Johnston, and his wife Natasha. He had become Ambassador to Jordan in 1956 at the time of the Suez Crisis. A fascinating weekend was spent in Beihan, situated in the Western Aden Protectorate, wedged between the Hadhramaut and the Rub' Al Khali (the Empty Quarter). Beihan was ruled by Sharif Hussein Ahmad Al Habieli in conjunction with his son, the Amir. The family are a branch of the Hashemites, proud of their descent from the Prophet and their relationship with the Jordanian royal family. Sharif Hussein had striking features. He was bearded, hawk-faced, and had flashing eyes. He had distinguished good manners and an uncontrollable sense of humour. We stayed in the Sharif's modestly constructed white and pink-hued palace, situated on a hillock in Wadi Beihan. This was an oasis of occasional palm trees with a vivid green carpet of young wheat and barley. There were a number of mud-walled huts, and strings of camels were seen padding off in different directions. Traditional desert dwellers in their black tents were a common sight.

The ancient trade route that ran from India to the southern Arabian coast, turning northwards towards the Mediterranean, traversed the state. We were privileged that weekend to have been taken by the Sharif to see a working salt mine. There were probably more than 50 workers, who greeted our arrival by kneeling and kissing the hand of the Sharif. Salt had been chipped away from that cliff face for hundreds of years, and bags of salt continue to be transported by camel along that very same trade route today.

In 1967 the collapse of the South Arabian Federation marked a tragic and dishonourable ending to 128 years of British administration. Britain's hasty withdrawal left the newly formed Federation of South Arabia and its peoples to the mercies of competing socialist radicals, who after a period of murderous civil war established, with Soviet backing, the Arab world's only communist state, leaving a further 27-year legacy of impoverishment and subjugation. In 1990, South Yemen and the Hadhramaut were united with North Yemen to become the Republic of Yemen. Since 9/11 the US, in support of the Republic of Yemen, has found itself locked in armed conflict with Al-Qaeda and ISIS-linked groups, remaining bent on establishing safe havens, training militants and spreading their influence throughout the Arabian Peninsula. British rule in this part of the world is now but a distant memory.

14

VISITS TO HADHRAMAUT, KUWAIT AND THE FAR EAST

Of all the places in the south of Arabia, the one in which I could have been persuaded to stay for a prolonged period was the Hadhramaut. In short, the word 'Hadhramaut' refers to the historical Qu'aiti and Kathiri sultanates, originally within the Eastern Aden Protectorate, and overseen by the British Resident, a government official, in Aden. It sits between Oman in the east, the border of the original Aden Protectorate to the west, the Empty Quarter to the north and by the Indian Ocean to the south. These states were abolished when South Yemen became an independent communist state in 1967.

The C-in-C's tour was to include Mukulla, the Qu'aiti capital and the Wadi Hadhramaut itself, which according to a well-known travel website is the most famous wadi in Arabia, and one of the most renowned valleys in the world. It had been celebrated in antiquity for the production of frankincense. Part of the territory was Qu'aiti, and part Kathiri. Some of the state boundaries at the time were still under dispute. We flew to Riyan, some 300 miles north-east of Aden. It was a coastal RAF staging post, used also by Aden Airways, built on a strip of sand bordering the sea 20 miles east of the sea port of Mukulla, which linked Britain to India and the Far East.

We drove from the airstrip by Land Rover along the beach, and on rounding a headland Mukulla came into view. The brilliant glitter of whitewashed palaces, mosques, houses and towers in different shapes and sizes offered a magnificent contrast of colour against a setting comprising the near vertical pink sandstone cliffs of Jebel Qarat and a vivid blue sea. From a distance of about 3 miles, it was rather reminiscent of Monte Carlo, which I knew well, but my vision of the Côte d'Azur soon evaporated in the high humidity. There were no signs of millionaires' yachts here. Instead, the harbour was crammed with dhows, some about to depart, hoisting their triangular lateen sails, to join the trade route stretching all the way from Bahrain to Zanzibar. On the harbour front were camel trains loading and unloading, Mukulla being the hub for a vast network of caravan routes.

ABOVE: MUKALLA HARBOUR.

RIGHT TOP: HADHRAMI WOMEN WORKING IN THE FIELDS.

RIGHT BOTTOM: KATHIRI SULTAN'S PALACE IN SAIUN.

Trade was Mukulla's principal industry, although fishing could have been. The latter was the most important economic activity along South Arabia's 750-mile-long coastline. Large shoals of sardines were traditionally harvested with seine nets, which are designed to hang vertically in the water by means of floats at the top to keep them vertical and weights at the bottom. The sardines, which are called *wasif*, are laid out to dry and provide a staple food for the local population as well as many camels. *Wasif* were also used as a fertiliser for vegetable production. In a good season, these fish are found piled up on the beaches for hundreds of yards. A subsidiary industry in the export of crayfish had just started when I was there and consignments were collected and transported away by Aden Airways. Tuna and shark were also landed and sold for local consumption as well as export. Dry shark tails and fins fetched high prices in China and the Far East. Other varieties of fish brought ashore included barracuda, kingfish, mackerel, sea perch, rock cod, as well as Moray eels. Soviet and Japanese fishing fleets, equipped with modern refrigerated ships, were already active in the Gulf of Aden, yet the potential of Mukulla's fishing industry had not at that time been realised.

Apart from the coastal Arab population, there was a cross-section of Baluchis, Pakistanis, Somalis, Africans, Javanese, and above all Indians, who were prominent because the government of India had administered the entire territory until 1937 and many Indians had remained. In the early nineteenth century, large-scale Hadhramaut migration had established sizeable Hadhrami minorities all around the Indian Ocean, Hyderabad, South East Asia, East Africa, Malabar, Java, Sumatra, Malacca and Singapore. The grandson of one Hadhrami emigrant, who moved to Saudi Arabia at the beginning of the twentieth century, would leave his imprint on world history: this was Osama Bin Laden.

The Colonial Office appointed a resident adviser for the area, based in Mukulla, alongside nine political officers called assistant advisers. All were dispersed through the nearby regions, providing the sultans with political and economic guidance and also assisting in maintaining peace and security at local level. During our five-day visit I had ample time to have in-depth conversations with several of the political officers. As well as being absorbed by their work and responsibilities, I became fascinated and more and more intrigued by my new surroundings. Steeped in time, this civilisation had a unique tribal culture, many individual customs and values, but also suffered massive disputes.

Wadi Hadhramaut, cut into a high plateau, is of global geographical and as already indicated, historical interest. Flying on from Mukulla, I gazed down on high rugged cliffs of limestone that glowed golden in the sun. This stretch of land measures 97 miles in length and roughly 5 miles in width; its soil is sandy but fertile. Whilst the wadi has an enviable winter climate, we were warned that the summer heat could be almost unbearable. Some geologists hold the theory that originally this valley was formed by floods running between the high plateaus of sandstone, forming a sparse network of deeply sunk wadis that act as seasonal watercourses. Flooding is by no means regular and varies from one to three times a year, perhaps the perfect setting to have inspired Paul Torday to write his novel *Salmon Fishing in the Yemen.*

Bedu tribes have inhabited the Wadi since biblical times. Some are said to be descended from the sons of Noah. The Hadhramis live in densely built towns alongside traditional watering stations. We saw the inhabitants of a typical local village gathering their wheat and millet. Round about, grew fields of lucerne and sorghum, a type of sweet grass. There were date and coconut groves, and even some coffee plantations. Higher up on the plateau itself, Bedouins grazed herds of sheep and goats. The women, who worked possibly harder than the men, were threshing the grain with palm logs, winnowing with flat baskets and tilling the land with hoes. From top to toe they were clad in black and wore pointed straw hats like those worn by mythical witches.

To reach Saiun, the Kathiri capital city, we flew further on to a small airstrip at Ghuraf some 15 miles distant. The *shamal*, the arid wind that blows from the desert, together with the brightness of the sun, forced us to land downwind, requiring our pilot to exert considerable skill in keeping to the short runway.

The allure of Saiun lies in its architecture. Owing to the lack of stone, all buildings are constructed out of bricks made of mud and straw, dried hard under the hot sun. After the buildings are completed, there follows a process of whitening with limestone. This is smeared on like putty and the effect when dry is a smooth glaze. Without doubt, for me the fairy-tale sultan's palace in Kathiri outshone any other building in the wadi. It is the biggest in the world made from mud bricks. This magnificent structure stands seven storeys high on a small hill in the centre of Saiun. From a distance, by virtue of its shape and appearance, it resembles a multi-tiered wedding cake in square form. Although the current facade was completed in 1874, the original structure dates back to the Sultan Badr Abu Twiriq in 1411.

On our last day there we visited Shibam, known as the Manhattan of the Hadhramaut because of its mud skyscrapers, which I concluded was an excellent example of early town planning based on the principle of vertical construction. It is now a World Heritage Site. At the time of our visit, it had a population of 3,400 and the inhabitants were squeezed into 485 houses in an area measuring only 275 square yards. For reasons of refuge and protection, there was no land for new development. Thus, every time an old house was demolished, it was replaced by a new skyscraper. Although the city was built on a mound, during flood time it could almost be surrounded by water. The population since the time of our visit has since doubled.

Life in this part of the world seemed to move at a wonderfully slow pace and the atmosphere was accordingly peaceful. I realised I had a growing respect for a culture about which I was not only fascinated but also eager to investigate more. I wondered how I would fare as a political officer under the aegis of the Colonial Office. My last evening in Saiun I spent alone, relaxing in a verdant roof garden just watching the sunset, wondering at its beauty and enjoying the tranquillity of the evening. What happened then is difficult to describe. For a fleeting moment, I felt a sudden pulse of overwhelming goodwill and harmony, leaving me feeling surprised and somewhat overcome. I found myself in a state of great calm and humility, unusual for me, and I asked myself whether perhaps there could be a depth to my life that I had overlooked. What if I followed my own star after all? Where would it take me?

Looking back now over the years, there were in my life a number of opportunities to change course. Maybe, even in these beautiful surroundings, my father's advice rang in my ear dictating that I should pursue an army career. Perhaps I got cold feet because the assistant advisers that I had just met were university graduates, had passed the Civil Service exam to qualify for colonial service and were already fluent Arab linguists, none of which I could claim. So iron logic prevailed. I was not at this point in a position to change career. Within a relatively short time of our return, British forces were called upon to support the independent State of Kuwait. We would all soon have to leave the Hadhramaut, and I needed to turn my mind to practical matters on behalf of the C-in-C.

Kuwait had been a former British protectorate. General Qasim, the self-imposed prime minister, responsible with others for the murder of King Faisal of Iraq and his pro-British prime minister, Nuri as-Said, had been busy building up a close relationship with the Soviet Union, strengthening his army with T-55 tanks and heavy Russian artillery. This force was now theoretically strong enough to capture Kuwait's oil fields. Whilst in our lifetime we may have witnessed two Gulf Wars fought for the same objective, it was the original collapse of the Ottoman Empire after Turkey's defeat in the First World War that prompted Iraq to claim sovereignty over Kuwait. Qasim reignited the claim but his expansionist ideas were supported neither by President Nasser in Egypt nor by many of the other Arab states. By the time the British forces had arrived in strength in defence of Kuwait, Qasim had withdrawn his forces from its border. The situation then reverted to a war of words. Qasim claimed he feared a British pre-emptive strike and accused the British of discrediting him. The 'Kuwait Crisis' became merely a war of words. Two years later the Ba'ath Party, most likely influenced by Saddam Hussein, forcibly removed him from power and after a short trial he was executed, like Saddam himself would be in the fullness of time.

The 11th Hussars were amongst the first troops to arrive. Their assignment was to carry out a traditional armoured car role, covering troops on the Kuwait-Iraq border. This task was to be performed jointly with the Kuwait armoured car force. I found myself, within the first 48 hours, flying to Kuwait City with the C-in-C, who was to mastermind the whole operation. As he had more staff officers looking after him than he could possibly need, I sought permission to rejoin the regiment for the duration of the operation.

My plea was accepted and I set about finding their exact location. Freddie Wills, who had just completed an air-portability course in England, suddenly found himself responsible for loading Saladin armoured cars and Ferret scout cars into an RAF Beverley aircraft in Aden. On completing this mission he too flew to join me and the regiment in Kuwait City. It was not going to be a problem finding the regiment in daylight, as we knew it to be sitting astride the main Kuwait City to Basra road.

With us, attempting to cover news of the impending battle, was a *Time Life* magazine journalist who had flown in from New York. There could be no better place to report on this battle than with the force protecting the Kuwait-Iraq border. I insisted that he join us. We hitched a lift with an obliging Iraqi driver, whose pantechnicon truck was loaded with goods from Kuwait to be sold in Basra, and who was oblivious of the fact that he might be passing through a possible war zone. Some 50 miles towards Basra, we found the 11th Hussar tactical sign on the side of the road and so alighted. An 11th Hussar trooper conducted us to the commanding officers' tent. He was Lieutenant Colonel Philip Lauder, a veteran wartime soldier who had fought in the North African desert campaign. He had a pronounced stutter, and he would stroke his nose as though it would help to extract some word that he found difficult to articulate. He was clearly under some pressure.

Freddie and I entered the tent, saluted smartly, saying, 'Reporting for duty, Colonel, with a guest.' Sitting at a trestle table and stroking the end of his nose vigorously, all he could say was 'How did you f...f...f... find your way here?' After this warm and reassuring welcome, followed by laughter, we were made liaison officers for the short time we were in Kuwait, communicating for the most part with the Kuwaiti armed forces and the administrative staff of the resident oil companies, which suited us well.

Philip Lauder and the *Time Life* magazine journalist spent considerable time together and formed a strong bond of friendship. The journalist was asked to stay on for three days and wrote a very positive article about the regiment's responsibilities for the next publication. Most of us will remember Kuwait for the intense heat, the sandstorms, the salamander lizards and the scorpions. General Qasim's tanks never left their concentration areas. It was rumoured, but never authenticated, that the SAS managed to remove many of the wheels from the tank transporters. Had it not been for such a build-up of British forces in such a rapid time, this operation might have been the prelude to the later Gulf or Iraq wars.

My 13 months as ADC to the C-in-C passed all too quickly, the term of office lasting only as long as the 11th Hussars remained in Little Aden. When they returned to England by troop ship, I flew back with the RAF. Nevertheless, before my departure I took part in an official C-in-C's tour of the Far East Command. The entire staff of the C-in-C wished to be included and the Hastings was filled to capacity. My responsibility as far as the travel arrangements were concerned was to ensure that the entire planeload of passengers and their luggage reached each destination en route. We were to fly via the island of Gan and then on to Singapore and Hong Kong. The return journey was to be via Bangkok and Bahrain.

After two entertaining days in Bangkok, a friend, Mark Schreiber, many years later to be ennobled as Lord Marlesford, asked me a favour. Mark was working for Fisons, the pharmaceutical and chemical giant, and he asked if on our departure from the hotel, I could possibly transport two extra suitcases to the Air India desk at the airport. These belonged to a friend, and her take-off to the UK was an hour after our departure to Bahrain. I saw no problem. I had 18 cars at my disposal. The Aden hierarchy consisting of the C-in-C, the general, the air vice marshal and their wives were to be transported in Cars 1 to 3. The entire luggage for the Hasting's flight was to be loaded into cars and vans numbering 4 to 10, and to include the two extra suitcases. The remainder of us were driven in cars 11 to 18, into which convoy I had foolishly placed myself. I had certainly not thought through the possible implications of cars 11-18 being delayed.

As it happened, there was a serious accident on the dual carriageway to the airport, causing a huge tailback. Cars 1-10 managed to circumvent the wreckage at the scene of the accident and duly reached the airport but the remaining cars, all of which alas lacked any form of air-conditioning, were laid up for some 40 minutes in what seemed like a Turkish bath. Bangkok airport in 1961 could scarcely have been classed as either international or secure. The Hastings had been placed in a parking bay in front of a two-storey VIP lounge. The cars and vans carrying the luggage were permitted to drive straight on to the concrete apron to the aircraft for loading. It was quite clear what was going to happen. All suitcases would be loaded on to the Hastings, including the two suitcases belonging to Mark's friend. On my arrival, I was prevented from reaching the Hastings by armed guards standing in front of the crowd barriers. Despite my gesticulations and sign language, I watched helplessly as the last suitcase was loaded into the hold.

Finally, a policeman who spoke limited English escorted me to the VIP lounge, where the Elworthys were relaxing with a cup of tea. I had just built up sufficient courage to admit my predicament, and the scenario looked increasingly grim. Firstly, The C-in-C was a stickler for punctuality; secondly, it was now likely that a firm promise to a friend might be unfulfilled; and thirdly, a passenger on an Air India flight to London might arrive without as much as a toothbrush. My prayer for a miracle was heard. At that very moment, a high-ranking Thai airport official came into the VIP lounge to apologise to the C-in-C: refuelling for the Hastings had not been completed on time as the tanker's pumping mechanism had failed, and they were awaiting a replacement tanker. The delay might well be another hour before departure. Wiping the sweat from my brow, I waited till half the luggage had been unloaded from the Hastings before the offending two suitcases appeared, which were swiftly delivered to the Air India desk to be reunited with their owner in time for her check-in. It was an anxious moment but my guardian angel certainly saved the day.

With sad goodbyes to the Elworthys at Bahrain, who continued in the Hastings to Aden, I returned to England on an RAF flight. It was not long afterwards that I loaded a car with luggage, took the ferry to Zeebrugge and drove across north Germany to the regiment's new base at Hohne, where I was to be stationed for the next six years.

15

GERMANY

Hohne Camp is located between Soltau and Celle in German Westphalia. It is also close to the original site of the Bergen-Belsen concentration camp. When this camp was liberated by the British 11th Armoured Division in April 1945 the stories of its scenes of horror and depravity sent shock waves round the world. Inside the camp were some 53,000 people, half-starved and seriously ill, and another 13,000 corpses lying around the camp unburied. There followed an agonising process by the British troops of trying to save the survivors, many suffering from typhus, starvation and dysentery, most of whom would die unless they received medical attention. With the war still raging, only the most primitive drugs and facilities were available. It was often said that until well after the war, no bird could be heard to sing near the site. Whilst I cannot vouch for that, I can say that I had a horse that refused to be ridden down a tree-lined ride some 200 yards from its western boundary. It would rear up and turn its head for home. It clearly sensed an unknown and fearful energy from those mass graves. The humanitarian disaster of Belsen still presents a challenge to the conscience of the world.

In the early 1960s, entire divisions of the British Army on the Rhine used to partake in autumn manoeuvres. The German authorities would designate a large area in northern Germany where training could take place without any restriction on troop movements. This decision was not popular amongst those who lived in small towns and villages around the area, but to the farming fraternity it was manna from heaven. The slightest sign of tank tracks or wheel marks across their land, whether seeded or ploughed, was going to qualify for worthwhile compensation. Before any of these exercises ever started, British troops would gather in a concentration area. The dark nights prior to the exercise beginning were regularly illuminated throughout by the headlights of farmers' tractors, ploughing up as much land as possible.

My regiment had by now fully converted from armoured cars to Centurion tanks. I had not yet attended a conversion course and was therefore somewhat green about taking command of a tank, which I found very large and cumbersome. Whilst on a regimental exercise in October I instructed the driver of my tank to slowly drive parallel to a series of small fields that were interconnected by a wire fence, the top strand being barbed wire. I had told my gunner to traverse the gun barrel to the left at the imaginary enemy threat. This meant that the barrel was sticking out at right angles to the direction in which we were travelling. It was a lovely sunny day and I was day-dreaming, admiring a horse that had been nonchalantly rubbing its neck against the wire, and noticing six blackish cows which jogged my memory of farming days in New Zealand.

All of a sudden this reverie was rudely interrupted by an ear-splitting crash. I had not noticed a concrete electricity pylon just inside the fence. As the tank rolled slowly forward, the 12-foot long solid metal gun barrel sliced straight through the concrete like a knife through butter. The pylon was supporting two cables, each carrying more than 15,000 volts. These remained intact and came to rest on top of the barbed wire fence. I watched, frozen, as a gigantic electric fire was created and within minutes every wooden fence post started to smoulder and burst into flames. The old horse had now wisely moved into the middle of the field to avoid the crackling inferno and the billowing smoke. But one cow panicked and ran straight into the fence where it met instant death by electrocution, landing with all four feet in the air. My brother officers later could only see the funny side of this drama. When I resumed radio contact I was inundated with calls about the time of the barbeque and requests for the beef to be underdone rather than cremated. The locals had good reason not to be pleased with this incident as it plunged the nearby town of Bockenheim into total darkness for three weeks.

I was not, however, the only tank commander to cause serious out-of-order damage that year. Two brother officers in their in their respective tanks arguably topped my performance. One hit a swing bridge over one of the busiest canals in Europe. As the bridge had been knocked out of kilter, it could neither be opened nor closed for days, which must have adversely affected the German economy, whilst rows of barges, as far as the eye could see, remained motionless on the canal in both directions. The other shed a tank track whilst driving at night across a very steep slope. With the threat of rain, it was feared that the tank itself might slide to the bottom of the hill of its own volition and it was going to be safer to leave it there till the summer months, when the Royal Engineers could build a road from the bottom of the hill. It was recovered three months later. Exercises involving heavy-tracked equipment inevitably caused some considerable collateral damage over the period of exercise training, for which the British taxpayer footed the bill.

In May 1963, it was announced that the regiment would train at La Courtine in France. This was a historic moment as it was the first time that British troops had returned there since 1945. La Courtine is about 300 miles south of Paris in the *département* of Creuse. This area of France will always be remembered for the lively activities of the French Resistance, and equally for the courage shown by the people of Creuse under constant duress of Nazi occupation lasting throughout the Second World War. It is further renowned for the manufacture of tapestries, for which the town of Aubusson is the most well known. Another town close by is Felletin, which was responsible for making the famous Graham Sutherland tapestry in Coventry Cathedral called 'Christ in Glory'. This piece of needlework measures 75½ feet high by 38 feet wide. It was completed in three years and used a tree trunk as a roller. It was made in one single piece, and until the 1990s was the largest vertical handmade tapestry in the world.

As I purported to speak some French, I was sent with an advance party to receive the tanks on their arrival accompanied by their drivers, which would come all the way by rail from Hohne. The 18 Centurion tanks were loaded onto what were known as flats, simply reinforced railway wagons without sides but strong enough to carry the dead weight of a 52-ton Centurion tank. It was likely that during a three-day journey across Germany and France the load bearing would prove too much for some of the flats, thus a spare flat was added to the train in case of emergency. On the particular Saturday morning the train arrived at La Courtine with 17 tanks and one missing. I immediately reported the noted absence to the French liaison officer, Colonel Dupouts, who with tongue in cheek muttered that French officers responsible for that sort of loss would face a firing squad at dawn the next day. In fact, the only spare flat had been used within an hour of leaving Hohne. A second flat had broken down when the train reached Châlons-sur-Marne, where the tank was unhitched from the train, pushed into a siding, and the 11th Hussar tank driver left to his own devices. Three hours later the train with the remaining 17 tanks plus drivers sped through Chalon-sur-Saône, some 160 miles away. It took the whole weekend to find out in which of the Chalons the tank and its driver were now hiding. Early the following Monday morning a heated argument ensued between the stationmaster, French railway police and French army movement control, all wishing to avoid taking responsibility for the lost tank. The tank driver could not speak a word of French, but using his initiative took the opportunity of establishing Anglo-French *entente cordiale* by enjoying the hospitality of a local demoiselle and her family. He was in no hurry to join us in La Courtine, and was rather *désolé* when he was picked up by Land Rover two days later.

Romance was blossoming in my own life too. Celia Mann was a great friend of my sister Sarah. They had attended the same school in Wellington, New Zealand. Her father, John Mann, had left England in 1957 to become managing director of the Unilever enterprise in New Zealand. The surname Mann is synonymous with cricket: John's brother George, and their father Frank T. Mann, had both captained England for MCC tours of South Africa, in 1948-49 and 1922-23, respectively. John himself had played for Middlesex but his business career somewhat curtailed his sporting activities. We had met the family in New Zealand and when they returned, Sarah's friendship with Celia continued and she would stay for weekends at my parents' home near Wantage, often when I was on leave from Germany. Celia herself was then working for a London art dealer. Over the next 18 months we saw as much of each other as we could. I finally took the plunge and we were married in Holy Trinity Sloane Street, London in April 1964. Celia was only 20.

We began our married life in Hohne with the regiment, where she found herself to be the youngest officers' wife. As a junior captain I had to wait and accrue more qualifying 'points' before being allocated an army quarter. The only available rented accommodation was a minute one-bedroomed flat over the top of the local BP service station on the Hohne Camp ring road. Whenever a squadron of tanks rolled past, the cups and saucers shook on the kitchen shelf as if there was an impending earthquake. Finally we were allocated a married quarter after 18 months: a first-floor flat in a two-storey block, used by the SS during the Second World War.

It was reputed that our flat had been visited by Ilsa, the wife of Karl Otto Koch, the SS German commandant of Buchenwald concentration camp, who had allegedly made lampshades from human skin. However, during her war crimes trial the evidence was considered inconclusive, and she was acquitted. Celia was mercifully quite unaffected by such a horrendous history. This was just as well, since our spacious three-bedroomed flat was perfect for anyone wishing to start a family. Celia was enjoying her new friendships with other young army wives and was in no hurry to have children. However, a year later, in May 1966, Clare was born in the British Military Hospital in Hanover. We transformed the second bedroom into a nursery, and the third was soon occupied by Clare's new nanny, Bessie. I thoroughly enjoyed early parenthood, and even pushing the pram.

Within 15 months of our marriage, Her Majesty Queen Elizabeth the Queen Mother was to visit Hohne to present the 11th Hussars, Prince Albert's Own, with a new Regimental guidon. The year 1965 coincided with the 250th anniversary of the formation of the 11th Light Dragoons. It also fell within nine days of the 125th anniversary of the colonelcy of the Prince Consort, Prince Albert of Saxe-Coburg. The official parade took place on 13th July in full sunshine after 21 days of continuous rain. As editor of the regimental journal I had written, 'drill has been a mystery for most 11th Hussars until the spring of 1965', although from April that year, under the instruction of a drill sergeant and another senior NCO of the Coldstream Guards, the standard of drill for us all was greatly enhanced. As was usual, there were endless rehearsals for the guidon parade itself.

I provided my two polo ponies, Luchia and Cockrobin, for the mounted detachment. Their docile temperaments were considered suitable for participating in the ceremonial parade. Cockrobin was my docile Somerset cob, unfazed by any situation – except in the autumn. When the leaves fell he would skip and dance to avoid them touching his fetlocks. A picture of the parade, by the artist Terence Cuneo, was commissioned by the regiment. This depicted part of the guard attired in their crimson trousers, prominent against their khaki tunics, with Her Majesty taking the salute. Cuneo had the habit of painting mice in his pictures and in this case he included a mouse standing to attention in the floral display, dressed in cherry-coloured overalls with double golden stripe, mirroring the guard of honour. Many old comrades attended the parade, making this a special occasion for us all. Among these, watching with pride, were the three distinguished 11th

Hussar generals of the Second World War, Major-Generals Combe and Spears, together with my father.

Several days after the guidon presentation, the commanding officer Lieutenant Colonel Dick Sutton, my first cousin, and Trooper Fryer, his driver, died on duty following a car accident. Dick's wife Sally was badly injured in the crash. The party, were at the time, accompanying a strong regimental detachment which paraded the new guidon at Prince Albert's birthplace at Coburg. News of this very tragic event much dampened the earlier celebrations.

My father remained at Hohne for an extra three days and was keen to know what I had been up to, particularly in my sporting activities. I greatly enjoyed the opportunity to ski, which entailed at least one month's training in Austria before taking part in the army championships in St Moritz, Switzerland. My two polo ponies gave me some amusement. One of these enjoyed jumping and was sufficiently versatile to take part in hunter trials. I am sure that my father was proud of seeing me actively engaged at regimental duty, while being simultaneously concerned about my further progress. He had brainwashed himself into believing that in due course I would automatically command the regiment. For this, attending Staff College was a virtual prerequisite. Though there could be exceptions from this, provided the candidate was 'staff qualified', at least three of us would be competing for one place.

I now began to ask myself whether I was up to it. In my confusion I asked myself if I would be wasting my life. Supposing I passed the exam, I would then be contracted to remain in the army for several years to come. If, however, I failed, it would mean a major disappointment to my father and could risk my being shunted from one unfulfilling staff appointment to another, for the rest of my career. If, alternatively, I did not sit it, searching questions would be asked, calling into question my ambition and commitment to provide the best for my family. I felt imprisoned. There seemed no easy way out of a dilemma that was fast, I feared, becoming a personal crisis. I seemed to have been dealt a favourable hand of cards, that was for sure: a privileged upbringing, a lovely young wife, the blessing of a lovely daughter and the opportunity of career progression, if I passed the exam. Celia was gaining in confidence in herself as a wife and home-maker. My head was not with the army, and my heart was now following suit, yet I could not shake off a profound sense of guilt for wanting a card I felt had not yet been dealt out to me: my own choice in the matter. I always had a choice whether to stay in the army or leave and live the life I wanted; it was just that I kept on putting off exercising that choice, playing for time in the vain hope that something would simply turn up to save me from deciding for myself.

Change of a sort was on the way 18 months later. I was to be appointed as a staff officer to 4th Guards Brigade for two years. Our new army quarter would be upgraded from a flat to a semi-detached house with three bedrooms, and a much-welcomed garden. Just as well, as our second daughter Julia was born in London two years later; a rather easier arrival than Clare.

After my first year at Iserlohn, the Brigade moved to Munster, where my new boss was to be Brigadier Michael Gow, later General Sir Michael Gow. Over the move I would have the overall responsibility of transporting all classified documents to the new HQ. On completing the move, many of these documents were no longer relevant and had to be destroyed. Shredders were not yet widely used and classified documents were burnt in an incinerator. To my horror, a few days later, one partially burned document marked 'Top Secret' was found smouldering on a rubbish tip within the compound. The bonfire had been lit by a civilian janitor. How this document ever got there I shall never know, but the loss or partial destruction of such an item is a very serious security matter. When the janitor was interviewed by the Intelligence Corps it turned out that he was of Polish extraction, had been there since the end of the Second World War and could neither speak nor write a word of English! As I was overall responsible for this breach of security, I felt that if anybody should be sacked, it should be me. Luckily it was deemed that there was no breach and my apology for the incident was accepted by my new boss, with relief for both of us.

On ending my two-year secondment to 4th Guards Brigade I decided to make my official departure mounted on horseback in full 11th Hussar dress. This prompted the next publication of the *Guards Magazine* to describe me as 'The only line cavalry officer ever to have served with the 4th Guards Brigade'. My official departure needed preparation, and a dress rehearsal. Cockrobin had to be coaxed up the steps of the brigade HQ building and into Mike Gow's office. This try-out was arranged for the Sunday afternoon prior to my ultimate departure at midday on the Monday. Cockrobin was led up the eight steps at the entrance without flinching and, though a little rotund, he managed to pass through the metal security grille before walking down the long passage towards the brigadier's office door, through which he could just squeeze. Matthews, my groom, had thought of something rather important. The change from the freezing outside temperature to a highly centrally heated environment would have an immediate effect on Cockrobin. Matthews was in the corridor in readiness with an army issue tin waste-paper basket when Cockrobin lifted his tail and deposited what was expected: a welcome addition for the garden compost. The rehearsal was a resounding success, and luckily the bin was not needed for my official farewell on the Monday. The colourful occasion marked the end of a most enjoyable two years.

My growing family stayed behind in Munster for a further nine months while I served there with the 10th Hussars, with my brother Guy as adjutant, prior to the amalgamation of the 10th and 11th at Tidworth the following year. By serving once again at regimental duty I found myself in the same position as before, feeling under enormous pressure and obligation to remain in the army to support the new amalgamated regiment. Celia preferred the way things were, and this did not ease my uncertainty as I weighed up the situation.

There was now my financial state of affairs to consider. The army paid me a salary and provided a house for us, and paid for part of the children's education. They offered gratuities and inflation-proof pensions according to length of service. Also on offer were numerous other financial perks such as motor mileage allowance, first-class rail warrants for officers on duty and also overseas allowances. Overheads such as water and electricity were free. All these points reinforced my father's argument that I should remain in the army until the pensionable age of 55. The thought filled me with a sense of doom. I began to grasp at straws to find any opportunity to leave the army. Choices made under such circumstances are inevitably fraught with difficulty.

IMAGES ON THE FACING PAGE:

TOP: THE AUTHOR ON COCKROBIN, BIDDING FAREWELL TO THE BRIGADE COMMANDER, 1969.

BOTTOM: WINNERS OF THE REGIMENTAL POLO AT TIDWORTH, 1970. THE AUTHOR EXTREME RIGHT.

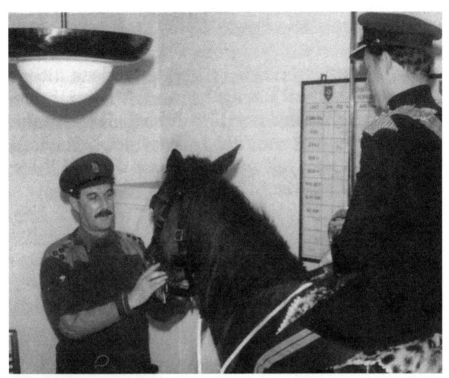

16

THE UNCLIMBABLE MOUNTAIN

My parents returned from New Zealand and they settled close to the town of Wantage in Berkshire. I met up with the managing director of one of the car dealerships with whom my parents did business, and out of this I reached an agreement with him which resulted in my being presented with the possibility I had been looking for: of a career change

The idea of buying into the motor trade as a shareholder and director rather appealed to me, despite my complete lack of commercial expertise and knowledge of this field. I told my father that I had been asked to become a director of the business. He and our family solicitor from London were diametrically opposed to the idea on principle. Obstinately disregarding my father's will, I nevertheless instructed the solicitor to prepare a suitable contract. I always recall him saying, 'Then we will have to make the best of a very bad job.' This comment unnerved me. Why had he said that, I wondered? My unease was compounded when his searches revealed that there were outstanding loans charged against the company that were not reflected in the annual accounts. I had missed this. The business was, in fact, insolvent, and I withdrew in relief. It was a timely escape. I realised I had used the whole exercise as an excuse to leave the army.

This having failed, and licking my wounds, I felt obliged to be seen preparing for taking the Staff College Exam. I can only say that I paid lip service to it. To give a somewhat pathetic impression of my effort, I had enrolled for several correspondence courses, which involved posting off my work intermittently for correction. Two weeks later, my papers would be returned replete with comments in red ink, including candid explanations as to why they were given such low grades. I allowed myself to believe that I would not pass, thinking to myself, my father thinks I will fail, and

I will make sure he is right. My poor grades merely served to confirm the certainty of his impending disappointment. I continued to play the part of a serious candidate, attending courses in military law, military history and current affairs. When the Staff College results were announced, my failure only went to reinforce my motivation to leave the army. I realised that becoming a senior army officer was not a calling that I had ever chosen. It had now become a mountain that I could not climb, even if I wanted to, and at last I accepted it. From then on, my attitude began to change. Any guilt about letting anyone down evaporated completely. It was time for me to move on, and there could be no turning back.

Having committed myself irrevocably to this course of action, I realised that many challenges would undoubtedly lie ahead. Celia was understandably unsure and suspicious. Our army life was secure and had cushioned us from the competitive business of earning a living. To cap it all, the Vocational Guidance Association based in London, from which I sought advice and whose test I completed, concluded that I possessed the qualities and aptitudes sought in a good officer. The test however also showed, to my great interest, that I would be happier connected with a career on the land. This confirmed what I already knew from my six contented months of livestock farming in New Zealand. I now had my key, but as yet no lock in which to put it. I would not commence the formal process of leaving the army until the next step was clearer.

During ten days' leave 'undercover', I set up job interviews for various posts in England, ranging from merchant banking to estate management and farming. Merchant banking would have proved an unsuitable profession, which is precisely what my father told me after I unwisely informed him of an impending interview with Flemings. He was on the case within seconds, informing Flemings that I had failed maths O level at the first attempt! In spite of this perceived weakness, I was offered a three-month internship, but declined their generosity. After that, I kept the other interviews a secret.

Having ruled out both estate management and agriculture, through lack of qualifications, I was finally offered a glimmer of hope by the personal assistant to Frank Sykes of Sykes Chickens. 'For all forms of farming now,' she said, 'you require a great deal of capital. One industry that requires less would be horticulture. Have you ever considered that?' No, I hadn't, but was nevertheless sufficiently enthused by her suggestion to look into it. The general economic climate seemed bleak. The pound was weak. Fewer people were travelling abroad, choosing instead to stay at home. Upon further research, gardening emerged as the third most popular leisure activity after sailing and angling. Also, there seemed to be an increasing demand for landscape gardeners and designers. The latter seemed an interesting market to investigate.

My first impression was that this would be a simple managerial exercise. In my naive way, I imagined that a good sergeant with a few loyal 11th Hussar troopers could carry out this sort of business effectively and with ease. I soon realised, with the English weather, how hazardous garden maintenance could be. Part of my 'undercover' leave was spent with Allan Alexander, a well-respected landscaper and plantsman running a garden business from Hermitage near Newbury. The summer of 1970 was a wet one, which made grass-cutting much more difficult. To gain first-hand experience, I had offered to cut a client's lawn with one of Allan's rotary mowers. As I mowed and came nearer to the house, I ran over a small Dinky toy that shot out of the machine sideways and through the large bottom pane of the dining room French windows. This incident somewhat dampened my interest in garden contracting, fearing as I did further unforeseen accidents and so having to pay soaring premiums for public liability insurance cover.

By 1970 the popularity of garden centres was growing throughout the country. I became increasing interested in the relatively new phenomenon of garden centres. ICI, Fisons, Murphys and PBI were spending millions on marketing and promoting their products, helping the nursery and garden centre trade. At the forefront of this new venture was the new Waterers centre at the Twyford Floral Mile near Reading. Its layout and operation struck me as being very impressive. Judging by a seemingly full car park, the new garden centre trade was drawing a large number of customers. My investigations in Germany had revealed the same trend: I visited a large garden centre at Bochum in the Ruhr which, like Waterers, displayed an enormous range of ornamental trees and shrubs, with a vast expanse of glass given over to garden furniture, tools and accessories. There was even a thriving cafe-restaurant. This was exactly how I had imagined a garden centre could be. My heart and mind were now in harmonious accord, and it was clear how I should proceed. I would plan a nursery and garden centre based on the Bochum model that could be developed in easy stages over several years.

When I was 25 years old and still in the army, my father had generously given me a small inheritance invested in stocks and shares. These were administered by Cazenove, the London stockbrokers. Stephen Carden, a partner of my age, had been designated to look after my affairs and by 1969 had become an expert on investment opportunities in the Australian stock market. As a staff officer in 4th Guards Brigade, I had been allocated a German civilian telephone in my house. The monthly bill in Deutschmarks was passed to the army paymaster for settlement and, provided it was not excessive, was never queried. No prying eyes ever noticed the five-weekly international telephone calls dialled to London Wall 2828 in the City as the Australian stock market began to reach its peak. By selling at the top of the market, Stephen had quadrupled my inheritance. Furthermore, gains on the original share prices were not subject to capital gains tax: I had already spent sufficient fiscal years as a resident on German soil to become exempt. The total asset was not reinvested but remained in cash. It would later buy a market garden, provide collateral for working capital to finance a nursery and garden centre business, and purchase a small Georgian farmhouse with 5 acres as a family home.

Having set a plan for the future I now had to face my commanding officer with the intention to resign my commission. I was aware that the application and process would take three months to be formalised, during which time the 10th and 11th Hussars were to be amalgamated at Perham Down near Tidworth. The newly formed regiment, the Royal Hussars, was not technically born until the amalgamation parade on Balaclava Day, 25th October 1970. For different reasons, the conventional parade grounds had been discarded and the tattoo ground, which doubled as the Tidworth rugby ground, was chosen for the parade. Although it had a large covered stand for spectators, the parade would take place on grass, which in the event of rain might become a quagmire. The risk was taken and a drill sergeant from the Irish Guards drilled the new regiment into shape. The new guidon was presented by HRH Princess Alice, Duchess of Gloucester. It was, indeed, a proud moment for the Norries. There had been a long association between the two regiments, as previously described. On this occasion I commanded one of the guards, my brother Guy commanded the 10th Hussars mounted escort and our father, commissioned as an 11th Hussar, who had commanded the 10th Hussars in India, proudly led the march past of old comrades from both regiments. I was there in body, but in truth, although the event was indeed memorable, my mind was drifting elsewhere.

Soon after the amalgamation, Allan Alexander rang to say that a 9.5-acre modest market garden with a four-bedroom house and three small greenhouses was for sale on the outskirts of Hermitage. It was called Fairfield. The owner, Mr Tuersley, and his family grew vegetables for the wholesale trade with the excess being sold from his garage shop. The quality of his bunched carrots, grown on greensand, had gained a reputation for being the best in the county. A priority for me before contracts were exchanged was to find a first-class accountant who knew about the nursery and garden centre trade. Allan Alexander introduced me to Oswald Harmon-Smith, accountant to Blackwells, a well-known grower of house plants, perennials and annuals. They were also owners of a large garden centre at Stratton St Margaret near Swindon. First priority solved. The second priority was to find a knowledgeable manager, with a view to an eventual partnership. I had always been convinced that I should find a Dutchman who had been trained in horticulture, and when with the regiment in Germany I had driven to Holland for the weekend and visited the horticultural college in Boskoop. The principal's secretary kindly composed and typed out an advertisement in Dutch, inviting any Boskoop graduate wishing to pursue a career in the nursery and garden centre industry in England to make contact with me. The advertisement appeared in several editions of the college magazine, but to no avail.

Ron Lousley, senior partner of A.W. Neate, estate agents in Newbury, was acting on my behalf in the purchase of Fairfield. He knew of Hans Overeynder, a Dutchman who was managing another local nursery. Hans and I were soon introduced to each other over a drink at Ron's house and he said he was interested in the proposal. Could such a 'marriage' work, I asked myself? Our characters, temperaments and training were completely different. A little voice told me not to throw that advertisement away, and I have always kept a copy: it is a reminder that whereas things may indeed turn out as we hope, how they do so is not necessarily as we expect!

My vision for some time had been a combined nursery and garden centre with a string of franchises, whose businesses in the leisure industry complemented those in the garden industry. I could also see that the site of Fairfield was advantageously placed, being within a mile of the A34 Southampton to Birmingham trunk road, which in turn was to have an exit and entry onto the planned M4 London to Bristol motorway. I felt that once Fairfield became known, potential customers living within a 25-mile catchment area would find it an easy garden centre to reach once the motorway had been built and the trunk road improved. My scheme for starting a successful business seemed realistic.

Hans agreed to become manager of Fairfield with a view to entering into partnership when the time was appropriate. Celia and I were still living at Tidworth at the time and used to come over to Fairfield some 25 miles on Saturday mornings to help sell Mr Tuersley's produce, which was set out on simple trestle tables covered with green plastic grass mats in the garage shop. Celia was still not confident that I had made the correct decision on a career change. Clearly fed up with the constant filling of packing cases, she announced that my gardening capabilities were thoroughly suspect. She reminded me that the first time I had planted lettuce seeds in our vegetable patch in Germany, the plants struggled to break surface on the last day of October. Not only had the cabbage patch and flower border at Tidworth been neglected, but in mowing the lawn I had scalped several areas by placing the rotary blades at the wrong level. What hope, she wondered, was there for a new career in horticulture? She had a point, but I had a vision.

In the meantime, someone had whistleblown me to the Ministry of Defence. I had received a somewhat stuffy official letter explaining that it had come to their notice that I was running a business before the resignation of my commission had been gazetted. In essence, there was probably an overlap of three weeks. So I took no notice of the letter and never heard any more about it. Hans, who had handed in his notice to his current employer, generously gave up some of his annual holiday to join me in visiting garden centres in Holland and Germany. Six months later he and his family moved to Fairfield House, the premises vacated by Mr and Mrs Tuersley.

Although I was nervous about the future I do recall a strong feeling of freedom and, unusually for me, a measure of self-confidence despite the fact that I was aware that many new businesses failed within a year or two. I had a young family to support, a home to buy, a career to build. I could not spend the capital that was available to me twice, so I had to be as sure as I could possibly be that I was doing the best thing for all of us. I was sure. The contract was signed, Hans came on board and a new life was about to begin.

17

HOME AND GARDEN: FAIRFIELD

Celia, Clare, Julia and I left Tidworth for a cottage at Brimpton belonging to Celia's father, before buying Henwick Old Farm, which Ron Lousley had negotiated to purchase on our behalf. The 6-acre property in the hamlet of Henwick, 3 miles north-east of Newbury, consisted of a pretty Berkshire four-square farmhouse in red brick close to an attractive thatched barn, well hidden by high hedges and thick planting of trees along the roadside. I was in a good position, now that I was in the trade, to plant the garden with some unusual trees and shrubs, not to mention maintaining it tidily as a decent advertisement for Fairfield.

The farmland to the east of Henwick was owned by Henry Billington, a former 1930s Davis Cup player. Ladbrokes would not have offered long odds on him winning the Mens' Singles at Wimbledon during the Second World War years. However, the event was cancelled over that period. It is no surprise to know that his skills passed to his grandson, Tim Henman, a Wimbledon semi-finalist and also former Davis Cup player. In line with the Berkshire Structure Plan, several hundred acres of Henry Billington's land on the north side of Thatcham were sold for housing development. It took several years for the housing estates to creep up on Henwick, but it was a sign of fundamental change in the countryside. It was issues such as these, concerning the environment, that would become the first focus of my future parliamentary career.

New housing, however, would prove to be a boost to the garden centre trade, so my loyalties were somewhat divided. What was noticeable at Henwick in the years to come was the constant hum of activity that had begun to replace the silence of the countryside. The red glimmer of street lighting illuminating the night sky, and an increase in traffic on a narrow country lane outside the main gate, were now unalterable facts. I decided that Henwick would be much improved by a water feature which would add interest and value to the property. In the field below the house, a large-tracked JCB landscaped a 1½ acre pond up to a depth of 6 feet in the shape of a leg of mutton. I had originally planned to stock it with trout. An existing top pond in the garden fed by a spring was connected to the new excavation by way of a narrow channel. The work was completed only hours before the onset of five days of continuous heavy rain. Clare and Julia had each won eight goldfish at a fair, and unknown to me released them into the top pond. Water flowed in a continuous spate down the channel, and so did some of the goldfish. Years later the leg of mutton on a bright day would show hundreds of shimmering red and yellow silhouettes. Not even the visiting herons could keep the goldfish population down. I was not sure about the compatibility of trout and goldfish living together in harmony, so I decided upon pinioned ornamental duck instead.

A decorative house was installed, protected by high wire to keep out predators such as foxes. We chose several different varieties of duck, including Carolina, mandarin, pintail, pochard, teal, and shovelers from the Argentine, tufted and widgeon, all of which fed either on special floating pellets or on handfuls of wheat spread on the bank. Some time later we suffered another period of intense rain. Both ponds overflowed, more goldfish disappeared down the channel, and several of the ducks were last seen leaving Henry Billington's swimming pool about 500 yards away before disappearing down a culvert under the road. This eventually connected to the River Kennet, where I am sure they enjoyed a better life.

The business was much affected by the weather as well. On 31st May 1975 came a prolonged and unpredicted frost, the worst for 50 years. Fairfield lost hundreds of boxes of bedding plants. Loss of stock was further exacerbated by having to find and buy in replacement from other growers, many of whom were struggling with the same problems. The following year was probably the most testing. In January, hurricane-force winds caused massive and expensive damage to glass and crops, to be followed by the infamous relentless summer of 1976. Our water supply, although adequate under normal conditions, could not sustain all the growing stock, and the Fairfield soil is light and sandy and thus unable to retain sufficient moisture during the heat wave. Hundreds of conifers were lost as a result. I had allocated what I had perceived as sufficient working capital but quickly had to persuade the bank to increase this figure by 20 per cent to meet the rising costs and avoid a massive overdraft. We tried to make light of our economic trials but a rather unhelpful reply from the bank provoked the following response:

Ode to the Overdraft

Whether Midland or Lloyds or Natwest
They'll convince you their service is best
On exceeding your ceiling
You'll soon get the feeling
That Barclays are just like the rest.

With this in mind I continued to remain on the look-out for new and exciting investment opportunities. One was to prove less than wise. The Wilson government had imposed exchange control regulations on UK citizens. It was therefore illegal to buy land abroad. Nonetheless, a friend who had joined a particular US property company and taken advice believed that investors could avoid breaking the law by exercising their right to buy land in the US. Lehigh Acres was a small town on the west coast of Florida. It enjoyed a perfect climate and was an ideal location in which to choose a retirement home. The scheme had attracted US citizens of retirement age and particularly those who were living in the colder states of the continent. I was shown an elaborate map of development plots near the proposed shopping centres, golf courses and marinas. It was an impressive development. I exercised the option to buy several plots, which would be allocated exclusively to me. I proceeded to pay a monthly cheque to an account in a respectable bank in Pall Mall. What could possibly go wrong?

Six months later a car arrived at the Fairfield Nurseries car park. Out stepped a man whose official government ID card showed him to be a senior officer from Her Majesty's Treasury. He said that he had come specifically to find me in person, and once settled in the office he asked, 'Do you know that you have contravened the exchange control regulations?' I had not a clue what he meant. 'No,' I answered. It transpired that cheques paid into the London bank were being laundered through the Free Bank of Kuwait, an action which was fraudulent and illegal. He told me to expect a summons for a court hearing. Indeed, two days later the local policeman knocked on the door to deliver it. This came as a sharp intrusion into our busy but otherwise constructive family life. I was troubled that if I were to admit to my father what had happened, he would probably pretend to himself that the offence would carry a prison sentence. To avoid this charade I did not tell him. I did tell Patricia, who was as discrete as she was understanding. She promised to keep it all a secret until the matter had been resolved.

Once again I found myself in the hands of the family solicitor, who was all too aware of my earlier garage fiasco. 'It will all be in the *Evening Standard* – "Peer's Son Contravenes Exchange Control Regulations in Bid to Buy into Florida Property Boom"', he warned. One of his most valuable assets was his knowledge of the legal profession in London. He not only knew the stipendiary magistrate at Bow Street who would preside in court, but could also recommend suitable barristers to defend me. He accordingly chose one who later became a High Court judge and was knighted on his retirement. He was certainly a knight in shining armour for me that day. In court, he simply asked the senior officer from the Treasury whether he believed I knew that I had committed an offence. The answer was 'No'. Did he also doubt my integrity and honesty? The answer was 'No!' The three reporters in the press box quietly dispersed for a cup of coffee, as the case against me was clearly falling well short of being a national scoop.

The stipendiary magistrate stated that mine had been exposed as a test case by HM Treasury, since I had broken the law, albeit unknowingly in his view. I was fined the minimum amount for the offence, which was £50. After leaving Bow Street I visited my father to explain the outcome. How would he react? I need not have worried. I gave him the full story and he showed immediate relief that his eldest son's escapade had not appeared in the tabloid press. When I later viewed the legal fees in total disbelief, it struck me that I might still have chosen the wrong profession. At least the US property company repaid me in full for my monthly instalments. The daydream of becoming a property tycoon evaporated into thin air. Lehigh Acres would not, as I had hoped, provide further security against borrowing from Barclays to support development at Fairfield. I once again had to learn an important lesson: if something looks too good to be true, then it probably is!

As part of Fairfield's development plans we aimed to have a wide range of items for sale in the garden centre, but Hans and I decided to draw the line at selling plastic gnomes. Fellow garden centre operators had no qualms about lowering the tone, and reported massive sales. One year, when the Chelsea Flower Show committee decided to ban the presence and sale of gnomes – a ban lifted only in 2013 – the principal manufacturer and supplier to the horticultural trade chained several life-size stone gnomes to the iron railings outside the main entrance. It was a brilliant piece of publicity. Before they could be removed, the national newspapers had picked up the story, with photographs publicising the horrendous ill-treatment of the gnome species. As a result gnome sales that year almost doubled. As if to rub salt into the wound, at the same time I had written to the adjutant at the Royal School of Military Survey, Hermitage, located across the road from Fairfield, asking to take advertising space in the camp magazine. Frustrated at being unable to read my illegible signature, which looked like Gnorrie, and taking the double 'r' as an 'm', he responded by writing 'Dear Mr Gnome'. The story must have been on his mind.

Fairfield was in the meantime progressing steadily, more by word of mouth than through advertising. Hans was already well known in Newbury circles, first and foremost as a knowledgeable plantsman. As a member of the Newbury Round Table, he had a mass of contacts and friends, many of whom became loyal customers. I knew a lot of people within a 25-mile radius of Fairfield, many having large estates or gardens, and kept abreast of the new housing developments. With such an extensive local awareness I could easily have moonlighted as an estate agent.

Whereas most of my energy had been directed at building up the business and creating a garden as a worthy advertisement for the business, I was ever conscious that my father, Patricia and Nanny were entering their twilight years. My short visits to see them had become more frequent and more appreciated, and after all they only lived a 30-minute drive away. The Ham, bought by my parents in 1958, is an attractive large red-brick Georgian country house wedged between Wantage and Letcombe Regis. It was described in *The Times* as an 'Oxfordshire Treasure', dating from 1740. It has a Victorian wing around which are clustered several outbuildings on the north side forming a square around a tarmac backyard, in the middle of which was a stone monument. With King Alfred's historical connection to Wantage in mind, we used to tell our friends it marked the spot where Alfred burned his cakes. In fact there was no historical significance at all, and its location was a perfect menace, claiming damage to many cars whose drivers had inadvertently reversed into it.

136

Within the grounds, the Letcombe Brook meanders through the fields dividing into a millstream and small lake before rejoining below the mill and continuing its flow towards Wantage. The garden was substantial and the walled garden had been run as a commercial venture, its produce being sold to two vegetable and fruit shops in the town. Thus, when the house was bought by my parents, there were two resident gardeners, three part-time ladies who worked in the house, and a butler. All were keen to keep their employment.

After 13 years of Government House life it was understandable that my father in particular wished to continue to live in the comfort and lifestyle to which he had become accustomed. By contrast, Patricia and Nanny had each become competent and innovative cooks. At weekends, cordon bleu cooking friends of my sisters Sarah and Annabel assisted in the kitchen, adding their own culinary expertise to supplement the weekend menus.

The butler, or 'Jeeves' as I shall call him without divulging his real name, had no pressing desire to move with his previous employer. He and his wife were happy living in the lodge at the main gate and their children attended the local school. On the face of it, the decision was of mutual benefit, and over the following years Jeeves served my father with devotion. Apart from duties as butler, he attended to my father's every need as his valet. He ironed his shirts and suits, polished his shoes, woke him with a cup of tea in the mornings and served him whisky and sodas with two cubes of ice late at night. House guests who came to stay loved him too. Jeeves was the perfect butler, except for one secret flaw, which holding the key of the wine cellar did not help. Until one particular incident, no one in the family was aware that, after washing up after lunch, Jeeves might surreptitiously slip into the cellar, lock the door and fortify himself before bicycling down the drive home.

Without local knowledge, it would have been difficult to believe that the cellar existed at all. It had been built onto the end of the 'Long Room', a reception room only used when large numbers of guests were entertained. The door itself was hidden in the bookcase which stretched the entire width of one wall. The books that appeared on the four shelves were false but the covers gave the impression that my parents were collecting an old and valuable set of first editions. When unlocked, the heavy door swung open to reveal a cellar on two levels with wine racks secured to the walls in every possible space. It was not only a perfect place to store wine, but also an ideal space in which to hide and drink it.

On one dark December evening my sister Rose and her husband Humphrey had driven down to stay for the weekend. When they turned into the drive their headlights illuminated a rather vacillating cyclist steering an erratic course towards the house. The closer they drove, the wobblier the movements became. Suddenly the bicycle and rider veered off left at right angles through a gap in the bushes and into the millstream. Some moments later, silhouetted in the headlights, a sodden and dishevelled figure emerged from several feet of water, wearing a black short coat, white shirt, black tie, and black and white pinstripe trousers. Without acknowledging my sister and brother-in-law, the figure of Jeeves skulked away into the darkness, gingerly pushing his bicycle back towards the lodge.

Although the table had been set that evening, Jeeves did not return to serve dinner. My father, wild with rage, rang the lodge. Mrs Jeeves answered. Managing to control himself, my father insisted that Jeeves be in his office on the dot of 9 am the following morning. Jeeves arrived uncharacteristically late, in clean dry clothes, sporting a very swollen black eye. Mrs Jeeves had evidently not been pleased with him. My father announced that he would not tolerate drunkenness from any member of his staff and therefore would no longer require his services. Looking very disconsolate, Jeeves bicycled back to the lodge, this time in a straight line.

By 10.30 my father had thought through the consequences of his actions. The remains of breakfast for eight had not been cleared away. There was to be a lunch party for 14. There was no one to lay it or polish the silver. There was no one to receive the guests at the front door, serve the drinks before lunch or to open the wine. And who would bring him his cup of tea in the following morning? The truth was, he had realised, that Jeeves was indispensable. He was telephoned at the lodge and told to return to the office immediately. After accepting an apology for his behaviour and a promise to visit Alcoholics Anonymous, my father reinstated him. The cellar key was handed back and entrusted to Jeeves only when necessary. By Christmas, relationships had returned to normal and my father gave Jeeves a watch as a present, together with a card that said quite simply: 'Happy Christmas and a punctual New Year'.

Years later, after Jeeves retired, my brother Guy and I had recourse to check through the cellar. We soon noticed that some of the bottles of white wine had been opened and the corks were protruding. On emptying the contents of the first bottle into a jug, we discovered that it was filled with water. So was the second. Jesus may be remembered for miraculously turning water into wine, but Jeeves will be recalled affectionately by the Norries for reversing the process. Later, we found a duplicate cellar key in a drawer in the pantry!

18

STEPPING OUT OF MY COMFORT ZONE

By 1977 my father's health had begun to deteriorate. Up until then he had accepted his age and its limitations with grace. Long gone were his interests in wandering around antique shops, attending the sales of fine art at Christie's and Sotheby's, or just playing nine holes of golf. Luckily, however, his pre-eminent interest in horse racing remained. I have described earlier in this book my father's equestrian skills as a young army officer, becoming an accomplished rider, among other things winning point-to-points and steeplechases. Whilst he served as Governor of South Australia and later as Governor General of New Zealand, he also always enjoyed being a successful owner. His horses frequently appeared in the frame at race meetings. Perhaps his most talented horse was Cardigan, who was only narrowly beaten into second place in New Zealand's most prestigious race, the Auckland Cup.

He was highly knowledgeable on breeding horses and was one of the very first owners to import a New Zealand thoroughbred mare into England. Zizette suffered a terrible sea voyage on the way over. She was heavily in foal and therefore bedded down in a specially constructed loose box on the open deck. The ship was caught in a hurricane in the Pacific, an ordeal she manage to survive. Later, on arrival at Southampton Docks, she was unfortunate enough to be dropped inside her crate from a height of 10 feet. As a result of this nasty and fearful experience she slipped her foal. Happily, she herself recovered and produced further foals in later years at Sir Cecil Boyd-Rochford's stud in Ireland.

When living at The Ham at Wantage, my father had always kept one or two horses with local trainers. George Todd, Bob Turnell and Arthur Budgett, who looked after his valuable brood mare Daring Dolly, were all in easy reach, as were many of the local racecourses. Enticement and Miss Pokerface were two of his more successful horses in training over this period of time. Miss Pokerface was sold and was retired to stud where one of her progeny, Master Oats, would later be the winner of the 1995 Cheltenham Gold Cup.

My father's interest in racing, alas, was reduced all too soon to television viewing. By now he was finding it difficult to keep his weight down and was ever reluctant to take any form of exercise, apart from a gentle walk around the garden. He spent much time dozing in his armchair in the hall, facing the front door, hoping some local friends might call. In the evenings after dinner he would adopt the same position, quietly watching the television with a glass of whisky in his hand. Patricia did her best to keep him mentally active. She would always encourage my two younger sisters to return from London for the weekends with their friends. My father could not resist prodding his daughters about any possible relationship, nor commenting on the suitability of the young men as possible sons-in-law. Not surprisingly, close liaisons were kept secret.

Patricia also hosted small lunch parties in the hope that my father would not lose touch with his many friends and interests. Two of his racing friends who would often come on such occasions were Fred Winter and Dick Francis, both former champion jockeys. Fred was the only person ever to have won the Cheltenham Gold Cup, Champion Hurdle and Grand National as both jockey and trainer. As a jockey he also won the Grand National four times. Fred's wife Diana, before her marriage, had stayed with my parents at Government House in Wellington during a world tour. Dick Francis will always be remembered for riding the Queen Mother's horse Devon Loch in the 1956 Grand National, falling inexplicably on the flat just short of the winning post. The racing correspondent for the *Sunday Express* for many years, he then became very well known as an author, writing more than 40 international bestsellers. Both wives were keen gardeners and later became frequent visitors to Fairfield.

Another regular and always welcome visitor was Penelope Betjeman, wife of Sir John Betjeman, the Poet Laureate, who lived nearby. With more than a trace of eccentricity, she would ride to the front door on her pony and ring the long-handled doorbell. Jeeves would open the door and in she would ride. From the saddle she would immediately engage in conversation with my parents without any thought of dismounting. A carrot would be brought for the pony and a glass or two of sherry was served all round. There was little consideration given to health and safety in those days! I had always remained friends with Candida, John and Penelope Betjeman's daughter. Before her death in 2014, she had become a well-known author, journalist, TV personality and knowledgeable gardener, sharing her father's passion for conserving England's architectural heritage.

Monitoring my father's health all the years since he arrived at The Ham, Dr Hawkey warned me of my father's impending death. Though he remained mentally alert, my father was fast deteriorating physically, and within a few months died in Wantage hospital. To me, perhaps, the measure of his life is best summed up by Earl Spencer, father of Diana Princess of Wales and former ADC to my father in Australia, in an obituary he wrote in *The Times*:

Willoughby Norrie was a man who achieved greatness, yet always retained the common touch; never pompous, never patronising. His time as governor of South Australia and governor general of New Zealand represented a high peak of British prestige in that part of the southern hemisphere.

He was always individual in his methods and during his years in South Australia he held, in a most remarkable way, the affections of all the people in all parts of that vast state. He travelled thousands of miles, often in primitive conditions, to meet the country people and when this famous cavalry officer was bucked off his camel in the far 'outback', his popularity knew no bounds.

As governor of the most English in character of the Australian states he brought to his office a strong sense of duty, unswerving loyalty to the sovereign, and the strength of a devoted family life. He treated his staff, whether high or low, with great consideration, and was rewarded by their loving friendship. His wife and family gave him constant and unflinching support.

He was a superb ambassador for his country, one of a long line who have given much of their lives to strengthening the links that bind us to our Commonwealth brothers in Australia and New Zealand.

In these egalitarian days we should recall with gratitude the goodwill and affection he personally engendered for the home country in those distant lands.

So many of the questions I had, I never dared put to my father until just before his death. I wanted to ask more than anything about my mother Jocelyn, that childhood loss still coming to the surface as I looked back on my life. How did she compare to Patricia, I wondered? He explained that they were clearly different people. Jocelyn had led a quiet early life on her parents' farm near Bracknell, at home amongst horses and county life, whereas Patricia's life was more in the public eye. Jocelyn had very little experience of any other world except meeting young cavalry officers through her elder sister. She was a gentle and sensitive young woman. In her late thirties, as the wife of the commanding officer of the 10th Hussars at Meerut, my mother was the perfect sounding board for the officers' wives, who turned to her for advice on private family issues. On arriving back at Aldershot at the end of the tour, she widened her counselling to the soldier's wives at the welfare centre. In fact, her services were so much in demand that those wishing to see her without an appointment would chance their luck by walking directly to Anglesey House with their children. Would she perhaps have become somewhat lost in the diplomatic and political world of Government House life? She died soon after my birth, so we shall never know into what fullness she might have blossomed.

Patricia was more self-contained. She had spent time in France and spoke the language well, she knew a wide section of people from many walks of life and was running her own house and farm before my mother died and she had met my father. Such responsibility was more unusual for a woman. After marrying my father, there were aspects of public life that she did not enjoy, making speeches for instance, but her natural shyness diminished as her confidence grew. In the book by Gavin MacLean, *The Last of the Ten Thousand Pound Poms – Norrie, Cobham, Fergusson and Porritt*, the author intimated that the scales tipped in favour of my father's appointment as Governor General of New Zealand because he had a very sensible and supportive wife! Patricia always had a clear vision of what should be done, and saw how she would accomplish it. She helped my father enormously, being gently persuasive without obviously interfering.

I have the impression that perhaps Jocelyn had very been close to Nanny, who as recorded in an earlier chapter, lived in Meerut over the same three-year period as my parents, whilst being nanny to the Vaughan family. The families were great friends and the polo ground in the cool of the evening was very much a social meeting place for wives, nannies and children. It was here, I believe, that the two of them began to know each other. This regular honest communication was to be of great comfort to my mother when she received the horrendous news of Diana's death at boarding school. I am sure that much remained confidential between them and will never be known, and in that sense my mother remains frustratingly out of reach for me. There are so many things that I would have asked her had I been able to.

My father was an attractive man, a flirt, brimming with charisma, whose presence immediately filled any room. He took great pride in his appearance, hair always trim, fingernails well manicured. Women were drawn to him, particularly in India – although Nanny would say no more than that! He and Jocelyn made a handsome couple in the inter-war India of the British Empire. Jocelyn would have been comfortable within the military enclave she had always known; they would have enjoyed doing the social round, and the impression that remains for me is of a happy young couple in their prime enjoying army life to the full. The sentiment I choose to associate with them is joy rather than regret.

About the time of his death, the Henwick Country Club, opposite Henwick Old Farm, became a nightclub open for business six nights a week alternating with live bands and discos, attracting a seedy crowd from London and the Reading area. The volume of the subliminal beat of the music until two or three o'clock in the morning was a nightmare, as was the noise from the now inadequate parking for up to two hundred cars revving up for the drive home. There had been a number of incidents when the police had been called in. On one occasion a drunk had beaten a fellow guest over the head with an iron railing. A man later died in hospital and his assailant was later convicted of manslaughter. One night when Celia and the children had gone to the Isle of Wight to stay with friends, I awoke about 3am.

The night sky had turned to daylight and there was an eerie silence. There was no noise of cars or music, not a breath of wind, but simply a strange noise of crackling. I ran to the bedroom on the west side of the house that overlooked the club. Flames were shooting 30 feet high above the club premises, moving slowly from left to right away from my thatched barn. Thankfully no sparks were flying in its direction. The fire brigades from Newbury and Thatcham arrived within ten minutes but by this time the entire building was engulfed. There were no human casualties. Luckily, the club had been closed for two weeks' holiday at the end of August and the only occupant was a resident caretaker.

It was at least four years later that five executive modern houses were built on the site, which remained an eyesore until construction had ceased. Two weeks after the blaze, some local itinerant travellers made a reconnaissance of the wasteland used as an overflow car park. It was clearly being eyed as an alternative site to the one they had set up at Greenham Common. Caravans and trucks began to take up occupancy in a matter of hours and a JCB removed part of the hedge and bank to make easier access. The travellers asked if I would provide water as I had an outside tap on the wall of the barn.

I thought it prudent to do so as I discovered that this particular gang already held a bad reputation for theft, although nothing was ever stolen from our property. The only minor incident concerned a piebald pony, which was either hobbled or tethered in the campsite. One night it broke loose and careered around our garden. The travellers denied it was their piebald pony that had been responsible for the damage to the lawn. The damage, they said, must have been caused by a horse belonging to the farmer in the adjacent field. Celia and I had both seen the piebald on the lawn, silhouetted in the moonlight. There was no mistake.

This episode was repeated the night before the travellers were finally evicted from Henwick by the local enforcement officer and returned to Greenham Common. As I watched the cavalcade of trucks and caravans leave the following morning, I noticed the last vehicle to leave was a tractor pulling a caravan. The large rear-window had been removed and the caravan had become a converted horse-box. The piebald held a commanding view of its final eviction from Henwick. How it ever entered and exited through a narrow caravan side door with metal steps remains a mystery. This episode and the development opposite Henwick Old Farm galvanised me into thinking about finding a new property in a less urban environment.

As it happened, John Bennett, a friend and successful property developer, was developing a small hamlet at Craven Hill near Hamstead Marshall, some 4 miles west of Newbury. The project formed part of some old buildings of the Craven Estate and included part of a Grade I listed Georgian wall. Outline planning permission for a house had been granted for part of the site, outside the original walled garden, where the only tree standing was a majestic 300-year-old Lebanese cedar. John's brother, Tim Bennett, was an architect of repute and an ideal choice for designing such a project taking in to account both the walled garden and the stunning views across the Kennet Valley and North Hampshire Downs.

As the walls were Grade I listed, English Heritage was obliged to offer its opinion on any plan presented. The planning committee of the Newbury District Council were so fascinated by the project that Tim Bennett had drawn up that they held their meeting on site and voted for its approval. English Heritage initially disapproved of the plan, but when Eastgate House was completed eighteen months later and the garden had begun to take shape, they agreed that the project was very exciting and avant-garde. The garden was landscaped from scratch and, as I had all the contacts in the horticultural trade, I was able to secure some large and unusual plants as well as some pot grown semi-mature trees.

Because of the height of the walls, which were about 14 feet, the house was designed upside down. The drawing room and my office were upstairs to get the view, whilst the principal bedrooms were on the ground floor with the dining room and kitchen. I would have expected at least one miscalculation in the design, but I have to say that it all worked perfectly with state-of-the-art heating and even the massive glass atrium deflected the rays of the sun and was self-cleaning in the rain.

Looking back at the time when I lived at Henwick Old Farm and at Eastgate House, a common thread running through my life was dogs. I had twenty-four years of enjoying the company of faithful black Labradors, none of whom survived more than eight years. I always had bitches and they were all spayed, and so I was never involved with breeding. All came as semi-trained gun dogs. On arrival, they could all retrieve obediently and would sit when told. I have to admit, however, to being a poor disciplinarian. At the end of their first shooting season, their behaviour had become so unruly that they had to be tethered with a metal corkscrew.

If Meggan, and her successors, Maggie and Gnat, were not tethered, they would creep away. Gnat finally achieved fame by being written up in *The Field* as one of the worst behaved gun dogs in the south of England. An article written by Duff Hart-Davis described Gnat as arriving as three-quarter trained. At the end of the first shooting season, he described her training as having been reduced to one quarter. Gnat, once un-tethered, would suddenly disappear at the end of the drive. She clearly had no confidence in the ability of other dogs to find birds. She would go back to the cover or game crop from which the birds had been driven. If her searching was not to her satisfaction, she would sniff out an adjoining cover or game crop. Finally, she might even visit a cover belonging to the adjacent estate. She always returned with a bird in her mouth, alive or dead. I was always so relieved to see her return that I scarcely chastised her. It was just such a total relief that she had not ruined the next drive or been shot by an irate keeper from the neighbouring shoot.

The article in *The Field* caused great amusement to my friends, particularly those who owned Labradors. Gnat received considerable fan mail from other gun dogs, who claimed they were incensed by such a defamatory publication. They insisted that none of it was true and that a slur had been cast on the good behaviour and high standard of gun dog training in which the Labrador breed is held in such high esteem. Two other dogs played an important part in my life. Fudge, a rather rotund brown and white Jack Russell belonged to Celia. Sadie from Soho, rechristened Burble, a mongrel mix of poodle and sheepdog from the Battersea Dogs' Home, had belonged to my brother-in-law, who lived in London. When I saw Burble straining to spend tuppence on a sixth-floor balcony in a block of flats, I decided she should be offered a more congenial life.

Her immediate adoption was granted with regret but understanding. Burble would not have qualified as a possible prize winner at Crufts but had a generous nature and she doubled as an extra nanny on seaside holidays when her sheep-herding genes prevented the children from venturing too close to the sea. Fudge, on the other hand, was vociferous and completely devoted to Gnat. They were an inseparable couple – Little and Large. I admit to shedding many tears when they all departed this life. They were good friends and offered wonderful solace in moments of despair.

A NOW QUARTER TRAINED GNAT WITH THE AUTHOR.

19

BILLS, PILLS AND TILLS

Now that I had inherited my father's title, I wanted to honour the hereditary peerage he had been given in recognition of his distinguished service to King, Queen and country.

How could I best achieve this? I gave the matter a great deal of thought, given that I was in business full-time at Fairfield. The simple answer was to take my seat in the House of Lords and see how things would progress from there. That was a very straight-forward procedure. On the specified day just before Question Time in the House, I was to bring the writ of summons, issued by the Chancellor's office, to the Table in the Chamber. I was then instructed by the clerk to take the Oath of Allegiance, sign the Test Roll, go to the Woolsack to shake hands with the Lord Chancellor and leave immediately via the door to the Prince's Chamber. Custom dictated I was then to re-enter from the Peers' Lobby, the opposite end of the Chamber, and join the Conservative benches. From that moment I was entitled to vote on all issues if I so wished. Finally I had to think about choosing a subject on which to make my maiden speech, and my fellow peers had strongly advised me that I should do this as soon as possible. It was discreetly brought to my attention that there were some peers who had still not yet spoken, and was better for my reputation not to fall into that category.

The Labour government of 1979 was about to introduce a new Shops Bill (Sunday trading) in the House of Lords. On hearing this, I went to see Lord Ponsonby, the minister responsible for introducing the bill. He was delighted with my interest when I explained that, as a full-time working director of a nursery and garden centre business, my trade would be much affected. Sunday trading, and the opposition to it, with its long history, was an interesting topic for me. It was finally legalised in 1994 after 26 attempts, starting in the 1950s. There had been a major report in 1964, and over the years various amendments relating to closing hours had all proved very controversial. Many shops had in any case broken the law for years. Of the big stores, only Marks & Spencer, Waitrose and House of Fraser had held out, opening on a Sunday for the first time ever in their trading history in 1994.

Under this new law, all shops are free to trade in whatever goods they like within the time limits set out – these do not apply to smaller shops – although there are still restrictions for Easter Day and Christmas Day when they fall on a Sunday. Of course, later innovations, especially Internet shopping, mean that 24 hours a day, seven days a week, shopping is possible for anyone with access to a computer. In fact, it seems astonishing that the issue of Sunday trading was not resolved until as late as 1994, when shopping habits were beginning to change with the onset of new technology, 1995, for instance, seeing the launch of Amazon and eBay.

In 1979, opinion polls had shown that at least two-thirds of the population in England and Wales would welcome the freedom to shop on Sundays without restriction. What was agreed by practically everyone was that the anomalies of the current law should not be allowed to continue. The 1950s Shops Act forbade Sunday trading in England and Wales except for certain specified items. In Scotland, with the exception of barbers and hairdressers, the relevant section of the Shops Act never applied: Scotland opened on demand.

In 1979, statistics showed that 23 per cent of shops opened on Sunday and about twice as many people in Scotland attended church regularly compared with people in England and Wales. The view of church leaders in England on Sunday trading had always been a mixture of total opposition and compromise. In a later debate in 1989, the Bishop of St Albans described the campaign to remove restrictions on Sunday trading for commercial gain as a form of latter-day prostitution, whereas the Bishop of Manchester believed there could be a halfway house between the current law and total deregulation, allowing certain categories of shops to open for specified hours. As the debate continued, it was pointed out that the electronic tills of the cathedral shops on a Sunday afternoon were often near meltdown, selling items not covered by the Act. Thus the churches' approach to resolving the issue began to favour greater compromise.

Enforcement of the Sunday trading laws in England and Wales was left to the local authorities. In some areas it was strictly observed whilst in others it was openly flouted.

Items sold on a Sunday were often bizarre and it was all too easy to poke fun at the ludicrous aspects and uncertainties that were unenforceable and largely unenforced. The anomalies were well known: in those days, on a Sunday you could buy fish and chips from a takeaway but not from a fish and chip shop. You could buy a pornographic magazine but not a Bible. The monks of Buckfast Abbey could sell wine but not a crucifix or a religious book. Accessories for aircraft, agricultural machinery and mowers could be sold, but not the machines themselves. In the case of a garden centre, you could buy a standard rose but you could not legally buy a bag of peat, planting medium or rose fertiliser with which to plant it. You could buy neither a fungicide to spray for black spot or mildew nor an insecticide to spray for greenfly. You could not buy a stake or plastic ties to secure it after planting. Nor could you buy a spade to dig the hole, as this was considered to be unfair to the ironmongery trade. In desperation, one garden centre operator, it was rumoured, who quite legitimately sold vegetables on Sundays, attempted to make a number of dubious sales of a pound of carrots at £250 per pound, giving away a set of garden furniture free with them. When the local authorities received a complaint about it, they maintained a sense of humour. He was given a warning and avoided a large fine.

All the anomalies applicable to garden centres, such as mine, were raised later by me at the committee stage of the bill, as by tradition I was obliged to keep my maiden speech non-controversial. Instead, I illustrated how well Scotland was managing and what Sunday restrictions existed on the Continent. There were, I felt, two main issues to Sunday trading. Firstly, there was widespread fear that it would lead to higher prices and that if this was so, the general public would be resentful of the extra cost, which in turn would adversely affect the trader and his workforce. Secondly, there would be the grave possibility of family life being disrupted not only for the Sunday shopper, but also for the trader. There might also be unacceptable disturbance and noise experienced by those living in the immediate vicinity of the shopping area, and unforeseen problems arising for services like car parking and public transport.

As I had pointed out at my meeting with Tom Ponsonby, the nursery and garden centre trade in which I worked was much affected by the existing law. The Horticultural Trades Association and the International Garden Centre Group were pleased to find a peer in their midst who would rattle the political sabre on their behalf. At the beginning of my maiden speech it was also important to declare an interest as a full-time working director of my business. This would avoid any criticism being levelled later, but I was also more likely to be considered an expert in my own field and my arguments would therefore attract more attention. Eight minutes was the suggested limit for my speech but I increased it to 13. My friend Ronald Lousley acted as a mentor and helped to draft the speech from a mass of available material produced by organisations both for and against lifting restrictions on Sunday trading. Counting down the days until my maiden speech, I began to wonder whether my father would have been proud of my efforts. The day, when it came, turned out for me to be one of mixed emotions, which ranged from total fear to temporary euphoria.

★★★

At 6.34 pm precisely, on 13th March 1979, I would rise to my feet to make my speech in the Chamber. Arriving on that day at the House of Lords for the customary 2.30 pm Question Time, I was about to pitch myself into the unknown. My support group, comprising my family plus Ronald Lousley, arrived at about 4.30 pm. Public speaking for me had never come easily. My father-in-law had suggested I put myself on a course. This I had done in February, but it would not be truthful to say that it imbued me with great confidence. On the last day of the course it was suggested by my tutors that I could learn to be a little more theatrical by using my hands. The final speech that I made on the course, without notes, was recorded on video and played back. I gesticulated with my hands so violently that the film crew thought this was a serious flaw in my presentation. The recording featured nothing of me apart from the consistent movement of my arms and fingers by which I had attempted to emphasise the seemingly important points I was making. With the memory of that in mind, my nerves remained on edge with my bladder in disarray. However, one trump card remained in my possession. An osteopath in Oxford had promised me a special yellow pill which I was to swallow with an hour before my speech. But uncertainty lingered. How would I know what time to take the pill? Would the debate start on time? I was to be the fourth speaker, but for how long would the first three peers speak? The pill was supposed to give me confidence. Might it make me aggressive? Would a further glass of water force me to leave the Chamber prematurely? Would the effect of the yellow pill make me slur my words, causing me to sound as though I had consumed six glasses of champagne and was now without a care in the world?

At 5.57 pm Lord Ponsonby introduced the Sunday Trading Bill for its second reading. He said it now had more support than ever before, including approval from the tourist authorities. Changes in trading patterns had already happened, unrelated to the law, which removed some of the objections. The National Federation of Fish Friers, for example, had been dead against it until they realised that they were swimming against the tide, causing them to change their policy. Lord Ponsonby cited numerous surveys which showed support for the proposed changes, particularly amongst working people. The current legislation was often in any case ignored, and was also not being enforced because it was too complicated.

I took the pill, my bladder remained quiet, and soon I felt confident and carefree. I convinced myself the ordeal was no worse than reading the lesson in church. The first three speakers announced that they were looking forward to my maiden speech and I began to feel slightly less anxious about choosing such a controversial subject. Then my turn came. Clearing my throat, I managed to stand up, starting by telling the House that the proposed Act would not abolish general restrictions but would simply allow businesses already open to sell their whole range of goods, and it would get rid of the ridiculous anomalies that the various amendments had produced. Sunday trading would still be distinct and different from trading on ordinary days. I supported the legislation, declaring that reform would bring the law more up to date.

I explained how I was concerned about the potential for rising costs both to the trader and to the shopper. From my own experience I knew that at least 50 per cent of all retailing costs are due to labour. Sunday workers would need extra pay and there would be pressure on all the 'invisible' support services for shoppers: car park attendants, public transport, emergency cover for the utilities, security for takings which could not be banked until Monday, and many more, explaining my wish that these concerns would be explored during future debates on the bill.

The peers who spoke after me were complimentary about my speech, but the bill itself got a mixed reception. One aspect that needed to be explored was the exploitation of workers. The Union of Shop, Distributive and Allied Workers (USDAW) had of course been the main proponents of workers' rights. Lord Allen of Fallowfield, the general secretary of the USDAW, who followed me in speaking, said he was totally opposed to the bill, and his union had led a long and spirited campaign against Sunday trading on behalf of its members. Unfortunately for the minister introducing the bill, Lord Allen revealed to the House that he had until recently been part of the union's parliamentary panel. Lord Ponsonby had apparently supported USDAW policy on Sunday trading. 'Some of my friends are saying that the conversion of my noble friend Lord Ponsonby within most recent years makes the conversion of St Paul on his journey to Damascus pale into insignificance,' Lord Allen said. Lord Ponsonby brushed this off in his final remarks, saying that some modification was necessary and many of the other peers had supported him.

My short-lived euphoria and relief at having delivered my speech satisfactorily stayed with me until the end of the debate. Lord Jellicoe, leader of the Conservative Opposition, who incidentally was a supportive client of my garden centre, stood at the bar of the House to listen. A few minutes later a congratulatory note arrived from him. This was very reassuring, but after the very last celebratory drink had been consumed in the Guest Bar, it became clear the effects of the pill had worn off, and with this my lack of confidence had returned.

I had survived my first ordeal, but clearly the future could not depend on swallowing yellow pills. There had been a moment in the Chamber when I imagined my presence there to be pure fantasy, and now I was feeling uncomfortably apprehensive. Was this really to be the beginning of a parliamentary career, I asked myself? As a result of this lack of confidence I remained for the next ten years a reluctant parliamentarian, attending very little unless persuaded by the government whips to appear and vote. Apprehensive about making a fool of myself, I allowed public speaking to remain anathema to me. Aged seven, I can remember the terror of playing the piano at a school concert. Although wanting to overcome my lack of self-confidence I was not sure how best to do it, but felt that if I changed my attitude then hopefully confidence could grow.

Trading on Sundays was a difficult issue that Hans and I had to face, as the nursery was already open six days a week. We both had young families and worked alternate Saturdays. Hans had the added stress of living on the premises in Fairfield House, which afforded very little privacy. Also, some of the staff stated that they were unwilling to work on Sundays as they were not in favour of taking a weekday off. A new Shops Act Sunday Trading Bill had still eluded the statute books so we ran the risk of breaking the law and being prosecuted ourselves if we traded on a Sunday. Integrating one's work and home life satisfactorily is always a challenge for those who are self-employed. I found it a temptation to work hard, and then work harder, without giving due attention to anything else. It had always stuck in my mind that, according to a former president of Coca-Cola, we juggle five different balls in our daily lives, four of which are made of crystal and will smash if we drop them. The fifth is made of rubber and will always, relentlessly, unerringly bounce back. The five balls are family, friends, health, spirituality ... and work. With our eyes fixed exclusively on the fifth, we agreed to open on Sundays.

Very soon we attracted hundreds of people at the weekends, and then found we were caught out as car parking for 200 cars at any one time was still insufficient. The Fairfield site was now hosting seven different franchises including garden buildings, a thatching centre, a patio centre for paving and fencing, an area for coldwater and tropical fish, swimming pools and saunas, mowers and garden machinery and a cafe-restaurant. On the whole, these separately owned businesses became a further attraction, keeping customers on the premises to spend money for longer. The Thatcher government had passed the Housing Act (1980) which would result in 1 million council houses being bought by their tenants. More private home ownership inevitably led to more money being spent in garden centres. We were no exception, and as we grew to meet increased demand, our staff numbers grew too, to include young part-timers employed at weekends.

Fairfield had grown organically through Hans and myself as a family business. Hans held the operational management responsibility of running the business, especially the growing side, the nursery stock, the staffing and financial control. With the garden centre manager I had overall responsibility for all other merchandise, public relations, advertising, and the publication of the catalogue and promotional literature. I must have dropped thousands of coloured Fairfield brochures through letter boxes of potential clients. I became a reasonably knowledgeable plantsman. The catalogue was written in such a way as to help clients plan their gardens effectively. It listed trees and shrubs of different sizes, colours, suitable positions for planting, flowering times, toleration to certain soils and their hardiness, plus many other features. I familiarised myself each week with the trees and shrubs in the display beds. I attended most trade fairs with the garden centre manager and often persuaded him to buy selected new lines which I believed would sell. Importantly, I also carried out a lot of deliveries within a 25-mile radius of Hermitage, enabling me to meet clients in their own environment and take time to look at their gardens to advise and suggest further additions. Fairfield occupied nearly all of my time and energy during the ten-year period between 1979 and 1989.

An independent publicity consultant, Alan Mercado, and I devised the Fairfield Nurseries Conservation Colouring Competition and Quiz to promote the urgent and important message of conservation to school children within a 35-mile radius of Fairfield. In 1988 nearly 10,000 children took part aged between the ages of five and eighteen. Providing that the schools had more than 20 entries each, they qualified for a pot-grown elm sapling, resistant to Dutch Elm Disease, to be planted in the school's grounds or neighbourhood. They also received a 50-year term-by-term diary in which to record the tree's progress. It was a small attempt by us to repair the extensive damage caused by the recent ravages of the incurable Dutch Elm Disease by which the shape of the countryside was being radically altered.

A mature elm is a magnificent tree and for me it was heart-breaking to see parts of the countryside becoming reminiscent of the Somme battlefield, where hedgerows and trees had been ravaged by shelling, their broken trunks and misshapen branches offering a stark contrast to their former beauty. My father's bravery at the cavalry charge at the battle of Néry came to mind, and the tragic death of his younger brother, my Uncle George, two years later.

The judges took a fortnight to complete the task of selecting the prize winners, each of whom received home computers. Professor David Bellamy presented the prizes and later that evening, at his invitation, I attended a London event hosted by the Conservation Foundation which was, although I didn't then know it, to be the prelude to a far-reaching life change for me. Professor Bellamy had orchestrated that during the evening, I would meet as many UK representatives of environmental charities as possible. Had he earmarked me as a future protégé who could fly the green flag in

Parliament? The British Trust for Conservation Volunteers (BTCV), with David as a vice president, was the most attractive organisation to me. It promoted environmental conservation through practical tasks undertaken by volunteers. Another group, the Campaign for the Protection of Rural England (CPRE) explained that much of their work involved lobbying MPs and peers, and expressed their concerns about the impending legislation to privatise the water, electricity and coal industries. The Campaign for National Parks (CNP) described to me the future challenges confronting the National Parks of England and Wales, particularly the relationship with local authorities and funding. This already gave me much to think about. The Tree Council also expressed the importance of the planting and conservation of trees and woods. Even the Royal Society for the Protection of Birds (RSPB), a charity already well known to me, emphasised their need to secure a healthy environment for birds and wildlife. All of this made me feel somewhat less reticent about possibly representing environmental issues as my chosen speciality in Parliament.

I had actually recently been involved in my first act of conservation. As president of the Newbury Branch of the Royal British Legion, I had gone on record to complain about the neglected state of the war memorial, stating, 'It would be shameful for me to lay an Armistice Day wreath on a memorial which is covered in graffiti and green slime.' I had gone further, turning up with a bucket and mop to clean it up as best I could. The story of this complete with photograph appeared in the Thursday edition of the *Newbury Weekly News* and again in some of the national newspapers at the weekend.

Some of my fellow guests on that evening with David said that they had just seen the write-up with photographs of the Newbury event in the Sunday tabloids. Bad news tends to sell newspapers, but positive stories in my view can raise the spirits and heighten awareness of matters that ought to be of concern to the public. The war memorial episode highlighted for me the power of the press to draw attention to something that was so obviously neglected, and thereby gain public support to remedy it. Even before the advent of the Internet, procedures in both Houses of Parliament were recorded for the press, radio and television, now known collectively as the media. I saw at once how important it would be for the media to receive good news stories about the environment.

My head was spinning! For two hours I felt I had been comprehensively briefed better than any government minister. I was quickly beginning to form a fuller picture of what makes up 'the environment' and how it could be blighted by carelessness, greed and apathy. When I left I knew I had some hard thinking ahead of me. If I were to make a meaningful contribution, could I divide my time effectively between Fairfield and Parliament?

GRAFFITI REMOVAL FROM THE WAR MEMORIAL AT NEWBURY, 1988.

20

A TOE IN THE WATER, A FINGER IN THE DAM

On the night of 16th October 1987, a severe depression in the Bay of Biscay moved north-east, causing havoc across London and the home counties. The devastation of what has since become known as the Great Storm was truly shocking: 15 million trees were felled at a stroke; 4 million cubic metres of timber was littered over roads and railways; hundreds of thousands were left without power for two weeks; and worst of all, 22 people lost their lives. Some of our most iconic landscapes were changed forever. Much of the destruction centred on Kent, where one of the national newspapers had described Sevenoaks as becoming 'One Oak' overnight! It was bad news once more for the insurance industry, which would have to cover losses of £2 billion. But it was better news for a number of wild boar which escaped from captivity during the storm, after their enclosures were damaged by falling trees, allowing them to breed and establish populations in woods across southern England. For me, The Great Storm would mark my very first contribution on environmental matters in the House of Lords.

By way of pure nepotism, Lord Maclean, my uncle by marriage, Chief Scout and Lord Chamberlain of the Household, had told me that he wanted to stand down from his various charitable responsibilities. He was at the time president of the BTCV. 'Why don't you take over the presidency?' he said. 'After all, you know a bit about trees. You also know David Bellamy. I am going to tell them you will replace me. No argument.' So in the spring of 1987, I accepted the official invitation to do so. BTCV played an important role in the emergency clear-up. As their new president, I was able to inform the House that some 4,000 volunteers had worked on more than 330 sites in the storm-ravaged areas, and that funding for the continued effort was crucial. I felt a good case had been presented, and I was delighted that extra funding was indeed secured.

BTCV started life 50 years ago as the Conservation Corps, under the patronage of HRH the Duke of Edinburgh. Since then it has been harnessing the efforts of willing and committed volunteers into practical conservation work. From 1988 I have watched with great admiration and enthusiasm how it has become one of the UK's largest and most influential environmental charities (now known as The Conservation Volunteers, TCV), its vision continuing to create a better environment where people are valued, included and involved in something both socially worthwhile and individually fulfilling.

Visiting one of the ongoing projects in the Chilterns, one of our local volunteers asked me over lunch if I would be interested to see a fine display of wild orchids. She believed that she had found a new site of *Orchis militaris* (the military orchid) which has a pale lilac hood formed by the sepals, giving it the appearance of a military helmet of bygone days. I happily agreed to be driven to a secret spot by the village playing fields. Whilst I was admiring this variety of rare species at close quarters, suddenly bearing towards us at great speed came the council tractor, pulling a set of gang-mowers.

'Over my dead body!' screamed our guide, who then prostrated herself in front of its oncoming path. The tractor came to a shuddering stop. A heated dialogue between the gesticulating driver and the prostrate female then ensued. When tempers had cooled, the tractor driver began to see the funny side of the situation. Even after being shown the delicate beauty of the wild orchids he admitted that he could scarcely tell the difference between a daisy and a dandelion. A compromise was reached and he agreed to leave the narrow strip uncut. He was true to his word the following year, and I hope has remained a converted environmentalist ever since.

'One less of them; one more of us,' as Spike Milligan might have said. Spike enjoyed being a volunteer for us on several BTCV working holidays in the early 1960s. He later became a very supportive vice president. Not long before his death, he accepted an invitation to speak to a large, admiring audience about his reminiscences of the sort of work that was carried out. Being Spike, however, his talk turned out to be more to do with the extracurricular activities in the evenings, the affections of the ladies he had won over, a vivid description of their natural assets, vital statistics and personalities. His talk overran by 45 minutes, raising many laughs and considerable funds for the raffle!

TESTING NEW SHEARS: THE AUTHOR
WITH THE CONSERVATION VOLUNTEERS
NORTHUMBERLAND, 1988.

The year after the storm I hoped to get my teeth stuck into environmental issues more fully so I wrote to Earl Cranbrook, the distinguished zoologist, who chaired the House of Lords European Commission Environment Sub-committee. I asked whether I could attend some of their meetings as an observer, as they had a remit to scrutinise a whole range of environmental issues and report back to the European Commission with their recommendations. Twelve hours later, and not really knowing what the committee actually did, Gathorne Cranbrook presented me in front the committee members, saying, 'I have co-opted a new member of the committee – Lord Norrie – who has been very busy last week successfully securing funding to repair damage caused by the Great Storm. We are pleased to have him join us.' Fait accompli, I thought. 'Thank you,' I said, making a mental note to exercise greater care when showing enthusiasm for anything that might entail extra work, as I had only ever intended to sit quietly at the back.

My commitment in the end was to play a fuller part on the committee chiefly by carrying out my own research in the light of advice given to me by the various non-governmental organisation (NGOs) that I supported. They fully briefed me with information, data and statistics on particular subjects that the committee was investigating. They led parliamentary enquiries into environmental topics including rural policies, forestry in the UK and the tropics, management of hazardous wastes and nuclear waste disposal, science in local government, noise pollution, air quality, and EU biodiversity legislation. Given the breadth and depth of expertise, the European Commission took note of our deliberations and it certainly helped them in the process of making decisions.

In our 1989 Report on Habitat and Species Protection, the committee lamented the biological losses which were depleting our natural heritage. We were horrified to have evidence of the colossal extent of environmental damage to flora, fauna and topography: large-scale shooting of migratory birds in Southern Europe, the wide extent of illegal trade in wild-collected plants, complex problems caused by poor land management, including lowering of water levels for agricultural irrigation, not to mention the fight for survival of recently endangered species. The statistics were grisly: in Belgium, for example, about 50,000 song birds were legally trapped each year, whereas further south in Corsica seven firms were producing 5,000 kilograms of pâté from thrushes and blackbirds annually. Imagine how many of those tiny birds were killed to produce that quantity. To give a further illustration of the task ahead, of Europe's 380 species of butterflies, 96 were threatened, with 15 of them on the brink of extinction.

Happily Europe was not silent. It produced a torrent of environmental legislation in the late 1980s and 1990s that flooded into the UK and onto the statute books. At the time the main legislation protecting wildlife was the Wildlife and Countryside Act 1981, but the proposal now was to introduce a 'Habitats Directive' which would shift the equilibrium towards Europe. An important role of the committee was to scrutinise the proposed legislation. As a Conservative, the question of whether legislation was 'national' or 'European' posed a dilemma for me. We are all concerned with habitat destruction and threatened wildlife; the question is whether protection policies should be implemented at national or community level. As an environmentalist, however, any insistence on better environmental protection – wherever it came from – was more than welcome. I was grateful that at least someone was insisting on cleaner beaches, pure water and a better-protected countryside. The EU Habitats Directive was eventually adopted in 1992, protecting 220 habitats and more than 1,000 species.

Sometimes I felt that the environment had become little more than a political football, more often than not being kicked into the long grass. The committee had found much evidence of very poor implementation and enforcement. Moves to massively improve things had been blocked or delayed. In my view, I felt, it could not be left to chance. Although we now had interdepartmental committees on environmental issues, 'green' ministers and an annual check-list of commitments, I believed that progress was still far too slow. Extending environmental assessment to government policies, plans and programmes was the major leap forward that was needed. Nowhere I felt was this more pressing for the committee's remit than tropical rain forests, whose fate was and remains a key issue for global environmental quality. To this the committee now turned.

Lord Cranbrook had been to Sarawak in Malaysia to see forestry operations first-hand. Evidence provided to the committee put us on red alert. Tropical forests now cover only 5 to 7 per cent of the earth's land surface yet still contain more than 60 per cent of all species. Since 1980, an area of tropical forest greater than the size of India has been felled for plantations, agriculture, pasture, mining and urban development. Every year commercial logging operations encroach upon 50,000 square kilometres of tropical rain forest; an area roughly the size of France. My stated view was that the short-term interests of loggers, ranchers and consumers in industrialised countries were taking priority over the protection of forest peoples, species and the environment in general.

The main concerns in our Report on Tropical Forests were the import of tropical timbers by the European Community, international conservation, the contribution of the burning of tropical forests to climate change and human rights. The committee concluded that the primary aim of European Union strategy should be to support sustainable management of natural forests and surrounding areas with emphasis on long-term value for local people. In 1990 the International Tropical Timber Organization set itself a goal that by 2000 the trade from rainforests should be entirely sustainable. In what Greenpeace has rightly called a spectacular failure, in 2011 less than 10 per cent of tropical timber coming onto the market came from sustainable sources. Yet the protection of large expanses of rainforest has been identified by the Intergovernmental Panel on Climate Change as one of the most cost-effective ways of combating climate change. Clearly, we need far more concerted international action to address this complex problem, which may yet be our best hope for winning the battle against global warming.

My knowledge and love of trees was broadened when I was invited to join the Tree Council in 1990. This is the UK's leading charity for trees, set up to promote their importance in a changing environment. The organisation is best known for National Tree Week, which has become the UK's largest annual celebration for trees and woods. Trees have been planted for many years as part of a winter festival on behalf of the Tree Council. Most members of the royal family, including the Queen and the late Queen Mother, every prime minister when at Chequers, and many more public figures have played a part in this.

The tree warden scheme is another of its enterprises. Eight thousand tree wardens all over the country form a national force of volunteers in local networks dedicated to their communities' trees. One of their important tasks is looking after newly planted trees in a challenging urban environment, and Boris Johnson as Mayor of London established a landmark beech to celebrate the fact that 10,000 trees had been planted on the streets of the capital.

There is a great sense of well-being where there are trees. We often make an emotional connection with the trees we plant, and can become personally attached to the ones that we see every day. I always look forward to the autumn. Living in Dumfriesshire on the hills above the beautiful Drumlanrig Castle, some 600 feet above sea-level, our stunning views to the south-west include coniferous plantations, mixed woods and some mature forestry, planted by generations of the Dukes of Buccleuch. During the autumn months, these woods remain resplendent as the leaves of ash, beech, birch, chestnut, oaks, sycamores and wild cherries offer a kaleidoscope of colour ranging through tones of red, purple, brown, yellow and gold. This is a superb contrast when highlighted against the dark green-black of Scots pine and Sitka spruce. In 2015 there was no need for autumn enthusiasts to visit Westonbirt or fly to Vermont to see 'the fall': it was all around us.

From temperate forests to tropical rainforests, deforestation is, however, an urgent environmental issue that is much underaddressed in this country. It jeopardises people's livelihoods, threatens species, and possibly even intensifies global warming. Evidence submitted to the commitee showed the equivalent of 36 football pitches is lost across the globe to logging or burning every minute of every day. Forests are the lungs of the world: we need them to breathe; without them, all that lives will perish. We cannot treat them solely as a form of income, by cutting them down with no replacement. Instead we must consider the world's trees as if they are our capital: once spent, gone.

This concept of 'environmental capital' was to occupy my time and energy during the social and economic turmoil of the 1980s. Margaret Thatcher declared to the Conservative party conference in 1986, 'Popular capitalism is nothing less than a crusade to enfranchise the many in the economic life of the nation.' Was she right? With my simple but suspicious mind, I wondered how this statement would relate to the commodity of water and its proposed privatisation. Maximising profits and respecting the environment do not easily go together. We cannot serve two masters. Meanwhile I was trying to serve three: family, business and Parliament. My life was becoming somewhat overstretched.

In order to attend at their Lordship's House on Monday to Thursday I had reduced my commitment at Fairfield to working just one weekend in two. I usually stayed two nights a week in London, saw little of my family, and felt increasingly guilty and weary. What to do? Hans and I had spent nearly 19 years building up the business, and he and his family had the added lack of privacy that living on the premises entailed. Although the business was a success, with an ever-increasing turnover, responsibilities and duties had increased commensurately. Hans and I both realised that a large capital outlay was always going to be needed to keep the garden centre in pristine condition. Considerable maintenance was required. After great deliberation it was decided to sell the business. Although there were a number of large garden centre groups that would be contenders as purchasers, we had always favoured selling to Hillier. We knew Robert Hillier as a friend and colleague, and he had long asked for first refusal should we decide to sell. A garden centre near Newbury was a natural geographical progression from Hillier's headquarters at Ampfield, near Winchester. My main concern was redundancy for the Fairfield staff, but Hillier kept their word and no one lost their job. Parliament and the environment could now become my focus.

In the 1990s there was a raft of environmental legislation in which I was actively involved. In the following chapters I have confined my coverage to the privatisation of the water, electricity and coal industries and National Parks legislation. Throughout my parliamentary career, I was privileged to be able to draw on the expertise and knowledge of three particular individuals: Evie Soames of Four Communications; Nick Herbert, MP for Arundel and South Downs; and Dame Fiona Reynolds, Master of Emmanuel College Cambridge.

21

PRIVATISATION: WATER

Edmund Burke, the political theorist and philosopher, wrote: 'Nobody made a greater mistake than he who did nothing because he could only do a little.' This sentiment seemed to resonate in the 1990 government White Paper 'This Common Inheritance', which set out the agenda for sustainable development in Britain. I sincerely believed then, as I still do now, that not only does each one of us have a contribution to make in life but we all must play our part, however small. I decided that my mission would be, if I possibly could, to inject greater environmental awareness into parliamentary debate, and perhaps a little 'greenery' into some major government initiatives.

One of the central doctrines of the Thatcher era was the need to privatise state-owned assets. The main reason was to raise money to fund the high levels of public spending without having to raise taxes. Once these budgetary pressures eased in the early 1980s attention then turned to the alleged wider economic benefits. These benefits were claimed to be higher productivity in the private sector, widening share ownership so as to create 'popular capitalism', and reducing the power of trade unions.

All this provoked concerns about potential impacts on the environment. When back in Parliament I began to investigate some of them as privatisation legislation began to pass through the Lords. At times this mission brought me into a certain amount of dispute with my own Conservative front bench, but I felt it was important that I did not compromise by meekly toeing the party line on aspects about which I felt strongly. I soon gained a reputation as a committed environmentalist.

The Conservative Prime Minister Margaret Thatcher had raised the stakes on the environment during eleven years in office from 1979 to

1990. It was her background as a scientist that, early on in terms of political awareness, prompted her to put climate change at the top of her agenda. It was not until the Paris Climate Change Conference of December 2015 that 195 governments finally reached agreement. It was hailed as a landmark deal committing the world to a low-carbon future. Back in 1988, in her headline-grabbing speech to the Conservative Party Conference in Brighton, she explained the issue well, saying: 'No generation has a freehold on this earth. All we have is a life tenancy – with full repairing lease. This government intends to meet the terms of that lease in full.' This was music to my ears and I hoped that, during the privatisation of the ten water authorities in England and Wales, the government would be receptive in safeguarding the environment.

There were about 16 peers from all sides of the House who joined in debates when environmental issues were at stake, aiming to get the very best legislation and to ensure that all the points and arguments for and against were aired. The Lords were more inclined to devote more time for these issues than the members of the Commons. Arguably, the Lords possessed more expertise because many of the hereditary peers came from land-owning and countryside backgrounds and therefore had first-hand experience of day-to-day land management. Some of them, like me, also had a business background in country matters, and most of us shared a common bond of involvement in environmental charities.

The water privatisation bill arrived from the Commons with few environmental safeguards. It was going to be a huge effort to make sure that what we wanted would be included. It was the policy of the NGOs not to lobby MPs and push for the changes they wanted to see in the Commons, knowing full well that any bill would be opened up for scrutiny in the Lords. Nothing in those days could easily be hidden or slip through unnoticed. Nevertheless there would inevitably be aspects in any bill that would stir controversy.

My premise in all this was to secure a duty for the new privatised industry in question to minimise environmental impact. Even when a bill was part of a major strand in the government's agenda – like the privatisation bills – it was accepted that although I was perceived as an authority on environmental matters, I could still be a maverick. I could therefore be a nuisance to my own side, though my own front bench was prepared to accept this situation as an advantage to them, since that discussion might well highlight loopholes.

In my quest to add some greenery to the forthcoming legislation in 1989 I drew on the support principally of those NGOs, such as the CPRE, CNP and RSPB, that I had met at Dr David Bellamy's reception. They were all up to speed with and at the forefront of environmental issues, providing briefings and advising on amendments I was to sponsor. These were crucial as source material for me, since they contained accurate information and specific examples to illustrate essential points in my speeches to the House. I felt it important that I understood every single argument and the supporting evidence in detail. Only then, I concluded, could I be robust in its promotion and defence. More often than not the simple message is the one that people will hear most clearly. To this end I endeavoured to deliver my speeches in straightforward language, so that the message was direct and plain, and easy to follow. Parliamentary lobbyists, working on behalf of clients affected by new laws, were keen to hear what I had to say too.

A bill can start in either the House of Commons or the House of Lords and in order to become law must pass through both Houses. Like a game of ping-pong in slow motion, it can pass back and forth between the two Houses, each House poring over amendments, particularly when there is a contentious issue with a great divergence of views. After the Queen's Speech, normally in November, it has been customary for the government of the day to choose a patently non-contentious bill to be presented in the House of Lords so as to make efficient use of vital parliamentary time. Alas, the water privatisation bill was a non-starter for this role. It was to start in the Commons.

The first reading is really a formal announcement explaining the publication of the bill. The second reading will offer an airing of the pros and cons, establishing benchmarks for further debate. At the committee stage there is detailed discussion of the fine print. At this point procedures in the House of Commons and the House of Lords differ. In the House of Commons at committee stage the debate usually takes place in a committee room and not on the floor of the House. In the Lords all stages of a bill, except under particular parliamentary procedural circumstances, are debated in the Chamber itself. The report stage involves the same detailed examination but amendments are likely to be pressed as there is little further opportunity after this to secure changes. The final reading involves last amendments and it is then either sent to the other House to go through all the stages again, or is sent for royal assent to become law.

I chose to table a searching parliamentary written question prior to a bill's first reading, to which the minister would have to respond with a detailed written reply within 14 days. This answer, published in Hansard, should give an indication of the points in a new bill which were potentially contentious. I worked out that if I grouped amendments together, I could introduce and speak to the amendments, without withdrawing them. This secured me a second bite of the cherry, enabling me to speak again and exert further influence on the deliberations.

My technique was to expose the weak points at each stage of the bill and give the minister a chance to reply. If it were at all possible to establish a relationship with the civil servants drafting up the minister's speech, then two or three questions that I would ask at the end of my speech would be faxed to the officials so that they could prepare a reply for the minister when summing up the debate. This often appealed to the minister because he or she could then show the House that questions of detail could be answered, confirming that they were in command of their brief.

Those of us who were environmentalists were inclined to act independently of party politics. When it came to pushing for environmental safeguards, as one of Margaret Thatcher's full repairing leaseholders, I considered that I had everything to gain and nothing to lose. There would have been much to lose, however, if the Water and Electricity Bills, which dominated much of 1989, did not address concerns on access, recreation and conservation in the countryside.

The second reading of the Water Bill outlined my fears, such as the potential environmental harm from development if Water Authority land was sold off. In those days, the existing authorities were the guardians of a substantial area of the country, adding up to an area slightly larger than Warwickshire which contained some of Britain's most spectacular landscapes, havens for flora and fauna. I strongly felt that the Water Bill was only paying lip service to protecting and maintaining this priceless natural amenity including areas of outdoor pursuits and water recreation, such as swimming, sailing and windsurfing, enjoyed now by more than 3.5 million people. What I felt was needed was a cast-iron guarantee that existing rights of access and recreational use of water authority land and water would be preserved.

Tabling two amendments to secure this guarantee, I argued that when less land is protected after privatisation than beforehand, it is hard to avoid the conclusion that the interests of the investor are being placed above those of the environment or the recreational user. I concluded that withdrawing the amendments at this stage, with the objective of engaging in further dialogue at a later stage of the bill, would be a better plan. By withdrawing an amendment rather than pressing it to a vote too soon, it was possible to persuade the government to draft its own amendment on the same point.

Sure enough, a month later the government brought forward its own amendments to the Water Bill which would bring National Parks and Areas of Outstanding Natural Beauty within a protective framework. This demonstrated to me the value of pressing that particular point earlier. The amendment failed, however, to protect Sites of Special Scientific Interest (SSSIs). There are more than 4,000 of these in England and they are the country's very best wildlife and geological sites. They include some of our most spectacular and beautiful habitats: large wetlands teeming with waders and waterfowl, gorse- and heather-clad heathlands, winding chalk rivers, flower-rich meadows, windswept shingle beaches and remote upland moorland and peat bog. In the 12 months prior to March 1988, eight sites had suffered long-term damage from development which had come through the planning system and seven sites had suffered partial damage. I suggested the example of the Blackwater Valley SSSI near Camberley, in Surrey, which had lost half its 100-acre area to a hypermarket development for Tesco and Marks & Spencer. Orchids and rare insects, such as the seed weaver and rove beetle, had lost their homes. Somebody, I felt strongly, should speak up for them! This was a pretty poor state of affairs.

I did my utmost to threaten the minister with sleepless nights if these special sites were not given the safeguards under the Water Bill that they needed. He eventually softened his position but refused to extend the protection any wider. It was encouraging a day or two later to read the headline in the *Daily Telegraph*: 'Lowland Beauty Spots Win Water Bill Safeguards'. Our alliance of environmentally minded peers, backed by environmental organisations like the RSPB, had made a real difference to the bill, and of course the environment. This support, in the last few years, has sadly dwindled.

Buoyed by this success, I could now address my further concerns about possible adverse effects the bill could have on the flora and fauna. It is difficult to delineate what lives on land and what lives in water. Otters, frogs and eels are examples of mammals, amphibians and fish equally at home in water or on dry land, and all need equal protection. I sought the inclusion of a protective duty in the bill that would compel the newly privatised companies to respect both. However the minister was more worried that this might extend the duties too widely. I was disappointed at the continuing resistance on the part of the government to taking this on board, so I put this important matter to a vote. There were 115 in favour, 121 against, a finely balanced result, which demonstrated the strength of feeling on the issue and even made the television news that evening! It was heartening that, on this occasion at least, the media took a positive and supportive approach, clearly supporting what I and others were trying to do. This went some way to making up for losing the vote.

I was dependent upon some stalwart supporters when the going got tough, and two deserve particular mention. Lord Renton supported me in almost every environmental debate. David Renton was a mentor *extraordinaire* and had been a Conservative MP and a government minister before being made a life peer. I was always very grateful for his support, counselling and wisdom, drawn from a political career going back to the 1930s. He died in 2007 aged 98. Baroness Nicol was my other supporter, a Labour peer and environmental expert. Wendy would speak up in support of most of my amendments and became my strongest ally from the Labour benches on environmental matters.

When it came to debating the subject of overabstraction of water, I knew that I could do so from first-hand experience. I explained that if water levels drop dramatically, and the flow decreases, this inevitably results in a drop in the water table level from massive silting. Deoxygenation is the result, followed by pollution from road salts and fertilisers which have not been diluted sufficiently. What happens then is that toxic levels build up in the rivers, nitrate levels and weed growth increase, and water temperatures rise. This causes oxygen levels to drop alarmingly and carbon dioxide levels to increase, the ultimate result being that fish, birds, insects and plants dramatically suffer, decline and disappear.

I had seen some of this damage for myself in my local rivers, the Pang and the Kennet. The Kennet had been flowing at 50-75 per cent below the norm in January that year and Thames Water had been taking groundwater at Compton to supply drinking water to Didcot since 1965. This now resulted in the average flow in the River Pang at Hampstead Norreys falling to no more than a trickle, and in the valley known as the Winterbournes, precious springs and flooded wetlands had been lost as a result of overabstraction for decades.

My amendment provided for a five-yearly review of water extraction licences so that the conditions could be varied, or in the worst case the licence revoked. The purpose was to maintain a viable minimum water level and flow. The minister was concerned about the bureaucracy involved in administering such a review system, but eventually accepted that the review should be on a 'from time to time' basis.

I later returned to this subject but the government would not give any more ground; a position that horrified me as I saw overabstraction as a major issue. I explained that having seen so much damage caused in my own local environment by overabstraction of water, which was perpetuated as a result of 23 years of inaction by the present Water Authority, I held out no hope of improvement under the privatised water industry unless an appropriate amendment was made to the bill. Nothing happened, and the bill was finally passed later that year.

Now, 26 years later, as of 2015, the available statistics show that windfarms may cause massive damage to wildlife, flora and fauna. In June 2015, *The Sunday Times* announced that Britain's largest onshore wind farm was being accused of contaminating private water supplies to at least 27 properties in west Scotland. Evidence of tests of drinking water taken after construction of the 215-turbine windfarm in 2006 revealed levels of bacteria more commonly expected in a Third World country! Industrialising large rural catchment areas with windfarm developments may not have been adequately considered by developers, planning authorities, health authorities, various water regulatory authorities and, in particular, the Scottish government.

The Water Act of 1989 privatised the ten public Water Authorities, creating ten private water companies in their place. In order to meet EU water standards and to make the sale more attractive, the government wrote off £5 billion of the industry's debts and provided a 'green dowry' of £1.6 billion for environmental investment. A flurry of further legislation followed, including the Water Industry Act 1991 and the Environment Act 1995, which absorbed the National Rivers Authority into the newly created

Environment Agency. I had always been quite sure that water was one of the most important issues of the time. If there were to be another major international war, I believed – and still do – that it was most likely to be about the availability of water, of all the Earth's natural resources.

22

MORE PRIVATISATION: ELECTRICITY AND COAL

The Electricity Privatisation Bill arrived in the House of Lords at about the same time as the Water Bill, raising similar environmental concerns. It also provided the first real parliamentary airing for the issue of global warming that would so dominate the environmental debate in the twenty-first century. In the course of the debates I claimed that we had to act now if we were to avoid creating insoluble problems for ourselves and future generations. The electricity supply industry was generating 233 million tonnes of carbon dioxide every year, along with 2.8 million tonnes of sulphur dioxide, the prime constituent of acid rain, and 809,000 tonnes of nitrogen oxides. As a result there was acid rain, which contributed to the greenhouse effect. This had already been shown to have adverse impacts on the forests, freshwaters and soils, and on insect and aquatic life-forms, damaging buildings and having a growing detrimental impact on human health. I felt the environmental safeguards in the bill were not explicit enough and needed immediate attention. At the committee stage I tabled a substantial amendment to the schedule at the back, which is where the environmental safeguards were set out. Some of my suggestions were accepted, so it was again a pleasure to read the favourable headline: 'Government Gives Way on Environment'.

Regard for the importance of natural beauty was added, which met my concern that low-voltage overhead wires and poles should be removed and put underground where possible, an imperative that is still being fought to achieve. In the opinion of many, the spaghetti-scape of the grid system ruins any beautiful scene. The only opportunities for improving matters, it would seem, are during the replacement of existing overhead lines. However, I learned that the high voltage National Grid lines could not be buried without considerable cost and environmental impacts, although there were opportunities to improve the regional companies' cables, particularly in designated landscapes. There have now been some major programmes in some of the National Parks and Areas of Outstanding Natural Beauty to bury the lower-voltage lines, thereby bringing huge benefits to the visual integrity of our landscape.

A responsibility in general for environmental issues made its way into the Electricity Act 1989. Thus, from starting with a 'very pale green' bill, those of us who were concerned with environmental protection edged the whole of the privatised industry into a safer place. But for how long?

The reform of the coal industry was one of Margaret Thatcher's flagship policies. The Coal Industry Bill of 1990 was therefore introduced as one of the ways of carrying out the capital reconstruction of the industry. Since the coal strike of 1985, British Coal – even after a surge in productivity – had been losing billions of pounds. This was down to falling coal prices internationally, and the restructuring programme, which together meant that British Coal had increased its borrowings to an estimated more than £5 billion. The calculation was that the majority of the collieries still operating would show a negative cash flow over their remaining lives and that at least half the industry's £4 billion assets would have to be written off. The demise of British Coal was largely due to cheap coal imports from other countries, particularly from the open-cast mines of South Africa and Australia. It was simply an unarguable economic truth that it was cheaper to get it out of the ground there and transport it here than it was to mine it in the UK. The bill would, however, allow for open-cast mining of high-quality coal such as anthracite in the UK, which would be attractive to private operators. Without safeguards, I said, whole landscapes could be altered and people's lives devastated.

My stated aim, as before, was to ensure that environmental considerations were given the utmost priority. Should not the environmental duties placed on British Coal, to include its open-cast operations, be extended to the private sector? I had recently visited an impressive BTCV-British Coal restoration project in County Durham and I was keen to ensure that the new arrangements would encourage similar joint ventures. The private sector open-cast operations appeared not to have such a good record on green issues. A 1984 report highlighted sites in Durham where environmental conditions had been breached and restoration conditions ignored.

We know that coal is normally extracted from surface mines using heavy equipment such as draglines, trucks, shovels and excavator machinery, requiring roads, thereby leading to soil compaction and erosion. Dust from the extraction process and stockpiles also causes significant degradation to air quality. Local biodiversity is destroyed and the erosion associated with open-cast coal mining leads to the transport of sediment to surface waters. The chemical composition of the water thereby changes due to higher concentrations of sulphur and soluble salts, leading to increased acidity. This polluted water is typically pumped straight onto the surrounding land, and into the watercourses.

I wanted to table an amendment giving provision for no licences to be granted for open-cast or deep mines until the operators had drawn up satisfactory plans to look after the environment. Legislative precedents in other Acts supported this. Although my amendment was supported by all sides of the House, the Government resisted, leaving me deeply disappointed. Viscount Ullswater had just taken over as the minister responsible for taking the Coal Bill through the House of Lords, but I still felt that the government was not listening to the wide support that my amendment had received. A good case, even an unanswerable one, is sometimes by itself not enough and so I decided on a more radical political approach.

Lord Graham of Edmonton, Opposition spokesman for the Coal Bill, confirmed that there was to be a Labour Party reception in the House of Lords that evening, indicating that there would be a strong body of support available to vote in my favour. I felt I was about to divide the House at a time when few Conservatives were present. At about 6.30 pm Lord Graham started to wind up for the Opposition in support of my amendment. Shortly afterwards, Viscount Ullswater summed up for the government. My instinct was proved correct and I won my vote. Support was clear: 80 in favour, 64 against. The broadsheet headlines the following day were highly favourable. This victory had been secured only with the help of the Labour Party, and I wondered nervously whether there would be a price to pay.

I have to say that I felt more than a twinge of conscience in defeating Nick Ullswater on his first appearance as a minister at the despatch box! He was after all only doing his best to see the Coal Bill reach the statute book with as little change as possible. He proved magnanimous in defeat. The following day brought another unwelcome example of climate change. I was summoned to see Lord Denham, the chief whip, who severely reprimanded me for my maverick actions, although forgiving me with his customary charm and wisdom. I left his office feeling humbled, but nevertheless unbowed. This was not the first time that integrity regarding what I believed in had brought me into a conflict of interest with my own party, but for me this was a matter of conscience. As has been said, it is neither right nor safe to go against one's conscience, and I knew that this was right.

Almost immediately a redrafted amendment was accepted by the government. The CPRE was particularly pleased, having successfully pressed for the original environmental duty on British Coal in 1957. Since then it had been in the forefront of organisations seeking to ensure the continuation of that safeguard in the privatised industry. The CPRE and I were the first to celebrate this achievement.

My work on all these privatisation and deregulation bills had a common strand: the need I felt to establish statutory environmental safeguards and explicit environmental duties on the newly created public bodies. During these years of campaigning, 'green' principles were of primary importance, I felt. When I began my parliamentary career I was 'green' in another way; now that I understood the nature of politics more clearly, I was learning that compromise did not necessarily mean abandoning principles. Politics is, after all, the art of achieving the possible.

My summons to the chief whip's office proved not to be my last. A few months later I received a message to come to Bertie Denham's office at midday. It was rather like being summoned to the headmaster's study, only on this occasion I was not clear what cardinal sin had been committed. I racked my brains for any clue, but came up with nothing, so later, taking a deep breath, I knocked respectfully on the door and went in. I could not have predicted would happen next.

Would I become a government whip and sit on the front bench, he asked. Well, would I? I was totally surprised. My record of voting with the government, after all, had not been unimpeachable. I was given 24 hours to consider. In shock, I found myself asking many questions. Was this really what I wanted to do to further my career in the House of Lords? Was I sharp enough to cope under pressure at the despatch box? What about unfamiliar briefs, such as pensions or social security, the likes of which were often given to newly appointed whips? Most important to me: was the freedom to speak without restriction on matters concerning the environment?

Mulling over it further, I thought that Question Time looked to be the greatest challenge. I had sometimes watched my fellow peers struggle at the despatch box. Briefs for ministers and whips, covering possible questions and suitable answers, are prepared by civil servants from the appropriate government department. The art of giving an acceptable answer to a loaded question rests very much in their hands. I had realised for some time that, ironically, the trickiest questions tended to come from my own side, the Conservative benches. This was because some would be in total disagreement with government policy and would wish to make their point accordingly, as I myself had done. For me, independent thought seemed the most important factor in reaching a decision; this I would lose, as I would have to toe the government line even if I disagreed with it. So in spite of being flattered to be asked to become a whip, I declined.

CARTOON OF THE AUTHOR: THE HOUSE MAGAZINE, WESTMINTER'S WEEKLY POLITICAL JOURNAL.

23

SINKING OR SWIMMING

As the years went on I felt I gained confidence in speaking and asking questions in the House on a regular basis. I was invited to sponsor a Private Members' Bill on swimming and water safety, drafted up by the Royal Life Saving Society (RLSS). This legislation would require maintained schools to teach to a standard which would ensure that their pupils could swim and also have an understanding of water safety. The Secretary of State for Education, within the National Curriculum, would be required to set attainment targets and programmes of study for those lessons. I liked the idea of this challenge.

Compared with other countries in Europe, swimming facilities in the UK rated poorly. In the preceding three years prior to the introduction of the bill, almost 200 British children under 15 had died by drowning, 80 per cent of whom could not swim. Being able to swim is a critical factor in reducing the risk of drowning. When my bill left the House of Lords, a similar Private Members' Bill was introduced in the House of Commons under the Ten-Minute Rule. An Early Day Motion welcoming the recommendation of the National Curriculum Physical Education Working Group was signed up by 240 MPs of all parties including five former ministers of sport. The bill I sponsored became law in 1994; its enactment, under statutory order, complemented RLSS's vision of safeguarding lives in, on and near water. We can never know how many young lives have been saved as a result of that Act. If it is even only one, then it will still have been worth it. As an old saying goes, 'for whoever saves one life, it is as if he has saved an entire world'.

At this time, there was one particular life that concerned me more than any other: that of my son (even though swimming was one of his skills).

Whilst I was fully occupied in London during the week, Mark had been preparing for A levels at boarding school, when, apparently inexplicably, his ankles began to swell up. Urine tests revealed a high level of protein and blood, pointing to a possible kidney-related condition. Before long, Mark was diagnosed as having a disorder known as Alport syndrome, which predominantly affects males in a family. The early symptoms can also include hearing and vision impairment. This renal failure disorder invariably appears in the sufferer's late teens or early twenties. This came as a wake-up call to the family and shocked us all. It meant that Mark would need to draw on his inner strength to get through both the trauma and the treatment, as would the entire family. The family prayed that he would pull through, though no one knew where this would lead.

Not knowing what else to do, I became involved with the National Kidney Federation, later becoming its president. The charity is run by patients for patients, aiming to promote the best in renal practice and treatment on behalf of sufferers. Some 40,000 sufferers in the UK are receiving dialysis or have functioning kidney transplants, which together are termed renal replacement therapy (RRT). When kidneys fail, the body is less able to remove toxic waste and excess water, which can result in premature death. Dialysis is the process to remove these wastes and water from the blood. It is estimated that well over 3 million people in the UK have moderate or severe kidney disease, many of whom display no symptoms. On awakening to the situation, the journey to recovery can be hard and painful, and very frightening, although nowadays acupuncture and other alternative treatments have been found to be highly successful in restoring the body's balance, greatly reducing the trauma and dangers of the disease.

In those early days, a consultant nephrologist concluded that Mark's kidneys might fail within the next 18 months. As it happened, they would fail within only nine. He was determined to put whatever time he had before then to good use, so after his A levels Mark went off to backpack around Australia and New Zealand, staying with old contacts of mine in both countries. Alas, his health was poor on his return and he had to abandon the estate management course he had begun at Cirencester Royal Agricultural College. Instead he lived at home, bought a car, enjoyed his friends and as full a social life as his condition allowed, and drove to the dialysis unit at the Royal Berkshire Hospital in Reading about three times per week.

ROYAL LIFE SAVING SOCIETY COMMONWEALTH
COUNCIL, AT BUCKINGHAM PALACE, 2001.
AUTHOR SEATED FRONT ROW, FAR RIGHT.

He was faced with disappointing restrictions on his diet and a list of forbidden foods. However, during the process of dialysing the restrictions were lifted and Mark was able to consume as many of his favourite Marmite sandwiches as he could swallow. There were times when the treatment made him feel very ill and one of us would have to rush him from home to the Royal Berks, where beds were at a premium and patients often packed in the Huntley & Palmer Ward like sardines. On several occasions there had been an unexpected death overnight. On one visit, he greeted the ward sister with the words, 'Not Death Row again!'

What was really needed, urgently, was a kidney transplant. By now Mark had waited for about seven years. All five of the family arrived to meet with the skilled Australian transplant surgeon, Professor Morris, in Oxford to discuss one of us being a live donor to Mark. None of our kidneys met the transplant criteria. As I was only a month short of my sixtieth birthday, my kidneys were considered to be somewhat beyond their sell-by date, although I was a marginal possibility. Mark immediately decided that he could do without either of my kidneys, which he described as 'pickled', preferring to risk waiting for the day when an organ in a more respectable condition might become available.

When the great day arrived, the donor kidney proved to be an excellent match and by 4 pm it had been transplanted and was performing perfectly. We all gave a collective sigh of relief. The greatest risk of rejection takes place during the first few weeks of transplantation, we were told. There were some tense moments, but all went well. Having to take a dose of anti-rejection drugs every day is a small price to pay, he feels, for the life that he now enjoys! As a wine merchant, he himself has always taken responsibility to balance the precious gift of a new kidney with his personal alcohol consumption and lifestyle. 'Don't worry about the new kidney, Dad,' he quipped, 'it is more likely that the liver will go first!'

Mark's years of ill-health were naturally a constant anxiety and concern to Celia and myself, not knowing very much about the disease. There were many times when I shed tears of desperation, and I would have done anything to bring him relief. By contrast he remained resolutely cheerful and optimistic. He was the embodiment of Burke's dictum already quoted in this book: just because he could not do what he had expected to be able to, that did not stop him from doing *something*. He got involved in all sorts of things. He raised some £21,000 for the Reading dialysis unit, and yet more by carrying out a sponsored tandem free-fall parachute jump from 11,000 feet, wisely harnessing himself to a parachute instructor first!

I, too, did what I could. I baulked at jumping out of an aeroplane, but I did have several meetings with government ministers in my capacity of president of the National Kidney Federation. Baroness Julia Cumberlege became the health minister in the Lords when John Major's government was still in power, offering a sympathetic ear and agreeing to be the principal guest speaker at the annual conference of the Federation in Torquay. Baroness Jay followed her after the change of government, and was equally supportive. Her brief covered both transplantation and organ donation. Margaret Jay suggested I should initiate a short debate. This I did on 19th November 1997, and I also spoke in another debate on the NHS in February 1999. There are two big issues which I tried to tackle as president: providing enough dialysis facilities for all who need them, and finding enough kidney donors. It is understood that end-stage renal failure is fatal unless a patient receives regular dialysis or a transplant. The number of people needing regular dialysis at that time was growing by 6.5 per cent annually, and the need continues to grow. One way of increasing the level of donation, I thought, might be if it was assumed that people would become donors at their death unless they had specifically opted out.

In 2008 the independent Organ Donation Taskforce published a long-awaited report for the Department of Health on the issue of presumed consent. This was a welcome development as I had helped the National Kidney Federation to press for an independent commission to explore methods of increasing organ donation. However, the taskforce did not recommend introducing a system of presumed consent. They judged that it would not increase donation rates and would be too complicated to implement. Most of the British Isles concurred, although the National Assembly for Wales has just introduced a controversial 'opt out' Human Transplantation Act (2013). Writing in 2016, after it became law, it still remains to be seen whether this will increase organ donation.

Remarkably, in 2014 Mark received his second kidney transplant. The first kidney, although still working, had become ineffective, and he was therefore due to begin dialysis for a second time. Perhaps there will come a time in future years when human stem cell applications will become a reality as a new resource for important organs and tissues, replacing the continuing need for transplantation. Scientists in Australia now, I read, have grown the world's first kidney from stem cells; a tiny organ which could eventually help to reduce the wait for transplants.

I was prompted to reflect on the painful early years during which the family wrestled with the realities of living with what we now know as Alport syndrome. Although unable to give him a kidney, there was something of value that I could give him, I thought: the freedom to decide what he wanted to do in life, along with the ability to achieve it and not be dictated to by his father, as my brother and I had been. By understanding and appreciating his assets, I hoped I could steer him gently into things at which he knew he would be capable. In other words, I wanted him to have the unconditional fatherly support and encouragement that I felt my early life had lacked.

Once more my thoughts returned to my early relationship with my father. There had been great lengths of time when I could not see him, and this obviously had a negative effect on me, one which I had no wish to repeat. As soon as Clare was born I determined to be with my own children as much as possible, but then found all too soon that much of the time that I would have liked to spend with them, particularly in later years, was often taken up by the unyielding demands of business and Parliament. I now realised that my father must have had similar pressures, so the two of us had shared a common dilemma: conflict between public duty and private life.

24

THE JEWELS IN THE CROWN: NATIONAL PARKS

I have to admit that my first two visits to a National Park were not enjoyed. In the late winter of 1958, I was posted by my regiment to Catterick Camp in Yorkshire to help organise some harsh training to toughen up potential officer recruits prior to their arrival at Mons Officers Cadet School in Aldershot. To describe the winter weather conditions in the Welsh Brecon Beacons and Otterburn in Northumberland as 'inhospitable' would be a massive understatement. However, this experience was fully compensated by some glorious summer sunshine, and I found time to visit the Yorkshire Dales as well as the Lake District a little further afield. This gave me space to reflect and to appreciate, probably for the first time ever, these wonderful areas of protected countryside where people live, work and shape the landscape. How important it was, I felt, that everyone should have the opportunity to appreciate them.

The National Parks of England and Wales were constituted as a gift to returning service men and women after the Second World War. They were to be 'national walking grounds', their natural beauty conserved for everyone to enjoy. They were established to complement the National Health Service, preventing ill health by promoting well-being instead. The minister introducing the Act of Parliament that set up National Parks said: 'The enjoyment of our leisure in the open air and the ability to leave our towns and walk on the moors and in the dales without fear of interruption are … just as much a part of positive health and well-being as are the building of hospitals or insurance against sickness.' In an increasingly sedentary and stressful age, I would not wish to add to this sentiment, but rather to strongly endorse it.

Ten National Parks were set up in the 1950s in England and Wales:

the Peak District, Lake District, Yorkshire Dales, North York Moors, Northumberland, Snowdonia, Brecon Beacons, Pembrokeshire Coast, Dartmoor and Exmoor. The names themselves are evocative of fresh air, muddy boots and glowing health. An eleventh – the Broads – was set up under its own Act of Parliament at the end of the 1980s. The New Forest joined the family in 2005, and the South Downs is the youngest member, joining in 2009 after a very long campaign. The highlight of 2016 has been the extention of Cumbria's 2 National Parks – the Lake District and the Yorkshire Dales. This has brought their boundaries to either side of the M6 and effectively join the Parks together to create a total of 1750 square miles of protected landscape.

No National Parks have been created in Northern Ireland. Further north, Scotland has two national Parks: Loch Lomond and The Trossachs, and The Cairngorms, created in 2002 and 2003, respectively. These were designated as such under the National Parks (Scotland) Act 2000 passed by the Scottish Parliament not long after its creation (or reconvening) in 1999.

It is easy to take for granted their characteristic appeal, ranging from the sweeping expanses and far horizons of Northumberland to the undulating moorland and rivers of Dartmoor. The sparkling meres and rugged mountains in the Lake District that so inspired Shelley, Coleridge and Wordsworth are world-famous. The addition now of the South Downs brings a new kind of national park, embracing rolling chalk downland, patches of heath and abundant woodlands of the Weald, as well as the iconic white cliffs of the Seven Sisters. But in 1991, all was not well.

Even as the National Parks were being designated, they were faced with many continuing pressures which threatened the quality of their existence. Some said that the increasing massed ranks of alien conifer plantations were akin to concentration camps for trees. New reservoirs were being scoured out to quench the thirst of industrial conurbations, flooding ancient valley communities and destroying sensitive ecosystems. Quarrying destroyed large chunks of green and pleasant hillsides, leaving raw, harsh scars behind. Even futuristic nuclear power stations, such as Trawsfynydd in Snowdonia National Park, were allowed to be built.

Although the first two National Parks were set up with independent boards, the rest had committees of county councils to oversee them, and they did not always put the interests of National Parks first. The county councils were also expected to part-fund the Parks, but often failed to come up with the cash on time. Furthermore, with the advent of so much noise from sports such as jet-skiing, motorcycle scrambling and banger racing, it was important to be more precise about the sort of informal recreation for which National Parks were best suited. The National Parks needed an updated framework and better tools to do their job. Something had to change, and quickly.

In 1990, the Countryside Commission (which had been set up by law to advise the government on countryside matters) established a panel to review National Parks. This was chaired by Professor Ron Edwards, who had been a Council for National Parks (CNP) vice president for many years. Originally a freshwater biologist, he held many public offices in England and Wales. The CNP greatly welcomed the publication of the Edwards Report, 'Fit for the Future', a year later.

There were four main recommendations. The first was that the purposes of what National Parks were for should be clear and brought up to date. The purposes were now identified as conservation, public enjoyment, and promoting social and economic development for communities within the Parks. Secondly, the Secretary of State was to be held accountable for ensuring that these purposes were met. A further recommendation was that certain planning applications for developments within the Parks should be subject to an environmental risk assessment. These planning applications would be scrutinised, lastly, by new independent statutory National Park Authorities set up for each park.

The government dutifully acknowledged the validity of the report's recommendations but still dragged its feet, with any new legislation continuing to be postponed. Other legislation which would impact upon National Parks, however, was in the pipeline. Under the plans for local government reorganisation some of the county councils which ran the Parks could disappear, causing, as I feared, much uncertainty and disruption. The Parks were in danger of being left in limbo, with an ambiguity as to who was to be responsible – and, more importantly, accountable – for their future funding and management.

Partly to address this anomaly and following a conference the CNP held in Tenby, the campaign for new National Parks legislation began in earnest in December 1992. My work as president of BTCV had already taken me to some of the National Parks in question. I recall witnessing

ABOVE: PROPOSED LOCAL GOVERNMENT
REORGANISATION WAS A THREAT TO THE FUTURE
FUNDING AND MANAGEMENT OF THE PEAK DISTRICT

BELOW: THE NATURAL BEAUTY OF SNOWDONIA

the first-class repairing, by volunteers, of the stone footpath from Gordale Scar to the top of Malham Cove in the Yorkshire Dales. In Snowdonia it was intriguing to see how other volunteers were involved in heather regeneration, by planting seed on newly scraped earth, which I learned is a necessary condition for successful germination. On one of my very first ever BTCV visits, I found myself in the Norfolk Broads and was amazed to see a volunteer, a young great-grandmother, becoming involved a little too deeply in her work. Even her all-embracing waterproof garment was no match for this wonderful lady's enthusiasm and I watched with some consternation as the water level exceeded the top of her chest waders.

On these travels I had often heard for myself how the present rules and regulations for the Parks were not fit for purpose. Please could I help? I was in a position, as a parliamentarian and a man with green credentials, to be an agent for change. I decided to take up the cudgel and become wholeheartedly involved with a campaign to reverse Burke's dictum: doing a lot rather than a little.

My career in the world of nurseries and garden centres had developed my interest in trees and natural beauty, thus my interest in the wider environment and beautiful landscapes was a natural progression. The president of the CNP in the late 1980s had been the Radio Four presenter Brian Redhead. I had taken on board the title of his book, *The National Parks of England and Wales, Not Ours but Ours to Look After.* I became another of CNP's vice presidents, formally taking up that position on 3 October 1991. I had many roles, mainly to help the CNP and influence policies and legislation for the benefit of National Parks. In acting as an advocate for them, I joined a group of people from all parties and from outside Parliament committed to the conservation and promotion of these beautiful areas. With other peers, I wrote to *The Times*, arguing that because of the pressing timetable of local government reorganisation, a short National Parks Bill should be introduced into the House of Lords after the Queen's Speech that November. There was a danger that unitary authorities would be set up in Wales without any adequate arrangements being made for the National Parks. In such a situation, who would take responsibility?

We awaited the Queen's Speech with very low expectations, and were proved right. The CNP had continued to be busy, however, and as a result of their ongoing campaign and lobbying, it became apparent that I could in fact promote the desired legislation myself. A draft would be produced by the civil service, to include the Edwards recommendations, which I could then sponsor and take as a Private Members' Bill in the Lords. This was an opportunity too good to miss. Such a procedure would allow controversial measures to be debated without damaging the government's agenda or credibility. Or perhaps, given the genuine lack of time for proper debate, it would continue to exert pressure on the government to bring forward its own legislation in the Commons at a later stage.

The first reading of my Private Members' Bill was on 3rd March 1994, a move welcomed by the magazine *Country Life*. Calling it a 'New Broom for the National Parks', the editorial said: 'For those who live and work in the parks, as much as for those who simply seek inspiration or relaxation there, these changes should bring a visible improvement'. That was precisely the publicity wanted. At the same time the publication *National Parks* had as its main headline, 'It's Norrie to the Rescue', alongside a picture of me captioned, 'Short, sharp and simple'. I am still a little unsure whether this referred to the bill or to me!

I had managed to visit many of the other National Parks on a fact-finding mission. In the cold of January and February, I visited the North York Moors, the Lake District and the Brecon Beacons with Baroness Nicol, another CNP vice president. In the North York Moors I met a farmer who was part of a National Park farm scheme in Farndale, an area noted for its wild daffodils and bluebells. It was an education to meet a Yorkshire farmer at his isolated home: on entering the cosy kitchen he exclaimed 'put wood in'th oyle, lad'. I looked around for the lad in question but all I could see was an open door. I then realised that I was being bidden to shut it! In his own Yorkshire brogue he said he had the nous to have used a jammy grant scheme to bring in a shed load of money by simply planting a few hedges. He was later amazed at the dramatic increase in birdlife and insects on his farm, telling me also how useful the hawthorn hedges were becoming as a windbreak for his livestock and other wild animals. It was possible, therefore, to have one's cake and eat it. Just what anyone wants, especially a Yorkshireman.

Visits to Exmoor and Dartmoor followed, and in all the National Parks I was warmly welcomed and briefed by the National Park staff and members, together with other local experts. We were in one such briefing session at Princetown in Dartmoor when suddenly Nick Atkinson, the National Park officer, jumped up from the table and ordered an evacuation

THE LAKE DISTRICT AT ITS BEST

– there was a blizzard brewing. The CNP's assistant director, Vicki Elcoate, drove me through heavy snow over the moor to our evening engagement. This turned out to be an exercise in lobbying by the local parish councils, who wanted greater representation on the National Park Authorities. I was soon the target of a letter-writing campaign by seemingly dozens of parish councils; every letter had to be answered in person, of course. This involved a lot of diplomatic effort, but I judged it would be worth it if it led to a more local and democratic representation.

I was not alone in being concerned for the future of National Parks. The acclaimed mountaineer Sir Chris Bonington had toured all the National Parks of England and Wales, winning support for the broad principles of my bill. I appreciated his input and support, and particularly his working with the National Park members and staff to understand the issues and communicate them to a wider audience. His role was to inspire people about the importance of National Parks; he would always say that it didn't matter where he travelled in the world, when he got home to the Lake District he knew he was in the most beautiful of landscapes that could rival any mountain area. Like many others, he did not want to see that threatened.

News of my bill was greeted by the Countryside Commission as 'a leap forward – we see this as an important step along the road to implementing the Edwards report'. The local government reorganisation clock was, nevertheless, still ticking. My spies were telling me that the last thing John Major's government wanted was for the arrangements around the National Parks to be unresolved. Although nothing was said, perhaps the government was relieved when what became known as the Norrie Bill had its second reading on 16th March 1994. I was encouraged that 23 speakers spoke broadly in support. The speakers came from all sides of the House and some contributions were most heartening, including that of the opposition spokesman, Lord Williams of Elvel, whose wise counsel during the passage of the bill was much valued. One of the speakers, Viscount Addison, the great-grandson of the Dr Addison who chaired the Addison inquiry into National Parks back in 1931, was a great help to me. William Addison helped with the research for the bill and acted as a very welcome 'runner' between my position on the Conservative benches and the CNP staff in guest seats at the rear of the Chamber. The CNP directors were there to help with specific points upon which I would have to comment in my final wind-up at the end of the debate. The rules of the Chamber do not permit passing messages or whispering, so I needed to ask William, who was sitting beside me, to leave the Chamber whenever I needed such information. When the time came we would signal to the CNP staff to meet up with him for a quick briefing, and supply him with a written reply. This manner of communication was somewhat tortuous, but effective.

At the committee stage that followed I was concerned about the make-up of members serving on the new park authorities. However, the Environment Minister, the Earl of Arran, provided a reassurance that the new authorities would reflect a reasonable mix of interests, including representation from those who lived within the Parks. There was much discussion on this point, but finally at third reading I successfully moved that 'the bill should now pass'. That evening I handed it to the Conservative member for Tiverton and Honiton, Angela Browning. In time-honoured tradition she literally carried it into the Commons to see what fate would hold for it there. If Virgil is to be believed, *fata viam invenient*, fate would find a way.

Lack of parliamentary time was the great obstacle that faced Private Members' Bills. In 1994, only Friday mornings were given up to these, and only the top six out of the annual ballot were actually likely to succeed. It only took a single MP to shout 'Object!' at second reading to stop a bill in its tracks, and that is exactly what happened.

Why did the bill fail? There was apparently a backlash from disparate quarters aiming to crush it, although I and others suspected a degree of collaboration behind the scenes. This opposition first emerged in an article in *The Field* by Lord Kimball with the entertaining headline of 'No to Nationalised Parks' and the even more entertaining strapline: 'In the belly of this Trojan horse lurks the socialist dogma of 1945'. Marcus Kimball was adamant that, because of the reforms to National Park Authority membership, there was a hidden agenda for them to be owned by the public and run as though the state were the landlord.

There was a valid argument lurking amongst the rhetoric: that more parliamentary time was needed for widespread debate than could be provided by a Private Members' Bill in the Lords. At committee stage of my bill in the House of Lords, Marcus Kimball compared it to the hurried and controversial Dangerous Dogs legislation: 'It gets us into trouble if we legislate in a hurry,' he pronounced. The only difference was that the

National Parks Bill had a fine pedigree which would stand it in good stead in the future.

Michael Jopling, (now Lord Jopling) then the MP for Westmorland and Lonsdale in the Lake District, proceeded to echo this in the Commons and was ultimately instrumental in its downfall. It may seem surprising that as a MP for a National Park constituency he would work to seek the demise of legislation that was so desperately needed, but he did. Angela Browning got early wind of this by overhearing him plotting for the bill to be vetoed by others on a Friday he couldn't attend.

Not seeking to hide his part in the bill's demise, Michael Jopling wrote a letter to the North Yorkshire Moors Association in October 1994, declaring that the 'Norrie Bill was dead'. He commented that it remained to be seen whether the government would deal with the 'issue of national parks' in the next session, apparently hoping that they would. His objection was not the content of my bill, but the injury he thought had been done to Parliament in the way it had come to the Commons. He was vexed that, in his view, the Commons could be expected to pass a bill without a single word being said, calling this state of affairs 'intolerable'. He had a point, I thought, but at least my bill had highlighted the basic principles for future National Park legislation.

Angela Browning was clearly disappointed at the failure of the bill. Although I had been right to have anticipated its likely collapse, I felt assured that the government's inclination for National Parks legislation still remained. I was convinced that it was only a matter of time before another door would open.

THE AUTHOR, TIM YEO MP, MINISTER FOR THE
ENVIRONMENT AND COUNTRYSIDE, AND SIR CHRIS
BONNINGTON. THE CAKE DISPLAYS A CLOCK SET
AT 5 MINUTES TO MIDNIGHT EMPHASISING THE
URGENCY FOR NATIONAL PARK LEGISLATION

25

THE ENVIRONMENT BILL

It was vital to keep the pressure on the government in order to force it to introduce its own legislation, which at the time meant getting it included in the Queen's Speech in November 1994. I made sure that I missed no opportunity to do this. For instance in March that year I wrote to the Environment Minister calling for a Government Bill to be introduced. Tommy Arran came back with what turned out to be a well-worn form of words: 'It remains our *intention* to introduce legislation to implement the policies set out in our January 1992 policy statement on the national parks as soon as there is a suitable opportunity.' Many letters from the public prompted this same stock reply.

In October, a draft was published. If there was to be legislation on this subject, then it would most likely be included in a wider Environment Bill, with Environment Agency clauses, but to widespread dismay there was no mention of it. In response to my question about the absence of the National Park clauses in the published draft, Viscount Ullswater, the newly appointed Environment Minister, replied: 'We *hope* to present the Agency provisions to Parliament, as part of an Environmental Bill, at the earliest opportunity. Whilst I am not in a position to say exactly what would be in that bill, you should not read any significance into the absence of anything on national parks in the published draft.' Nick Ullswater had replaced Tommy Arran's good intentions with his own hope, and hope is a good breakfast but a poor supper. Was his statement sufficient cause for expectation, I wondered?

In any legislative campaign, MPs like to know that there is a groundswell of support, so it is essential to focus on MPs who are also influential decision-makers. To maintain the pressure, many, many letters were written by our friends and supporters. When we knew at the beginning of November 1994 that the contents of the Queen's Speech would be discussed at Cabinet level, we asked all our friends in John Redwood's constituency of Wokingham to contact him. A member of the Cabinet and Secretary of State for Wales, he was already responsible for three National Parks, and we hoped he would respond by fighting for the inclusion of National Parks legislation in any government bill.

There was much celebration, therefore, when the Queen's Speech in November 1994 promised our eagerly anticipated bill. The Environment Secretary John Gummer confirmed on 18th November that it would include the four broad recommendations from the Edwards report included in my earlier Private Members' Bill. We raised a glass when he announced: 'This session we shall certainly introduce measures to establish new independent authorities for the ten national parks in England and Wales.' Excellent news, another road paved with good intentions had reached a happy destination.

This new and important bill was intended primarily to set up the new Environment Agency but it also included sections on National Parks and hedgerow protection. On National Parks it included clauses which addressed our main concerns: firstly, to update the National Park purposes of conservation and recreation; secondly, to place a duty on all government departments to have regard to National Park purposes; and finally, to set up new Authorities for the ten National Parks in England and Wales. The government had accepted much of the Edwards report recommendations, but it was the omission of what the CNP saw as essential measures for National Park protection that became the focus of debate later. We wanted an environmental risk assessment test in legislation that meant 'potentially damaging development' in the Parks would only be allowed if absolutely essential and without alternative. It all depended, of course, on the definition of 'essential'.

The bill began its passage through Parliament with its second reading later that month, and I welcomed it wholeheartedly. The original National Park purposes, set out in the 1949 National Parks and Access to the Countryside Act, were 'to preserve and enhance the natural beauty of the areas and promote their enjoyment by the public'. The Edwards panel had recommended that it was time for a change, and I thoroughly agreed. The recommended new purposes were much broader in scope: firstly, to conserve and enhance the natural beauty, wildlife and cultural heritage;

HADRIAN'S WALL, NORTHUMBERLAND

and then, to promote opportunities for the understanding and enjoyment of the special qualities of the areas by the public. All very good, but with one caveat: the omission of the word 'quiet' before 'enjoyment' was for me highly significant, and one not to be ignored. A sense of peace and tranquillity had always been inherent in the National Park concept in England and Wales.

Of course, new recreational businesses had grown up in places like Windermere in the Lake District, including power-boating and water-skiing, all of which meant added noise. The government had foreseen a battle ahead over this issue when in 1992 it stated that the Parks should provide a wide range of experiences for the visitor, emphasising too that positive management could allow for many activities to coexist without serious damage to the essential qualities of the Parks. Were they right? An innocent soul might have assumed that an essential quality of the Parks was peace and tranquillity. Increasingly, alas, this was not the case. I hoped that if I proposed an amendment that would enshrine the term 'quiet enjoyment', this would receive support from many.

The minister, however, replied that 'quiet enjoyment' was difficult to define and that my amendment might lead to unintended bans on all kinds of activities. Other opponents broadened their interpretation of what my amendment might exclude, such as Michael Jopling MP who wrote to the Friends of the Lake District at that time: 'My concern is that in the hands of over-zealous officials it could give rise to over-enthusiastic curtailment of legitimate activities. This would include timber management with chainsaws, and grouse shooting.' This was neither the intention of my amendment, of course, nor the likely outcome; I was not anticipating Trappist colonies or slipper-wearing visitors.

Meanwhile my pile of mail was growing, and did not always contain congratulatory pats on my back. Lorimer Farrell of the Association of Rural Communities roundly berated me for supporting these measures, which he took to be a stealthy strategy to remove military training from the parks. Twenty-three per cent of the National Park in Northumberland where this constituent lived is used as a training area by the Ministry of Defence (MOD). 'You may see Northumbrians as covered in woad but we can read Hansard!' he said. I was gratified that anyone would want to read it. He added: 'You should be aware that continuing efforts by anybody to frustrate the army, or calls for public inquiries to challenge the primacy of the military on their own land, will further strengthen the case for the separation of MOD-owned areas from national parks'. In a PS he even implied that I was an 'urban environmentalist' who wore green wellies and a Barbour jacket whilst drinking with 'rough farmers over a jolly pint at the village pub'! He was partly right, of course; during the National Park campaign I had been offered many a jar by environmentally mindful farmers in pubs and inns all over the country. The efforts to have the National Park designation lifted from military training areas came to nothing and National Park purposes and military training continue to coexist, if in a somewhat uncomfortable truce at times.

At the committee stage of the bill my amendment won an important vote (by 129 to 121), which changed the proposed new second National Park purpose to 'promote opportunities for quiet enjoyment and understanding'. It was clearly a good move for the populace, although unpopular with the government because of the drafting difficulties associated.

With the word 'quiet' included, the bill went to the Commons, although the government blocked further progress. The Secretary of State for the Environment, John Gummer, said from the dispatch box that despite there being no mention of the word 'quiet', the government would ensure that the tranquillity that was suitable for National Parks would be maintained while enabling the public to continue to lead their lives in a reasonable manner. Although the Act does not specify 'quiet' enjoyment, the principle is largely practised. Policies to support it are included in National Park management plans and it was upheld after a public inquiry into the introduction of a 10 mile per hour speed limit on Windermere. This effectively bans water-skiing and other noisy sports on the lake, allowing the vast majority of people to appreciate their surroundings in peace and quiet. In a real sense, the spirit of 'quiet enjoyment' lives on.

There was still the key and troublesome issue of protecting National Parks from major intrusive developments, such as projects involving public infrastructure proposed for remote areas, which could cause great environmental damage. Since the inception of National Parks, these have included the Snowdonia nuclear power station previously mentioned, reservoirs proposed for Dartmoor and the Peak District, major quarries and dual carriageways throughout the country. When National Parks were established it was recognised that they could not be a 'no-go' zone for such developments. The post-war Minister of Town and Country Planning

Lewis Silkin proposed a major development test, the principles of which have withstood the scrutiny of time. We felt it was appropriate for it to be enshrined in legislation, as recommended by the Edwards report. The government minister, Nick Ullswater, did not however support the move, feeling that it was best to leave the test in planning policy guidance only. A decision was made not to press the matter further, as I felt for my part that the point had been sufficiently aired.

It was truly a cause for celebration when the new independent Park Authorities in Wales were set up on 1st April 1996, and those in England a year later, just over five years since the start of the campaign for new National Parks legislation. As the Edwards panel termed it, they were 'Fit for the Future'. I myself only felt 'fit to drop'. It was my interests outside Parliament that kept me going.

During my time preparing for the Environment Bill I went with BTCV to visit a Summer Working Holiday in France. One of the projects was to improve a coastal footpath near Dunkirk, which had involved British and French volunteers in three weeks of hard but rewarding work. The project attracted EU funding because of its political importance. The visiting party was to attend a mayoral lunch where I was asked to make a speech. I had a bilingual friend who translated my speech into French before I left. For good measure she had also composed a list of short sentences in French covering the history of BTCV, the merits of volunteering, the ways in which environmental charities in England operated and how funding might be raised. Off I went, speech and notes safely in my pocket.

We had an addition to our party: Jessica Holmes, a BBC correspondent who broadcast a Sunday night radio programme on environmental issues and who, unbeknown to me, placed a tape recorder under the table to record my speech. Afterwards a French environmental correspondent, who represented Radio France, asked if he could conduct a live interview in French. The only possible way, I suggested, would be if he could devise a set of questions which would match up with some of the short written statements that I had brought with me. The interview went rather well and I came away feeling very pleased with my contribution.

Several days after I returned home, I was surprised, just as the answer-phone tape ran out, to pick up part of a recorded message from a fellow peer and former ambassador. 'George, I recently listened to Jessica Holme's weekly programme and then tuned in to your interview with Radio France.

I was *most impressed* by the way you answered those questions put to you. The Foreign and Commonwealth Office has asked me to approach you and other fluent French speaking peers to join an EU ...' I never knew what, nor did anything – luckily – ever transpire!

Environmental conservation and biodiversity was one of the ten categories for travelling fellowships sponsored by the Winston Churchill Memorial Trust of which I became a council member in 1992. The Trust is the national memorial and living tribute to Sir Winston. When he died in 1965, thousands of people gave generously to a public subscription in gratitude for his outstanding contribution as a world leader. Income from these funds, wisely invested since 1965, has provided more than 5,000 travelling fellowships for a wide range of projects. Churchill fellows can be of any age and in any occupation, provided they are a British citizen resident in the UK. Applicants must demonstrate that their project is feasible, worthwhile and of real benefit to their community once they have returned from their travels. Churchill wanted British people from all walks of life to experience the benefits of overseas travel and be inspired to make their own unique contributions not only to British life but to global understanding.

Undergraduate bursaries at Churchill College are also awarded every year as well as financial support being given for a postgraduate fellowship. The annual categories are chosen from ten broad areas which reflect Sir Winston's wide-ranging interests in the sciences, the arts, social reform and adventure, as well as anything that contributed to the improvement of the United Kingdom as a whole. Interviews are carried out by the council members, and for some applicants it is the chance of a lifetime. Exploration of their subject, their research, skills and dedication can be impressive and moving. As a council member I learned a great deal on matters about which I previously knew little, especially concerning lesser-known countries to which fellows had travelled.

Some people make their living by travelling. For many years, when in the nursery and garden centre trade, I spent long hours with commercial travellers and manufacturers' representatives both selecting or desisting from ordering their products. Saying 'no' was not always easy, but was essential to ensure that the shelves were not overstocked with items that never sold. In 1992, the boot became firmly placed on the other foot when I became president of the Commercial Travellers' Benevolent Institution

(CTBI), now known as the Salespeople's Charity. This was brought into being in December 1849 at the London Tavern to help commercial travellers, their widows or their dependants who had fallen victim to poverty and distress. The institution held its own fundraising activities, and prominent business tycoons of the day lent their names and reputations to support these appeals. The profession was headed up by a number of associations, though the principal help came from the United Kingdom Commercial Travellers' Association meeting monthly in every city and town in the country, to network and pass on information regarding outstanding needs of potential beneficiaries. In 1949, the philanthropist Lord Leverhulme bequeathed a legacy to the London Commercial Travellers Society, which merged with the CTBI in later years and from which the charity continues to benefit.

26

DIPLOMACY AND GEOPOLITICS

Concurrent with my parliamentary and charitable commitments, I was also involved with two businesses. The first of these was a small consultancy which sought new commercial opportunities in Eastern Europe in general, and Romania in particular. I had previously visited Romania in my capacity as patron of the Faure-Alderson Romanian Appeal (FARA). My second business was in the waste industry. I acted as a link and adviser on parliamentary matters to Grundon Waste Management Ltd, based at Colnbrook near Heathrow Airport.

My main responsibility as a co-director of the consultancy was to meet with London-based ambassadors representing Romania, Hungary, Poland, the Czech Republic and Uzbekistan, the purpose being to discuss the various opportunities for inward investment in these countries. The consultancy concentrated on prospective energy projects involving oil, gas, electricity or water. My co-director would assess each opportunity and identify national and international energy and water companies who might be interested in investing in those geographic areas. We then took the prospective clients to meet the ambassador in London and arrange a visit to the relevant country. The clients could then be introduced to the ministers responsible, and to potential partners. I visited Romania some eight times, as well as Hungary and Uzbekistan. Although we were retained by various prestigious companies, none were prepared to risk inward investment in Eastern Europe. The experience was nonetheless of great value to me, in understanding aspects of the relationship between politics and geography in particular.

At the outset, my co-director believed that US and UK energy companies would be attracted to expand their activities in Eastern Europe.

A member of the royal family who, like Prince Andrew later, officially promoted British industry abroad, was the Duke of Gloucester, whom I had known on and off for many years of my life. With his agreement, and blessing from the Foreign Office and sponsorship by National Power which had just bought an energy company in Texas, we organised a royal visit to the US. The itinerary included holding a dinner in Washington and a lunch in New York for presidents or chief executives of the largest US energy companies, and directors of some of the investment banks in New York. One of the larger law firms in Washington also supported the visit and we met in their offices. The visit was considered a great accomplishment by National Power, and with this valuable experience and list of new contacts, we thought our consultancy was now in a realistic position to invite energy companies to look at inward investment in Eastern Europe. All looked to be set fair.

We had specifically targeted Romania because a fellow peer, also a director of the consultancy, knew an influential Anglo-Romanian who moved in Romanian government circles and knew the then president, Ion Iliescu. In London we had developed a very close relationship with Sergiu Celac, the Romanian Ambassador. Sergiu spoke perfect English and had been the official interpreter to the infamous Romanian President Nicolae Ceausescu. Losing favour with him, Sergiu was removed from his post before Ceaucescu and his wife Elena were executed on Christmas Day 1989. Sergiu was subsequently appointed Romanian Ambassador in London, always making the utmost efforts to promote the interests of Romania.

I made two trips to that country with my fellow directors and our Anglo Romanian contact, who unfortunately died soon after. As a result Sergiu Celac introduced us to a new potential Romanian partner. We had been focusing on the refurbishment of power stations and oil refineries, of which Petromedia, near Constanza on the Black Sea coast, was the most modern. It had the latest cutting-edge Soviet technology and was a possible prize worth pursuing by any interested foreign investor. We therefore wooed any US, UK and European energy companies who might wish to invest in this new territory.

One project involved gas storage in underground caves. A West Coast American corporation went with us on a four-day mission to Bucharest, and the proposed joint-venture Romanian partner reciprocated and went with us to visit them in San Francisco. Hopes were high. The Romanians accepted the proposal, but never delivered. Perhaps, given my childhood experience of gas, I should have smelled something not quite right! Things then went from bad to worse. Our Romanian joint-venture partner reneged on the payments to our company, leaving it almost insolvent. I decided to pursue the matter through the High Courts at my own expense. Although the courts found in my favour, the Romanians were not able to extract the payment, which by now had mounted up. An enforcement officer appointed by our Romanian lawyers eventually located shares held in the name of our joint-venture partner. The proceeds from the sale of these shares scarcely covered the legal fees in Romania. In hindsight it was an expensive and unwise risk on my part, but for me the decision to go to court was a moral choice, although it didn't get me anywhere.

From 2003 onwards, we turned our attention from energy projects in Eastern Europe to projects in Canada that, I was relieved to hear, did not involve gas, but water. I have already stated my view that future wars might well be fought over this most precious commodity. The amount of available fresh water around the world was falling then at an alarming rate, and continues to do so. Something like 2 billion people still do not have access to purified drinking water. Restrictions are commonplace in Australia, the United States and Canada, and we need look no further than the hosepipe bans imposed in the UK during ostensibly dry summers. The simple fact is that there is no more water on the planet today than there was 1 million years ago, when the human population has been estimated as being only 18,500; now 6 billion people are vying for every drop.

We researched the municipal water utilities of the Canadian province of Alberta. This province continued to experience inadequate levels of capital provision, preventing the replacement and extension of public water transportation through a new network of large-diameter pipelines. Alberta's public water supply capabilities and economics remained a political issue. Mayors of outlying townships, for example, refused to allow either commercial or residential development to take place until they were reassured that the water supplies in the long term were guaranteed. This project, alas, never got off the ground, although we were told it had great potential.

In 1991 I became an adviser to Grundon Waste Management Ltd, thanks to Allan Mercado, who had been our public relations manager at the garden centre at Fairfield and was now working for them. Their management was intent on developing contacts at government level and Allan effected my introduction to Tony Mitchell, the managing director. For the next ten years I enjoyed a very happy and fruitful relationship with the company. Grundon is still a family-owned company and the largest privately owned waste management group in the UK. It remains at the forefront of waste management practice and innovation. I found it fascinating that a small local aggregate supply business should have developed so effectively into a national commercial group, in the industrial services sector, with many diverse interests.

The waste industry as a whole cuts across a number of different government departments with responsibilities covering business, health, energy, environment, farming, science and technology. Grundon was most particular about land use and protecting wildlife. As soon as landfill sites close, they are reinstated to an environmentally friendly land use which might be agricultural, composting, planting woodland and hedges, lakes or reed beds. In one case on a site in Gloucestershire a herd of willing alpacas assisted in managing the restored land, the site of which has many steep banks and grass fields. The alpacas reduced the need for mowing and strimming, vastly improving the visual appearance of the site and also provided natural fertiliser.

In 1996 the government introduced a tax on waste going to landfill sites. And a tax credit scheme was also introduced, allowing landfill operators to claim against a percentage of their landfill tax. I was heartened that the company contributed this credit to an environmental body that supports community and environment projects, such as those run by NGOs like TCV, or the County Wildlife Trust. My experience working with Grundon filled an important gap for me in addressing ongoing environmental issues, and served as a useful background to matters debated in the Lords Chamber and in committee. Even today I keep up with the introduction of new green technologies relevant to the waste industry and renewable energy.

There were important lessons to learn from my business involvements in Eastern Europe and Canada, as well as working with Grundon in the UK. One was that I was too naive and inexperienced to be aware of the potential pitfalls when dealing with large corporations and foreign joint-venture partners. Pursuing an expensive court case at home and abroad, primarily because I felt morally aggrieved, certainly lacked discernment:

learning to swim is best not done during a storm. I should have simply accepted the Romanians' way of doing things, learned from it, and moved on. Instead I listened to Mars rather than Minerva and picked the wrong fight! Grundon was different. There, I was dealing with a company whose integrity and transparency shone out in an industry often criticised for flagrant disregard of environmental law.

Following the return of a Labour government in 1997, my prospects as a business and parliamentary eco-warrior looked a lot less favourable. It had its sights on reforming the Lords.

27

PEERING OUT

As Providence decreed it, I was a member of the House of Lords during that momentous time in 1998 which would mark, after 500 years, the beginning of the end for the privileged lifestyle of hereditary peers. That provenance, guaranteed by birth, of a duty to serve the public was about to be removed from people such as me. The Upper House of Parliament had taken the shape with which we are still most familiar from the fifteenth century. The Lords temporal became known as peers with five ranks – duke, marquess, earl, viscount and baron – even though equal to each other. Together with the Lower House, or House of Commons, both Houses had legislative powers such that either could propose a bill. Only if the bill was accepted by both Houses would it then come before the monarch and, upon receiving royal assent, become an Act of Parliament. The relationship between the two Houses, however, has not always been an easy one.

Every time the Lords threatened, or were thought to threaten, the freedoms of the House of Commons, attempts at reform followed. In 1909, for example, the Lords rejected the budget and in due course had their right to reject Commons legislation removed. A couple of years later, legislation was passed making sure that, even if the Lords did not fall into line with the Commons on a bill, it would nevertheless become law anyway. Various previous attempts at more radical reform of the Lords had failed, however. As far back as 1886, the Commons roundly condemned the rights of hereditary peers to make laws, but nothing came of it. The 1968 Labour government pledged to eliminate the hereditary basis of the Lords, but the bill to achieve this was so delayed by both Houses that it failed to make any progress.

The Labour manifesto before the 1997 general election included a very similar commitment: 'as an initial, self-contained reform, not dependent on further reform in the future, the right of hereditary peers to sit and vote in the House of Lords will be ended'. When the leader of the House of Commons, Margaret Beckett MP, introduced the bill in February 1999, I knew I had some serious thinking to do, because this was a momentous historical turning point which would change the fundamental basis of our entire parliamentary system. I understood and to an extent accepted the propriety of what was being proposed. How could I defend what is indefensible in a modern democracy? Why should hereditary voting determine the passing of bills and rules of procedure in the House? It was nevertheless a concern to many of us that there was no clarity whatsoever about what would replace an arrangement that had served us well for centuries.

The Association of Conservative Peers appointed a law firm in the City to advise about peers' rights. With such far-reaching changes being proposed, was the legality of the bill sound, I wondered? I knew that if I were to take a personal stand, I would need the help of legal counsel. Although I already had experience of speaking in the Chamber and being subjected to public scrutiny, this time it would be different: I would inevitably be challenged by some of the sharpest legal brains in the country on this issue.

Support was just around the corner. A friendly cross-bench hereditary peer retained an eminent barrister whose professional services were generously offered to me, which was a welcome bonus. More providentially still, I had the benefit of the consultancy co-director who had expertise in constitutional law, having gained a double first at Manchester and Oxford. He was able to research relevant case histories in law and, as the bill progressed, draft up my amendments and speeches. There was going to be at least a fortnightly gap between the various stages of the bill, which would give time for him to study relevant legal points that appeared weak and hence could be challenged.

Back in the Lords, the warm-up debates had begun during the previous autumn of 1998, generating a huge amount of interest, as might be expected. It was hardly likely that we would give the bill an easy ride: 'turkeys voting for Christmas' was an analogy that was used quite frequently. Although the death knell was tolling, the quality of the debate, and the wit it provoked, went some way into relieving the dismal mood of the House. A 'Motion to

Take Note' was tabled before the bill arrived in the House. The Lords were then able to debate the situation without coming to any positive decision. When speaking to convey my own concerns, I tried to keep things as simple as I could.

I concluded, as I listened to the Labour government's case, that it focused on party politics and fairness. The party political argument was at first sight compelling: Labour members referred to the fact that in the 1997 election the Conservatives had won 34 per cent of the vote, yet they had 66 per cent of the membership of the Lords who took a party whip. Even a cursory scrutiny would, however, reveal that these figures did not include the cross-benchers, many of whom were hereditary peers. They also did not take into account the number of peers who were not active in the House for various reasons. The real proportion of Conservative members active in the Lords was more like 39 per cent; it was the largest party, but not one with a majority.

With regard to fairness, it was being alleged that the House of Lords was of insufficient quality since the hereditary peers were 'predominantly driven by self-interest and out of touch with everyday concerns'. In the Commons, Geoffrey Hoon MP had quoted Thomas Paine, who in 1791 wrote in *Rights of Man*:

> *The idea of hereditary legislation is as inconsistent as that of hereditary judges, or hereditary juries; and as absurd as a hereditary mathematician, or a hereditary wise man, and as ridiculous as a hereditary poet-laureate.*

I had no inclination to disagree. The main objection from the Conservative side seemed to me to be about the overhastiness of the change process. The bill would unravel the current system without any certainty of the nature of its replacement. A Royal Commission was by now being proposed, with a remit of drawing up plans for the composition of a new Upper House. This became known as Stage Two. The problem was that whereas Stage One was all about destroying the current arrangements, and that would happen immediately after the bill was passed, Stage Two was still on the drawing board. There were genuine misgivings, borne out by subsequent experience, that the reform train would leave the station but not have a destination.

Would a reformed House of Lords include *any* hereditary peers? The government had originally said it would not, but later conceded that it might reconsider that point, which it subsequently did. Would it have members appointed by the government, the Prime Minister or an independent body? Would it have elected members? What would be its powers? Would there even *be* a second chamber? As Lord Strathclyde, leader of the Conservative Party in the Lords, succinctly put it at the time: 'How are we to replace a chamber which is hard-working, inexpensive and effective?'

My experience of the House of Lords was just that: its active members – which included us hereditary peers – were prone to working long hours, committed to the ethos of public service. There was a strong sense of responsibility allied to a tradition of independent thought. It was hard to see how this might be reproduced in Stage Two, at least in a way that secured consensus. Lord Judd summed it up well:

Noblesse oblige is no bad principle; and whatever the changes that come, history will not smile on us if we underrate character and independence of judgement. We must not replace what we have with a grey, boring place made up of aspiring, over-compliant placemen, unduly beholden to their party managers.

It seemed to me that the bill would trample on the property and human rights of hereditary peers. The government appeared to be trying to sweep both aside for no higher reason than party political ideology. What were the rights of hereditary peers, I asked myself? My rights in the House, as I understood them, were provided by letters patent, originally granted to barons who would offer counsel to the sovereign. At this juncture letters patent, I was led to believe, could not be revoked by Parliament or indeed anyone else. They granted a right to 'hold, possess a seat, place and voice' in Parliament.

Every peer also had rights acquired by custom. When speaking during the bill on 22th February 1999, I stated that as a peer, I had the customary personal right 'to enter this palace, enter this chamber, to sit and speak in it'. This was a custom that had existed from time immemorial without interruption within that place, and had, I understood, the force of law.

With this in mind, and given that the government had received a mandate for reform, I wondered whether they would consider, at least for now, that hereditary peers might retain the right to vote in debates, but these would have no relevance to the final result? However, their property rights to attend sit and debate would be retained under customary law. The ensuing debate was long – seven hours – and this was only day one! It went far into the night and by the end of the two days of our loaded discussions, even at this early stage, more than 90 peers had spoken. It was clear that there was much to be settled before the bill could become law.

In March 1999, their lordships took further briefing on what powers we might have had to block or delay the bill. The first question was whether the Salisbury Convention meant that we could not oppose the bill at second reading. Under this, the House of Lords does not table 'wrecking amendments', or efforts to destroy the bill, at second reading to any government legislation. The advice we received was that the House was not bound by the convention, which meant that the Lords could, if they so chose, frustrate the government by delaying the bill for two years over three parliamentary sessions, and the government would not have recourse to employ the Parliament Act 1911 to force through the legislation. This provided some grounds for hope that we could at least slow things down until a more sensible plan for Stage Two had emerged.

Those in power, meanwhile, were determined to forge ahead with their simplistic cull; we had, of course, been banned from calling it 'hereditary cleansing' on the grounds that more complex approaches had previously been doomed to fail. The bill flew through the Commons and arrived in the Lords in March 1999.

For the second reading more than 180 peers had their names down to speak, including four government ministers, dozens of former ones, and me. Despite the resolute opening speech by Baroness Jay on behalf of the Labour government, there was already the hint of a compromise. The pledge to rid the Lords of hereditary peers was being insidiously undermined, with talk of a later amendment to retain temporary membership for 'some hereditary peers'.

Some time after one o'clock in the morning, when it came to my turn to speak, I tried to remain true to my original and rather measured proposal, which would seek to avoid a constitutional conflict. I simply asserted that to remove my right to sit and speak in the House was unlawful. Even peers who had been beheaded as traitors on the fields of battle, I said, were permitted by law to pass on their rights to their successors. Those in the House and Parliament who had sought reform by statute could only succeed by rescinding property rights granted by the sovereign which would amount to expropriation without compensation, even in law.

I hoped that I held two winning cards up my sleeve. The government had not yet consulted the 54 Commonwealth states concerning the abolition of the rights of hereditary peers. I had found out that since the accession of Henry IV in 1399, a reigning sovereign is also a hereditary peer. The Queen is the Duke of Lancaster and therefore it was being proposed that her rights would also be abolished. The bill would have the effect of changing the Queen's title, and therefore was it possible that the bill would be flawed? Under the Statute of Westminster, each Commonwealth parliament must consent to any alteration in the succession or the royal style and titles. Had the government not done its groundwork perhaps? To me this seemed to present a huge hurdle which would need to be overcome.

Rather than seeing the bill as renewing or strengthening the constitution, it might do just the reverse. As previously mentioned I proposed therefore a constitutional compromise which, devoid of partisan politics or class attitudes, would enable hereditary peers to sit and express their views, but have no vote.

Our collective concerns about the impact of the constitutional changes on Commonwealth countries were the subject of discussion outside the House. As a result I joined a meeting organised by Freedom in Action, along with eight high commissioners or their representatives from Commonwealth countries. As the son of a former Governor General of New Zealand, I felt particularly concern for hereditary peers who were citizens of any of the Commonwealth countries, feeling that there was little distinction between them and hereditary peers who are UK citizens. Both should surely be able to participate fully in the life of Parliament. I wondered if the bill would infringe upon the rights of citizens of independent member nations of the Commonwealth. It also seemed to me to be in breach of various international agreements and legislation. Should the bill succeed, it would surely interfere with the right of Commonwealth citizens worldwide to be considered for elevation to the peerage.

Having written to the Queen's private secretary, Sir Robin Janvrin, to let him know, I decided to raise the matter of abolishing the Queen's right as a hereditary peer and of the need to secure approval for the changes from the Commonwealth parliaments. I also involved two Canadian ministers, who in the event decided to view it as an internal domestic issue and agreed to observe rather than take part. During the committee stage of the bill I was concerned about possible legal challenges ahead. When speaking to the House I suggested that my amendments would avoid what I called 'traps and snares' that the government had set for themselves and for the Opposition, and which lay set and ready in the provisions of the Statute of Westminster and the European Human Rights Convention and laws. The debate – lasting two further sessions – was long and became surprisingly technical. There was dispute over what was meant by property rights, what having letters patent meant in terms of rights, and where sovereignty lay in relation to the rights of hereditary peers.

There can be little doubt that by allowing the subject of property rights to be aired, some concessions, were won for those hereditary peers whom the bill would have disqualified. These individuals would have the concessionary privilege of using the Peers' Dining Room and also the library, when the House was not in session, and the right, when in session, to sit on the steps of the throne in the Chamber. My insistence on pressing forward these technical points led at that time to perhaps my most difficult moment in Parliament.

28

IMPROVEMENT, BUT FOR WHAT?

The Statute of Westminster 1931 said that if there was to be any alteration to the 'style or titles' of the Queen, the Commonwealth countries would have to agree to it, so I set out prove this. The salient point was, I believed, that the sovereign possessed the right to create hereditary peers who then could become members of the House of Lords. The proposed bill sought to abolish that right. It might be that I have the right to stand at Speakers' Corner in Hyde Park and shout this message to the entire world, I said. The fact that I have not done so does not mean that I no longer have the right. Such rights do not fall into abeyance because of non-use. A right is a right, whether it is the citizen's or the sovereign's. Or so I maintained.

Had the government acknowledged the fact that passing the bill would change the sovereign's rights? I accused it of 'repeated dissembling', going so far as to say that the minister, Baroness Jay, was 'dissembling' when she said that the sovereign's right to create hereditary peers 'remained exactly the same'. The use of the word 'dissembling' was unfortunate. I had meant it in the strict dictionary sense of disguising or masking something, but Margaret Jay took it to mean 'lying', and accusing another member of lying is absolutely against the rules of the House. Lord Williams of Mostyn declared that I had abused the freedom of the chamber, and that I should retract my words at once: 'to say that someone *is* "dissembling" means that they are telling untruths'. However, I was quite passionate about what I was saying, since it appeared that through this bill, the government intended to deny to the heir, the Duke of Cornwall, access to the House, and asked pointedly whether that would leave the sovereign's rights precisely as they were before. Substantial support came from fellow conservative peers on this issue.

Margaret Jay stuck to her view that no consultation was needed. She contended that the relevant Statute of Westminster only applied to the Dominions, New Zealand, Australia and Canada, and that the House of Lords Reform Bill did not fall into that category. For further clarification she claimed that although, after the passing of the bill, it would be the case that the sovereign would no longer have the power to grant a hereditary peerage, carrying with it a place in the House, that did not in any way alter the style or title of the sovereign. Feeling at this point satisfied that the points had by now been aired thoroughly, I judged it appropriate to withdraw the amendment.

But the matter of dissembling did not end there. The next day, on the floor of the House, prior to the debate on aspects of human rights as they affected the bill, Margaret Jay saw fit to raise the matter again, referring to my 'extremely unfortunate remarks'. Had I perhaps added fuel to the fire in the way I summed up before the withdrawal of my human rights amendment? I had asked her if she was aware that there had been a case involving the Communist Party of Turkey, whose right not to be politically excluded had been protected by the European Court of Human Rights. Was not the government's bill based on the same principle? So by trying to exclude a Conservative majority from the parliamentary process, the bill consequently trespassed on the human rights of peers. Might this perhaps lead to legal ramifications and future action at a later date for the government of the day?

Quite promptly I received a rather stern letter from the government chief whip via Tom Strathclyde's office, requiring me to write a letter of apology. This did not come as a surprise. I did write to Margaret Jay, although it was to say I was saddened for any offence taken. Having checked my dictionary, I wrote that dissembling did not necessarily imply untruthfulness, lying or falseness. I was well supported. Furthermore, I used the opportunity to reiterate that it was incorrect for her to maintain that the sovereign's rights remained precisely the same.

As the bill progressed through the Lords, the Labour government, I suspected, were about to realise that the sea changes they had planned were not going to be plain sailing. Firstly, the gathering angry mood of the House began to show that any bill published on the government manifesto was likely to be deliberately opposed, or delayed for as long as possible. Secondly, removing all the hereditary peers from parliament would make the day-to-day running of the House of Lords almost impossible. Many hereditary peers were chairmen or members of House committees. Fifteen of the 25 deputy speakers were hereditary peers, whose responsibilities included sitting on the Woolsack in the absence of the Lord Chancellor.

Viscount Cranborne, at that time leader of the Opposition, had been in private negotiation with Lord Irvine of Lairg, the Lord Chancellor. With the approval of the leader of the Opposition, William Hague, an initial deal was struck. Until Stage Two at any rate, 75 hereditary peers would remain, elected pro rata by their respective parties. Fifteen deputy speakers, termed Servants of the House, would be elected by the members of the House. Only hereditary peers would be eligible to vote.

Two further hereditary inclusions would be the Earl Marshal and the Lord Great Chamberlain, both having duties at the State Opening of Parliament. The Earl Marshal is additionally responsible for the organisation of state funerals and the monarch's coronation in Westminster Abbey. The Lord Great Chamberlain, alongside some coronation duties, is also entrusted by the sovereign with the custody and control of those parts of the Palace of Westminster which are outside the jurisdiction of the two Houses. These responsibilities include the Queen's Robing Room and the Royal Gallery.

The total of elected places agreed at this stage numbered 92, being larger than originally expected, with a further adjustment of some hereditary peers being given a life peerage. Once the bill headed for royal assent, a date to elect the 92 hereditary peers was announced for 3rd and 4th November 1999, allowing minimal time for any preparation. I put my name forward, not least on account of the organisations whose views I had undertaken to represent in Parliament. One chief executive summed it up by writing: 'The removal of a large number of hereditary peers from their active participation in the House of Lords will lead to considerable difficulties for many voluntary organisations in securing effective leadership in understanding the maze of Westminster and Whitehall.' These protestations fell upon stony ground. The Labour government were just not interested.

It was quite obvious that there was going to be strong competition for the election of the 42 Conservative peers. More than 220 of us registered the right to vote. More than 100 stood for election. Each candidate was allowed to write a 75-word personal resumé. These resumés were available for the Conservative voters to read in the library. Blatant lobbying by those who had registered to stand in the election might result in disqualification. Thus we were warned in writing.

The few days before the election were an almost unbearable conflict of anticipation mixed with fear and confusion. What would I do if I didn't get in? Did I deserve to be elected? I remained at home, uncomfortable and deeply apprehensive about the forthcoming result; I did not believe in trying to influence others on my behalf. The day came, and I took the fateful telephone call.

The House had become the beating heart of my life. Although the argument was won for the hereditary peers to maintain their right to enter the House and even sit on the steps of the throne, for me there would be no going back. Being short of just one vote spurred me to reflect on how lucky I had been to spend so many years as an active member of the House of Lords, a privilege given to me entirely through accident of birth as a result of my father's lifetime achievements. I began to reassess my relationship with my father once again, wondering how he would have responded to his son just missing the cut. My honest conclusion was that he would have been disappointed for me, rather than in me. He would certainly have been incensed at the House of Lords Act: I could hear him saying to me, 'How can *that* be an improvement!', and I would have agreed wholeheartedly with him.

My new circumstances allowed me to reminisce about his twilight years, when for the first time we had lived near to each other. He had changed considerably from the active general I had known in my younger years. Taking any form of exercise was confined to moving at slow speed from the garden door across the lawn to the wooden bridge spanning the Letcombe Brook, leading to the lake. Even in old age he remained a creature of habit. He would change for dinner in the evenings, wearing his maroon velvet smoking jacket, white silk shirt, satin black bow tie, black dress trousers and a pair of black corduroy slippers. After dinner, especially if it was a fine warm summer evening, he was in the habit of shuffling off, still in his slippers, towards the lake with a trout rod in his hand.

On one such evening when I was there we wandered out, a cigar firmly clenched in his mouth as was his way. We walked over the lawn together, but just as we approached the side of the bridge he slipped on the damp grass and found himself sliding on his posterior at increasing speed down the steep grass bank, feet first into the brook. His feet and corduroy slippers anchored themselves in deep mud as the water covered his knees.

'Get Jeeves and come and pull me out!'

'Remain upright,' I shouted, 'and don't move!'

By the time Jeeves and I both arrived at the scene he had sunk a little further. How were we best to extricate this very large and heavy object from the mud?

'You will have to turn over onto your hands and knees,' I suggested. 'Get out of your slippers and steady yourself on this broom handle. Then give us your arms so we can pull you onto dry land.'

The abandoned trout rod was now floating downstream. Eventually, my father managed to turn himself around without collapsing. It was a shame that no one was there with a video camera as Jeeves and I really struggled to heave his 18 stones up a near vertical bank on to the lawn. Then, as my father's form slowly changed from vertical to horizontal, his braces gave way and his trousers fell down, exposing his extra-large pair of white knee-length underpants. It was the most incongruous sight, seeing him lying on his stomach in full evening regalia, exposing his hindquarters as he still resolutely puffed at his cigar, watched by myself and Jeeves.

I expected to see some emotion in Jeeves's face but his expression remained as correct as ever. The fishing rod was rescued but the slippers were never quite as pristine again. Since, to my relief, he was none the worse for wear, I could not resist saying as my father and I laughed together: 'It is a disgrace, Dad, that you, as a distinguished peer of the realm, should ever be caught with your trousers down!' The memory of that day still makes me smile; perhaps our relationship over the years had not been as difficult as I remembered.

29

AND FINALLY: OFF TO DUMFRIES AND GALLOWAY

The decade preceding my departure from the House of Lords had brought me some political success, but it also saw a large measure of turmoil in my personal life. My home went, my savings went, and along with that, my marriage. In the early 1990s, I was one of thousands hit with a substantial financial liability as an underwriting member of Lloyds, and was obliged to place my home on the market. This was naturally painful. This coincided with my separation from Celia. I had long been on a downward spiral, avoiding the uncomfortable issues in my life. To compensate I worked late in the Lords, and became stressed about Mark's kidneys and the well-being of both Patricia and Nanny, now in their late eighties. I felt that Celia dealt with our difficulties far better than I did. I couldn't cope with the reality of separation, and subsequent divorce. The house was sold. The business was sold. I paid my Lloyd's losses. Celia moved to Hungerford and I moved permanently to a flat in London to pick up the pieces.

Dolphin Square was a large complex of flats on the Thames Embankment, built in the 1930s. Many of the flats were used by MPs and peers. It was located within easy walking distance of Parliament Square. Whilst it offered every facility such as cafés, shops, restaurant and swimming pool, I did not relish becoming a bachelor again in my early sixties. My real consolation was finding Kenny Penny, a veteran and talented jazz pianist, who played in the restaurant on Thursday nights. He agreed to give me lessons. I bought an electric clavinova keyboard from him, which allowed me to indulge myself, armed with headphones so as not to disturb my neighbours as I practised late into the night. Throughout my life I have always been lucky in finding piano teachers. From my school days I realised classical music was too challenging. Playing by ear the melodies composed by such Broadway songwriters as Gershwin, Jerome Kern and Cole Porter was more my style, and still is. On leaving school, I had started in earnest with a band leader in Wellington, New Zealand and found, at various stages of my life, teachers in Carlisle, Enniskillen, Celle in Germany, Tidworth, Newbury and even in Aden, where my teacher was a gifted and charming Indian musician who played at a rather seedy servicemen's nightclub. Arriving in Scotland, at last I found a replacement for Kenny in Glasgow and music continues to be a nourishing feature in my life.

Annie McCaffry was brought up in Scotland and still loves the wind and rain in her hair as she walks the hills. We first met in Switzerland during our teens, our families having met through army life, although Annie's father, serving in the Black Watch, had been killed in 1942. We met again with our families when living in Berkshire. Annie has always had a radically different way of understanding disease and viewing life from anything I have ever known. Although she started by designing children's clothes for Grade One in London, she later moved to the country. She owned and ran an art gallery which was often used to host lectures by pioneers in the holistic field that she had come across on her travels. It was also used for yoga classes for the locals and was the venue for 'Joe the Toe' to give talks on his 'zone therapy', not akin to reflexology. Joe's clients included Chelsea Football Club, Barbara Cartland and also Annie's Aunt Mar, who had introduced him to all of us. Celia and I were among many friends who visited the gallery for these different events. Annie would then disappear abroad again and not be seen for months on end. Where she went was a mystery to most of us! Now, after her publishing three books, I know.

Annie and I were married in 1997, and kept her lovely Wiltshire chapel – our home until we later moved to Scotland. But a small flat in London was acquired as I was still attending the House of Lords. We share a love of music, the arts and wilderness, Annie later becoming a trustee of the Wilderness Foundation, which we have continued to enjoy in many forms both here and abroad. I was beginning to understand more about embracing the personal 'inner world'. Having spent so many years and so much of my energy seeking to protect the outer world, through my environmental work, I see I neglected my own inner world, on allowing it to become as a derelict garden, untended and undeveloped. Annie suggested that I attend to that unfamiliar territory within. Beginning an inner dialogue was never going to be easy for someone like me. I needed to learn to speak openly,

THE AUTHOR AND HIS WIFE ANNIE,
DRESSED FOR THE OPENING OF PARLIAMENT, 1998.

something frowned upon during my upbringing but also needed to listen, not just with my ears but with my heart. It seemed essential to discipline myself in order to experience stillness and silence; I still struggle.

Through Annie I met a former science and medical correspondent for *The Sunday Times*, who was now respected author and a senior member teaching at the Brahma Kumari global retreat centre. Radically influenced by this organisation, he became a mentor and great friend to me. I began spending weekends there and going on some of the courses they ran. Little by little I began to see how I could achieve a degree of inner peace for myself.

Nevertheless, I was still new to my inner world when the axe fell in 1999. Leaving the House of Lords coincided with a hip replacement operation that I had long known was required but, typically, had postponed. The subsequent immobility took away any distractions that could have helped me sidestep thinking about the next move. My head was spinning: I could not avoid reflecting on the 'what ifs' of my life. I took some comfort from words I had once heard, that errors are the usual bridge between inexperience and wisdom; but whereas a wise man might have acted promptly, I remained in a state of frozen indecision. As was my habit, I buried and denied my deep-seated emotions. Keeping busy in the House had helped feed that denial. Now I knew that I had some straight talking to do, and all of it with myself.

I felt paralysed by the apparent uncertainty that stretched ominously ahead. The overwhelming sense of disillusionment was profound, recognising that I had invested so much of my time, effort and passion in the House of Lords, leaving no space for 'me'. Was Annie just the catalyst I needed to jolt me out of my post-parliamentary stupor? In the course of the next three years we planned and plotted our future. Annie was clear that she was not going to die in England! Since I had always enjoyed Scotland, the appealing thought of a chance to cast a salmon fly over an attractive stretch of local river proved an irresistible lure. We pressed green for go – to Scotland.

We bought a derelict farmhouse and outbuildings belonging to the Duke of Buccleuch, completely captivated by the stunning landscape and panoramic views in all directions. With the help of wonderful local workmen, we set out our imagination to create not just a lovely home but a unique spot where we would act as custodians for years to come. Little by little we have totally renovated the house, and converted a large barn, now used for musical events and talks. We have landscaped a garden, to include features to attract wildlife. Annie has been the heart and inspiration behind the project, but she and I were agreed that we wished Holehouse to be more than simply a nice home in the country. We wanted it to tell a story, and become something worthwhile. Part of this message is promoting the benefits that come from active listening, and Annie has helped me to learn how to do that with my whole being and not just with my ears!

As I listened I gradually became reacquainted with parts of myself that had been dormant for far too long. In particular I was able to recall that moment sitting on a rooftop in Saiun in the Hadhramaut, transfixed and overawed by the beauty of the sunset. The fading light had turned quickly to a penetrating darkness soon to be illuminated by a myriad of stars glittering in the Arabian night sky. Whatever that experience brought me, it had connected with all of me, not just with my intellect. It had *meant* something then, and has continued to do so. I now wanted, indeed needed, to find out what that was. Accordingly I had set out upon another journey which would be – as the title of one of Annie's books puts it – a *Journey to Myself*.

Consequently I now make time for silence and reflection, journeying to the centre, as it were, of my deepest self. Such a journey is intensely personal, but most unexpectedly I found inspiration in a very public place: the labyrinth outside Norwich cathedral.

I had visited the early thirteenth labyrinth at Chartres Cathedral, century, but the one in Norwich, laid out on grass to commemorate the Queen's Golden Jubilee in 2002, had a deeper impact on me. Unlike a maze, which requires logical tools to escape it, a labyrinth is instead designed to guide you, the choice being whether to enter it or not. The paths within the labyrinth offer a continuous route from the entrance to the centre, and represent the journey to our innermost self and out again to the everyday world.

Last year I designed my very own labyrinth, based on the sevenfold concentric pattern of the one in Norwich, constructed of pink Staffordshire stone chippings, with the path marked by slate-grey paving. It presents a harmonious contrast, within its landscaped green hollow, to the adjacent pond, its sparkling burn and semi-circular broad-leaved copse. It is not only a functional instrument to aid reflection, it is also an object of unusual beauty. The property remains a work in progress, and for both of us a labour of love.

Having reached the age of 80 how do I view my life on this planet? I was asked by a grandson recently. My answer was to quote some wisdom from Satish Kumar's book *Earth Pilgrim*. He suggests that we view our lives on this planet as tourists or pilgrims. Tourists value the Earth and all her resources only in terms of usefulness to themselves. Pilgrims perceive the planet to be sacred and recognise the intrinsic value of all life. As a tourist most of my life, I am edging towards becoming a pilgrim.

LABYRINTH IN THE GARDEN